AXION
adidas

BLUE
& GOLD
PASSION

BLUE & GOLD PASSION

A HISTORY OF BOCA JUNIORS

DANIEL WILLIAMSON

pitch

First published by Pitch Publishing, 2020

Pitch Publishing
A2 Yeoman Gate
Yeoman Way
Worthing
Sussex
BN13 3QZ
www.pitchpublishing.co.uk
info@pitchpublishing.co.uk

A CIP catalogue record is available for this book from the British Library.

ISBN 978 1 78531 653 1

Typesetting and origination by Pitch Publishing

Printed and bound in India by Replika Press Pvt. Ltd.

Contents

For my three girls:
Greta, Frieda and Lottie.

Acknowledgements

THANKS TO Jane at Pitch Publishing for giving me the platform to write this book, and have it published. Duncan at Olner Design took a vague description of how I wanted the book's front cover to look and brought it to life in a way I could never have imagined.

The seed for this book was planted when I discovered that Steven Scragg was having a book published by Pitch. Seeing the promotional material for the excellent *Frozen in Time* inspired me to think about ideas for a book of my own. Steven has been a great help throughout the process, from my initial pitch to completion.

My wife, Greta, has been supportive, encouraging, and has remained patient throughout the process.

Although I'm the one that has dedicated countless hours to this project, and my name will adorn the front cover, there are many people that have contributed and with whom I have collaborated. It is common to encounter negativity on social media, but any time I have reached out dozens of people, often strangers, have offered their help, wishing for nothing in return.

Matt Evans has provided daily support and proof-reading. I look forward to reciprocating and helping

Matt with his book which he is currently in the process of writing.

Gabriel Aguero, founder of the Boca in English Twitter account and podcast, has also provided enthusiastic support and proofreading. I interviewed Gabi about his favourite player, Juan Román Riquelme. His Boca in English colleague, Buenos Aires-based journalist Francisco Aure, was also interviewed for the book.

Patricio Córdoba has been passionate about the project from day one and, crucially, was instrumental in introducing me to two former Boca Juniors players. His father, Carlos *Cacho* Córdoba, won the 1981 Metropolitano championship alongside a young Diego Maradona; Alfredo Oscar Márquez emerged from the famed youth system and was part of the squad that won the 1976 Nacional championship under the tutelage of the legendary Juan Carlos *Toto* Lorenzo.

Journalist Nick Dorrington gave me the mobile phone number of José Maria Suárez who won five trophies in six years in the famous blue-and-gold shirt, including the 1977 Intercontinental Cup. Suárez was interviewed for chapter five.

Jorge *Ruso* Ribolzi, who I contacted on Twitter, discussed his memories of his time at La Bombonera. In total he won ten titles with the club: five as a player and, later, five as part of Alfio *Coco* Basile's coaching staff.

Club historian Guillermo Schoua discussed the club's early years and his mind-bogglingly detailed website, Historia de Boca, was a vital tool during the research process.

Rio de Janeiro-based Englishman Tim Vickery has inspired me over the years with his passionate coverage of South American football. It was an honour to discuss some of Boca's Copa Libertadores clashes against Brazilian sides – from Santos in 1963 to Grêmio in 2007 – with Tim.

Lucas Guerrero (Muy Boca), Víctor Fucci and Sebastián Sellaro (Somos Boca), Diego Tomasi (author of *El Caño Mas Bello Del Mundo*), and freelance journalist Leandro Cordobez discussed Boca's history with me. Their words are also included in this book.

Thanks to Euan McTear (LaLiga Lowdown), Chris Lee (Outside Write), and Gabriel Aguero and Francisco Aure (Boca in English) for inviting me on to their podcasts in April and May 2020 to discuss Boca's history and the process behind the book. Thanks to Maxi Kronenberg from *Clarín*, Argentina's biggest daily tabloid, for interviewing me about the book for their website and taking my story to Argentina.

Thanks to Seth Burkett, Dr Marieke Riethof, Andrés Burgo, Información CABJ, Vicente Ponce, and everyone else who supported the project in any way. Last, but not least, I want to send a sincere and huge thank you to all of the people who pre-ordered the book, parting with your money during a bizarre period of economic uncertainty which, as you are reading this in September 2020 and beyond, I'm hoping is over.

Introduction

WITH TWO games of the 2019/20 Superliga Argentina season remaining, Boca were three points adrift of their fiercest rivals, River Plate. Marcelo Gallardo was odds-on to lead his team to what would be his 20th title with the club as a player and manager. Even if Boca won both games, River would need just four points from the last six available to be crowned champions.

In the penultimate fixture of the season River were held to a 1-1 draw by Defensa y Justicia. Meanwhile, 500km away in Santa Fe, a rampant Boca destroyed Colón 4-0 with goals from Guillermo *Pol* Fernández, Eduardo Salvio, Carlos Tevez, and Ramón Ábila. The lead was cut to just one point, but the destiny of the title was still in River's hands: they merely needed to match, or better, Boca's result on the final day of the season.

Standing in River's way were Atlético Tucumán, managed by Ricardo Zielinski, the architect of their downfall in 2011 when Belgrano sent them to the second division. Tucumán took the lead on 19 minutes but River pegged them back after 35 minutes through Matías Suárez. With Boca and Gimnasia goalless at La Bombonera, going into the half-time break River retained their one-point lead and were champions as things stood.

Following clever work down the left, the ball fell to Ábila whose outstretched foot prodded the ball in the direction of Tevez who was hovering around the edge of the box. Boca's captain took one touch before rifling the ball straight down the goalkeeper's throat, the power and swerve too much for the Gimnasia custodian to handle. Amidst the deafening noise in La Bombonera, Boca's iconic home since 1940, Tevez rolled back the years, scaling the fence behind the goal that separates the fans and the pitch, a replica of a celebration he performed earlier in his career.

Twenty nervous minutes later, and with no further goals in Tucumán nor Buenos Aires, Boca were champions, something which had seemed so unlikely a week or two earlier. The party spilled out of the stadium and on to the narrow streets of La Boca. As is customary, thousands of fanatics gathered around the Obelisco, a famous landmark in downtown Buenos Aires. A sea of blue-and-gold stopped traffic on the Avenida 9 de Julio, one of the widest thoroughfares in the world and a major artery through Argentina's capital city.

After returning from China to sign for Boca for the third time, Tevez was considered finished by many, yet he was enjoying a new lease of life in 2020. Miguel Ángel Russo, who coached the club to the Copa Libertadores in 2007, was back for his second spell in the hot seat. Before the game Gimnasia coach Diego Maradona was presented with a plaque containing the new replica shirt with 'Maradona 10' printed on the back as the fans in the packed stands sang his name in homage. Seconds before kick-off Tevez planted a good-luck kiss on *El Diego*'s lips and, as events in the 72nd minute showed, the gesture worked. Following the match Maradona was disappointed to be on the losing side but moved and humbled by the tributes in his honour.

In the directors' boxes, the biggest icon in Boca's history, Juan Román Riquelme watched on in his new role as vice-president, attempting to keep a poker face whilst sipping on his yerba mate but cracking a slight smile as the celebrations rumbled on. Riquelme was part of the successful ticket, headed by Jorge Amor Ameal, himself president between 2008 and 2011, which won the elections of December 2019.

Tevez, Russo, Maradona, Riquelme, and Ameal all shared one thing in common: they had left the club and come back in some capacity. Amongst hundreds of other key figures that have been touched by the club throughout its 115-year history, Boca is in their blood. The passion for the blue and gold burns for eternity. It is exactly this passion that I hope to harness in this book.

The journey of Club Atlético Boca Juniors began in 1905 when the club was founded by five boys of Italian stock. Soon, the legend spread beyond the borders of the *barrio*, throughout the capital city, and would later touch all four corners of the Argentine Republic. Today, 69 major titles later, the club is truly global.

The story of Boca's foundation, how the famous colours were adopted, the history of La Bombonera, the iconic players and managers, and the plethora of titles accumulated by the club, are all covered in this book, the most comprehensive English-language chronicle of the club's illustrious history.

My first personal encounter with Argentine football and Boca Juniors came in the 1990s via *Trans World Sport*, a show aired on British TV station Channel 4, which shed light on niche sports and far-flung places in the pre-internet era. Boca Juniors were also an exotic presence on Championship Manager 97/98, a computer game that dominated my teenage years.

In 2001, in what was a groundbreaking transfer, Juan Sebastián Verón joined my local team, Manchester United, from Lazio. Although he is more synonymous with Estudiantes in an Argentine context, many of the first images I saw of him showed him wearing Boca's blue-and-gold jersey rather than the red and white of the outfit from his hometown, La Plata. Although Verón's time at Old Trafford wasn't exactly an unmitigated success, he still had enough charm and flashes of sublime beauty in his play to further heighten the intrigue I felt for Boca Juniors and Argentine football in general.

In August 2004, a year after Verón had departed for Chelsea, Boca visited Old Trafford to take part in the Vodafone Cup, a pre-season tournament also featuring hosts Manchester United, PSV Eindhoven, and Urawa Red Diamonds. Thunderstorms, not atypical of a Manchester summer, caused the Boca match versus the Dutch side to be abandoned, although it still provided me with the chance to see the iconic club in the flesh for the very first time. It was just nine months since Boca had been crowned de facto world champions after beating Milan to lift the Intercontinental Cup.

In the summer of 2008, I made my first trip to South America, with Argentina and La Bombonera on the itinerary. Carlos Tevez had joined Manchester United the year before, and the taxi drivers of Buenos Aires were all up to speed with the transfer, enthusiastically shouting his name when they discovered I was from Manchester. It showed me just how much of a global sport football is.

After disappointing for Barcelona following a 2002 switch, Riquelme had wowed Europe by dragging unfashionable Villarreal to within a spot-kick of the 2006 Champions League Final. He had returned to La Bombonera in 2007 and I couldn't wait to take in a match at the famous amphitheatre, to see the maestro up close and personal, performing for the crowd and conducting his orchestra.

After a stadium tour a few days earlier, we took our seats for the league fixture against Arsenal de Sarandí. It sadly transpired that Riquelme, as well as many of the club's other big hitters, was to be rested with the second leg of the Copa Libertadores semi-final against Brazilian side Fluminense coming up. Boca beat Arsenal 3-1 on a cold but dry wintery night, with a hat-trick from future Wigan Athletic misfit Mauro Boselli, yet the absence of the major stars left me somewhat underwhelmed and with an itch scratch still to.

Three years later, in July 2011, Boca were invited to take part in the Emirates Cup, hosted by Arsenal at their London home. A two-hour train ride south to the capital provided the chance to finally see Riquelme perform, going some way to exorcising the demons from 2008. Also present in the ground were a small number of Boca fans, replete with blue-and-gold umbrellas, who provided much of, if not all, the colour and vibrancy to proceedings. The home side made it 2-0 through Robin van Persie and Aaron Ramsey, yet the stage was set for Riquelme to dazzle. By then in the autumn of his career, Riquelme pulled the strings and created the two goals, converted by Lucas Viatri and Pablo Mouche that salvaged a draw. The nature of both assists encapsulated all that was majestic about Riquelme: moments of genius despite his apparent languid style.

In 2012/13 I lived in Argentina for a year as part of my university degree course. Although I called Córdoba, Argentina's second city, home for the majority of my stay, I flew in and out of the capital, and whilst there made the pilgrimage to La Boca, and of course La Bombonera, on both occasions. La Boca, with the stadium at its heart, is a fully functioning neighbourhood, although some areas form a veritable tourist trap. The traces of the great football club are present on every corner, etched on every wall. Even living in Córdoba, some 700km north-west, Boca Juniors' nationwide appeal was obvious, with each goal scored by Boca cheered by supporters watching the games on TV. The club's *La Mitad Mas Uno* (the majority plus one) slogan is certainly not just empty marketing speak.

It would be disingenuous, and unfair to the millions in Buenos Aires, Argentina, and indeed globally, to call myself a Boca fanatic. Some of the voices within the book live and breathe the club. However, I'm massively drawn to it, enough so to undertake a huge project such as this, which has taken so much of my time and energy but has been a true pleasure. I hope, for those who have been devotees *desde la cuna* (from the cradle), as the popular terrace chant goes, I have done their wonderful club justice.

Chapter One

The Foundation

IT IS impossible to separate the characteristics of modern-day Argentina from the massive wave of immigration that inundated its Atlantic shores in the late 19th and early 20th centuries. Football, the most fervent passion in the country today, is no exception to this rule. Whilst the movement of people dominates much of the current political discourse, it was actively encouraged by the embryonic Argentine government in the early 1800s after it had won independence from the Spanish Empire.

The territory of the new republic grew exponentially with the controversial Conquest of the Desert but, with a sparse indigenous population, the burgeoning economic powerhouse lacked the manpower to work the lands and provide a tax base. Between 1857 and 1930 Argentina received net immigration of 3.5 million people, almost half of which hailed from Italy, many of those from the peninsular escaping the hardships brought on by the Unification.

Many of those Italians searching for a better life ended up in North America, yet a huge number also docked in Buenos Aires. By 1914, as World War I escalated across Europe, it was estimated that 30 per cent of Argentina's population of 7.9 million was foreign-born. Whilst this mass influx of bodies provided the labour needed to drive the economy, it diluted and influenced whatever culture existed. The new arrivals brought with them their traditions – customs, language, and food – creating a unique blend that is still evident to this day.

Argentina's industry in the late 19th century centred on agriculture, the Pampas among the most fertile lands in the world. British capitalists ploughed money into the nascent economy to improve the infrastructure – railroads, docks, warehouses, and public utilities – to boost the industry. Britain was the prime investor in young Argentina, helping to transform the new nation into a Latin American success story. By 1910, British companies all but monopolised Argentina's railways, and this remained the case until President Juan Domingo Perón nationalised the network in 1948.

The British also created institutions of their own – newspapers, English-language schools, hospitals, and businesses – and by 1890 the British contingent in Argentina numbered more than 45,000. British global expansion was far from an altruistic endeavour in nature, yet it did bestow upon Argentina its greatest export: football. One Brit in particular, Alexander Watson Hutton from Glasgow's tough Gorbals district, would have a profound effect on the future of the game in the emerging republic, and soon the new sport would spread like wildfire throughout the docks and *barrios* of Buenos Aires. Football thrived, in part, because it was less dangerous than other sports such as cricket and rugby, and the rules were simpler.

Born in June 1853, Watson Hutton graduated from the University of Edinburgh with a second-class degree in philosophy. However, his real passion lay in physical education, a love for sport brought on by the death of his brothers from tuberculosis. Watson Hutton ventured to Argentina, arriving in 1882, and two years later founded the Buenos Aires English High School (BAEHS), a bilingual institution where sport was a key pillar of the curriculum.

Although football existed in Argentina before his arrival, Watson Hutton formalised the sport. On 12 February 1893 the Scotsman founded the Argentine Association Football League (AAFL), the first organised competition of its kind outside of the British Isles. The teacher entered a BAEHS team for former students into the league in 1898 yet, soon after, school names were banned as it was deemed a form of advertising so, in 1901, the team's name was changed to Alumni Athletic Club.

Whilst Alumni were sweeping all before them in the early years of official organised football, winning ten league titles in 12 years, what would later become known as Argentina's *Cinco Grandes* (Big Five) – Boca Juniors, River Plate, Independiente, Racing Club and San Lorenzo – were established, with immigrants at the heart of their foundation.

After several days of debate in early April 1905, Boca Juniors were founded on the third of the month, on a pleasant autumnal night. Five young men – Esteban Baglietto, Alfredo Scarpati, Santiago Pedro Sana and brothers Teodoro and Juan Antonio Farenga – became the driving forces of the newly established club. The name referenced their *barrio* as well as paying homage to the pervading British influence in the burgeoning Argentine football scene. One of the founding members was also studying English at the time. A bench in Plaza Solís, a small park approximately 12 blocks from Boca's current home, is widely acknowledged as the club's official place of birth.

The colossal iron frame of the Puente Transbordador (transporter bridge) dominates the skyline of La Boca, straddling the Matanza River, also known as the Riachuelo, connecting the city and province of Buenos Aires. The low-income neighbourhood grew due to the influx of immigrants, primarily from Genoa and other northern Italian towns and cities, who crafted dilapidated buildings from wood and sheet metal close to the port. These buildings would later be brightened up using leftover paint from ships, adorned with striking pastel colours which gave La Boca an identity that is still evident today and attracts tourists from all over the world.

Thousands of miles from home, the newly established neighbourhood teams became the immigrants' de facto national team, giving them colours to support and stand behind in the absence of a national flag. The territory of the *barrio* became their new national border to defend, providing a sense of belonging for those detached from their motherland. Instead, identity was forged on the pitch through the universal language of football. The protagonists behind the formation of Boca Juniors shared a distinct Genoese flavour, hence the nickname *Xeneizes*, and were no different.

With Baglietto installed as the club's first president, and even lining up as goalkeeper, Boca participated in their first-ever official game on 21 April 1905. Wearing a white shirt with three vertical black stripes hand-crafted by Manuela Farenga, sister of Teodoro and Juan Antonio, Boca thrashed Mariano Moreno 4-0 on the field of local club Independencia Sud. Scarpati, the club's first official secretary, was responsible for spreading the word about the club within the local community and, to swell the coffers, a membership scheme was created, starting at 50 cents per month with an initial five-peso registration fee.

Until 1908, when Boca joined the Argentine Football Association (AFA), the club participated in minor leagues and friendly matches. Following a 4-0 friendly victory over Ferro Carril Oeste, the club were placed in the second division, where they performed admirably in what was their first official campaign since affiliation. Boca won their group and were only eliminated at the semi-final stage at the hands of eventual champions Racing.

In 1911 Boca participated in the Divisíon Intermedia, a newly created league sandwiched in between the first and second divisions. The club required a last-day victory to stave off relegation. Although Boca finished third in the 1912 Intermedia, the club were promoted to the top flight due to a restructure of the league, which expanded from 6 to 15 teams. Boca more than held their own in the top division, kicking off their campaign on 13 April with a comfortable 4-1 victory over Estudiantil Porteño. The season was most notable, however, for the first-ever official league meeting against River Plate on 24 August at the home of Racing. River, founded in 1901 in La Boca, won 2-1 in a bad-tempered affair.

After years of experimenting, 1913 also saw Boca settle on the shirt design – a gold horizontal stripe across the chest atop a blue background – which the club is now synonymous with. The colour combination was first worn in 1907 when club president Juan Brichetto, who also worked in the docks, was inspired by the passing of the *Drottning Sophia*, a Swedish ship sporting its national flag.

Racing went on to triumph in the 1913 Primera División, their first title signalling a seismic power shift away from the British clubs, such as Alumni, that dominated the early years of Argentine football. Alumni, the poster boys of the early days of the game in the republic, dissolved two years after their final match, beset by financial trouble and other major issues. A year after the AFA had Hispanicised its name, and with the game's rules now written in Spanish, the takeover was complete. Football became *fútbol.* The hegemony of the British clubs was over, and the remaining four members of the Big Five would all go on to win their first titles over the next decade.

Boca moved up to third position in 1914 before dropping down to 14th in 1915, participating in a bloated 25-team league due to the reabsorption of the dissident Argentine Football Federation (FAF) after three years of rupture. In what amounted to a terrible campaign, Boca had to wait until their ninth game for a win and were on the receiving end of some crushing defeats, including 0-6 against Racing and 0-7 versus San Isidro.

Another disappointing term saw Boca finish 13th out of 22 in 1916. After two years based in Wilde, 10km to the south, the club returned to La Boca after membership had plummeted from 1,500 to just 300. For the members, mainly humble Genoese inhabitants of La Boca, Wilde may as well have been the other side of the world. Boca could have genuinely ceased to exist during the wilderness years in Wilde. This showed that the club are part of La Boca, and La Boca is part of Boca Juniors. The two are inextricably linked to this day.

Guillermo Schoua, a 42-year-old collector and statistician who works with the club's history department, and also created the outstanding Historia de Boca website, explains further: 'The remoteness of Wilde caused a significant drop in the number of members, but it was only meant to be a temporary move anyway. There were very few available pitches in La Boca, so the club rented in Wilde knowing they would have to do everything to return.'

Boca put two disappointing campaigns behind them in 1917 by finishing third, losing just two games out of 20. *Los Xeneizes* flew out of the traps and were unbeaten in 15 games until a 1-0 reverse to Racing proved decisive. Boca finished third yet again in 1918 yet trailed a dominant Racing, winning their sixth consecutive title, by 12 points. A 1-0 victory over River, however, on 18 August, brought several years of miserable results in the rivalry to an end. There were wild scenes in La Boca that night.

Two solid campaigns in 1917 and 1918 hinted that Boca, now firmly ensconced back in their neighbourhood, were on the cusp of glory. The year 1919 saw the second major schism in Argentine football. After just eight games, the championship was annulled following a dispute between the association and 13 of its members, who were unhappy with the governance of the game. The dissidents created the Asociación Amateurs de Football (AAmF) and organised a breakaway league; Boca Juniors remained loyal to the AFA, participating in the reorganised championship which kicked off on 28 September.

Boca hit the ground running, opening the season with a 5-1 home win over Porteño. The wins kept on coming and Boca ended the championship with a 100 per cent record, being crowned champions and earning the first star that would later adorn the club's crest. Although not all of the fixtures were fulfilled, and only six teams took part, the tournament was officially recognised and Boca's performances in the coming years proved that the club were one of the best in Argentina.

Alfredo Garasini and Alfredo Martín shared more than just a first name: they scored six goals apiece in the process and were the league's joint top scorers. After emerging from the club's youth ranks, Garasini debuted for the first team in 1916 and the adaptable forward would play numerous positions across the front line. Martín, signed from Tigre in 1918, would ultimately win three championships in the *azul y oro*.

Pedro Calomino, a youth-team product who debuted as far back as 1911, chipped in with five goals in eight games. The tricky winger is thought to have been the man who invented the *bicicleta* (step over) to fool opponents. The 1919 title was the first of four Calomino won with the *boquense* club and amid that fruitful spell he even won the 1921 South American Championship with Argentina. 'The most important player in the early years, the club's first idol, was Pedro Calomino,' stated Guillermo Schoua.

At the other end of the pitch Américo Tesoriere was tasked with keeping opposition forwards at bay. The tall, slim goalkeeper was one of the biggest stars of his era. Despite his elegance, Tesoriere was fearless in attacking the ball and, distinctively, participated in games wearing a grey roll-neck pullover. Tesoriere won 37 caps for Argentina, winning the South American Championship in both 1921 and 1925.

Ahead of the 1920 campaign, eight teams were promoted to the top flight to augment the numbers. The distinct gulf in class between the existing teams and the newcomers, as well as the goals of Pablo Bozzo, allowed Boca to canter to back-to-back title success, losing just once in 24 games in finishing 12 points clear of newly promoted Banfield. In the AAmF league, River Plate claimed their first championship.

Despite losing just three games of the 1921 season, Boca were unable to retain their title and slipped to third amidst severe institutional and economic problems. Key players – including mainstays of the title-winning campaigns such as Tesoriere and Garasini – left before the season had begun, joining the unfancied Sportivo del Norte, who ultimately finished below Boca. Member numbers dropped to 600 and with just three games of the season remaining, Emilio Gagliolo resigned the presidency to be replaced by a temporary emergency commission.

The players who had previously defected to Sportivo del Norte returned, along with the addition of Domingo Tarasconi and Ángel Médici to the playing ranks. Tarasconi, a forward equally at home in the centre or on the right of the pitch, was famed for his long-distance goals and scored a handful shy of 200 in his decade in the *azul y oro*. Despite the new additions, in the 1922 championship Boca failed to improve on the third-place finish from the previous year.

After two relatively quiet years, Boca were back in the title hunt in 1923, dominating the league along with Huracán, the pair finishing a country mile ahead of the rest of the field. A play-off was organised to decide who would be the worthy champion and, after two legs, the sides were one apiece. The third play-off finished 0-0 so a fourth game was arranged, at the home of Sportivo Barracas. Two from the prolific Tarasconi, who scored 39 league goals in just 33 appearances, gave Boca their third title in five years.

Los Xeneizes continued to underline their dominance in 1924, finishing five points clear of nearest challenger Temperley and just one draw away from a 100 per cent record, even without the departed Calomino. Tarasconi was once again ice cold in front of goal for the champions, whilst newcomer Ludovico Bidoglio, a central defender with exquisite technique, provided the class at the other end.

As well as the fourth league championship in six years, 1924 also saw the inauguration of the club's new 20,000-capacity wooden stadium in La Boca. Under the presidency of Manlio Anastasi, the club rented a plot of land penned in by railway tracks on one side, and by the streets Brandsen, Del Crucero (later Dr Del Valle Iberlucea) and Aristóbulo Del Valle. On 6 June the new stadium was opened with a 2-1 win over Nacional from Uruguay, with President of the Nation, Marcelo T. de Alvear and many other prominent figures in the crowd. It was at this location where Boca's *bostero* (a person who handles horse manure) nickname originated, as the new stadium stood next to a factory that created bricks out of horse manure. The new venue became a social hub of the neighbourhood, hosting other activities such as basketball, paleta, boxing, and bowls. Soon the club boasted more than 8,000 *socios* (members).

Having acquired a stadium, and with four championships on the honours board, the club had already made massive strides. However, the events of 1925 would prove pivotal in spreading the name of the club beyond the *barrio*. The story began in September 1923, when three businessmen from Madrid sent a letter to the club, inviting them to embark on a tour of Spain. Football was on the up in Argentina, said the letter, and Boca were deemed the nation's greatest exponents of the beautiful game. Following the gold-medal success of neighbours Uruguay at the 1924 Paris Olympics, the AFA wanted to send an Argentine representative side on a tour of Europe yet failed to reach an agreement. This is where Boca stepped in to fill the void, becoming a de facto national team.

On 13 January 1925 Boca's *Comisíon Directiva* assented to the businessmen's request and finally agreed to embark on the tour, adding matches in France and Germany to the itinerary. The trip would take players away from their families for five months and, more importantly from an economic point of view, their jobs. The concerned players were appeased with an attractive salary of 300 pesos per month for the duration of the tour.

Boca's squad was bolstered by the addition of five guest players from rival teams and the travelling delegation also included Hugo Marini, the head of sports of best-selling daily, *Crítica*. This was a huge development and represented the first time that football matches would be covered by newspapers in such depth. One fan, Victoriano Caffarena, joined the party, paying his own way but also doubling up as the team masseuse and kit man. He was a popular member of the group and was dubbed the *Jugador Número 12* (Twelfth Man) by the players.

The party set sail from Puerto Nuevo in February, receiving a send-off from more than 10,000 people, including fans and players from other clubs. After more than three weeks at sea, the boat completed its transatlantic voyage, and the opening match took place on 5 March. Boca beat Celta Vigo 3-1 then spent almost two months in Spain – also historically beating Real Madrid 1-0 – before moving on to Germany. The tour closed with a 4-2 victory over a Paris XI in the French capital and the overall record was an impressive one: played 19, won 15, drew one, with just three losses.

Throughout the tour Boca were proudly representing not only La Boca, but Buenos Aires and indeed the rest of Argentina. The national anthem was played before each game and news of the tour spread across the country where events were followed keenly. New icons, whose faces adorned the front covers of some of Argentina's most popular daily newspapers, were created. The tour made a huge impact in Argentina and the group returned in July, almost five months after the initial departure, greeted by a multitude of people. Although the club's heart and soul remained firmly in La Boca, it was now a true national passion, from La Quiaca on the Bolivian border in the north, down to Ushuaia in the south; from the peaks of the Andes in the west to the Atlantic coast. The slogan *La Mitad Más Uno* was born on this tour and Boca became the most popular club in Argentina.

Guillermo Schoua is in no doubt about the importance of the trip to Europe: 'It was a tipping point in the history of the club. Boca were already growing, had won their first titles, and, upon finishing the tour, became the most popular club in the country. The tour transcended borders and put Argentine football on the map.' However, even before the tour, Boca were already more popular than River, who had moved out of La Boca in 1923. 'According to the first survey, taken in 1911, Boca already had many more fans than

River and had larger attendances,' said Schoua. 'The tour increased Boca's popularity and River's departure to another neighbourhood ensured their club's survival. They had to find their stage, their fan base.'

The knock-on effect of the tour was that Boca had to give up the chance of defending the title they had won in 1924. With the blessing of the association, the club postponed their league fixtures and planned to play catch-up upon their return. However, they were unable to fulfil the schedule and only managed to complete seven fixtures, resulting in a fourth-from-bottom finish. The AFA bestowed upon the club the title of 'Campeón de Honor 1925' in recognition of the club's efforts to help put Argentine football firmly on the map and rival Uruguay's claim to *rioplatense* supremacy.

Boca's focus was firmly fixed on domestic matters in 1926, and the formidable outfit regained the championship without losing a single game, conceding just four goals in the process with the impenetrable Tesoriere – collecting his fifth championship medal – in goal. Thirty-eight of the club's 67 league goals came from the potent partnership of Tarasconi and new signing Roberto Cherro.

Cherro, who came to the fore at hometown club Sportivo Barracas before moving to Ferro, had to work hard to maintain his playing weight, yet boasted agility and a level of football intelligence that belied his powerful frame. Such was his technical ability, the inside-left was nicknamed *apilador* (dribbler) by Borocotó, the pen name of the leading journalist most known for his writing in the hugely influential Argentine sports magazine *El Gráfico*.

The brightest star of the 1926 season was central-midfielder Mario Fortunato, elected as the league's best player. Sadly, his playing career would be cut short due to a knee injury, with Fortunato hanging up his boots before his 25th birthday. It wouldn't be the end of his journey with Boca.

After eight seasons of division, the two associations merged ahead of the 1927 season. President Alvear assisted in reuniting the two factions, one of the first of many examples of Argentine politicians meddling in football. It was deemed that the national game would be better developed with one single vision and everyone pulling in the same direction.

According to Guillermo Schoua, the fact that Boca's first titles came when many of their rivals were participating in another league in no way waters down the achievement: 'Boca held many records during this time, including the longest unbeaten run and biggest victories, and won various titles. The 1925 tour was the first undertaken by any South American team, including national teams. On the tour the club beat Real Madrid and Atlético, and drew with Bayern Munich. The base of the Argentine national team at this time was made up of Boca players and when the championships were unified the club continued to compete at the top.'

Ahead of the merged 1927 championship, which would feature 34 teams, Boca added Manuel Fleitas Solich, the first Paraguayan to play in Argentina, to the squad. *El Brujo* (The Witch) later became more famous due to his exploits in management where he led Real Madrid and also won three successive league titles with Flamengo in the 1950s, yet in the late 1920s he was a dominant midfielder.

In the 15th round Boca travelled to Lanús, the 2-1 defeat the first *Los Xeneizes* had suffered since March 1924, a run stretching more than three years and 60 matches. Boca bounced back from the disappointment and continued to perform strongly, beating River 1-0 in the last month of the season. Boca ultimately finished one point behind San Lorenzo, proving that the club's recent dominance was no fluke.

The 1928 season provided a real sense of déjà vu for Boca, who once again finished a point behind the champions, this time Huracán. Cherro and Tarasconi were customarily on fire, scoring a combined 61 as Boca racked up a century of goals. A 6-0 home destruction of River, one of the biggest margins in *Superclásico* history, proved symptomatic of the firepower on show, with four goals coming from Cherro's boots alone. Such was Boca's dominance in this particular derby fixture, the match ended early after the River captain had asked the referee for clemency. The home on Calle Brandsen was becoming a veritable fortress and defeat to Talleres in the unlucky 13th round signalled only the first home reverse tasted in 51 games.

A convoluted format awaited the 35 participants of the top flight in 1929, with the teams firstly split into two groups. Boca, minus the departed legend Tesoriere after more than 260 official appearances, and Garasini, winner of five league titles, finished joint top of their group, along with San Lorenzo, who were defeated in a play-off for the right to face Gimnasia in the final. The La Plata outfit were successful and for the third year in succession Boca had to make do with a runners-up spot.

For the first time since the reunification of the organisations Boca won the championship in 1930, finishing five points clear of Estudiantes de La Plata. The almost ever-present duo of Cherro and Tarasconi couldn't be stopped, plundering 64 goals out of Boca's 113 between them. It couldn't be denied that Boca were now Argentina's premier club.

The so-called Roaring Twenties brought unprecedented levels of prosperity to western society, and for Boca Juniors it was no different. The club gleaned six league titles between 1919 and 1930, settled on a location that would be home for at least the following century, and embarked on a pioneering tour of Europe. Despite the looming Great Depression, another seismic change was afoot, one that took the club, and Argentine football as a whole, to a whole other stratosphere.

Chapter Two

La Nuestra 1.0 – The Dawn of Professionalism

IN EARLY May 1931, 18 prominent teams broke away to create the Liga Argentina de Football (LAF), a new, fully professional, competition. Discontent had come to the fore as the previous campaign had stretched to a chaotically disorganised 13 months, not finishing until April 1931. The dissidents were disenchanted with poor governance of the Argentine top flight, as well as the bloated format which saw 36 teams competing for the 1930 championship.

The professionalisation of the game was inevitable as more and more money flooded in. Touring British teams attracted large crowds in the early part of the century and many players wondered why they weren't benefitting from increasing gate receipts. As the sport became more popular, players became aware of their ability to generate income, and international football also made them aware of what they could earn abroad. Under-the-table payments, which had been commonplace for years, were now legitimised.

The new professional league kicked off on 31 May. Boca made a slow start, drawing the opening match 0-0 at home to Chacarita before losing by the odd goal in five in La Plata against Gimnasia. Boca, coached by Mario Fortunato, then won 11 of the next 14 games heading into the first *Superclásico* of the professional era. After an injury forced him into early retirement, Fortunato turned to coaching and had become Boca's manager in 1930 at just 26. Proving age was no barrier, his first of three spells in the Boca hot seat would glean four league titles.

The anticipation for the match was huge, and thousands of fans arrived at Boca's stadium up to five hours before kick-off. River took the lead after 16 minutes through Carlos Peucelle, and 13 minutes later Boca were awarded a hotly disputed penalty. Jorge Iribarren, the River goalkeeper, was adjudged to have fouled recently arrived Francisco *Pancho* Varallo, Boca's first major signing of the professional era. The 21-year-old forward saw his spot-kick saved but managed to finish the rebound to equalise. Boca had been able to entice Varallo, who won the league with Gimnasia in 1929, with a salary ten times higher than the one he earned in La Plata, a real flex of the muscles and a show of the financial clout the bigger clubs now enjoyed.

River's players took offence at the penalty decision and three were dismissed due to their overly vehement protests. The match was later abandoned and Boca were awarded a 1-0 win by the AFA. Police entered the pitch on horseback to quell the simmering resentment, and supporters clashed inside the stadium as well as on the streets of La Boca.

The third-to-last fixture of the season, a 4-1 mauling away to Estudiantes, proved to be the last action of Ludovico Bidoglio's distinguished career. After just 23 minutes of the defeat, the ball-playing central defender was seriously injured in a clash with a rival forward and was unable to recover from his injuries. He retired having won five league titles – four as an amateur and one as a professional – in the blue-and-gold shirt.

Boca sealed the title in the penultimate game of the season, and in doing so created history by securing back-to-back titles; the last champion of the amateur age was now the first of the professional era, a unique *bicampeonato*. The final fixture of the season proved to be the cherry on the icing on the cake. A 3-0 win away to River, on Three Kings' Day 1932, ensured Boca completed the double over their rivals and finished five points ahead of second-place San Lorenzo.

Varallo continued to plunder countless goals in 1932 – now alongside Paraguayan forward Delfín Benítez Cáceres in the wake of Domingo Tarasconi's retirement – but Boca were unable to retain their title and finished fourth. In a keenly fought race, Boca won the last five games, including a 2-1 victory over River, to finish with a bang but ultimately it wasn't enough.

Despite Varallo's 34-goal haul in 1933 and a ten-game winning streak at one point during the season, Boca finished second, one point behind San Lorenzo. River gained a modicum of revenge for 1932, beating Boca 3-1 on the final day of the season. It seemed that clashes between the two super-rivals were decisive each time they met, with no margin for error.

Club historian Guillermo Schoua believes that the dawn of the professional era only served to heighten the rivalry between Boca and River. 'Undoubtedly, being neighbours in La Boca in the early years, the clubs and their fans would face each other on the local pitches and around the neighbourhood,' he began. 'There were already jokes made at each other's expense and discussions around who was the best, and this was enhanced by the birth of professionalism. Besides, each club began to represent a distinct audience: Boca were the popular club of the masses; River, more elite.'

Ernesto Lazzatti made his first-team debut as an 18-year-old in the third match of the 1934 campaign. The technically refined central-midfielder arrived as a relative unknown yet would last more than 13 years at the club and become an idol. The youngster, fondly known as *El Pibe de Oro* (The Golden Boy), enjoyed a solid campaign, featuring in 37 of the 39 fixtures as a rampant Boca won the league one point ahead of Independiente. Fortunato's men plundered 101 goals, with 60 of them coming from the trio of Benítez Cáceres, Roberto Cherro, and Varallo. Vicente Cusatti, promoted from the youth team, played more games than anyone else, bagging 14 goals of his own in the process.

After four years of running side by side, the LAF merged with the AFA's official competition ahead of the 1935 season. Argentine football was united once again, the latest schism over. Boca retained their title, finishing three points clear of Independiente, and in winning the title became the first *bicampeón* of the professional era. The back-to-back champions retained their ruthlessness in attack, scoring 98 goals, almost half of which came from Varallo and the prolific left foot of Benítez Cáceres.

The great 1935 side was also built on a foundation of rock, the defence conceding just 31 goals. Much of this new-found solidity was owed to 23-year-old Brazilian international Domingos da Guia who debuted on 17 March 1935 and improved the backline dramatically. In his three years in Buenos Aires, the Rio native proved himself to be a composed, elegant and stylish defender with impeccable timing in the tackle.

In winning the championship with Boca the intelligent defender completed an impressive treble, having won titles in Uruguay (Nacional, 1933) and Brazil (Vasco da Gama, 1934). Upon returning to his homeland he would go on to win three more with Flamengo. Juan Yüstrich, a goalkeeper from Swiss-German stock, was another key figure tasked with maintaining Boca's stingy defence and was the first man between the sticks since Tesoriere that the club could truly rely on.

The 1936 calendar was split into two separate championships: the Copa Campeonato and the Copa de Honor. Boca finished third and fifth respectively. Despite notching another century of goals in the 1937 league campaign – which had returned to a long format and now featured relegation and promotion – Boca finished third, 13 points behind champions River Plate.

The 1938 season proved to be one of transition for Boca, who finished fifth, 18 points behind Independiente. More than 12 years after debuting for the club, Roberto Cherro played his last competitive match for *Los Xeneizes*, unfittingly being dismissed for dissent in a 2-1 defeat to Racing in September. His marching orders were given by Isaac Caswell, a local politician from Blackburn, Lancashire, who was the first in an AFA experiment to utilise English referees to instil law and order on Argentine football pitches. The fans showed their displeasure by pelting him with missiles as he left the pitch. Cherro left the club having won five league titles – two in the amateur era, three as a professional – and having become the club's leading scorer of all time with 218 official goals, a record that stood for more than 70 years. The forward was a fine example of a player who straddled the two distinct eras, excelling in both.

The 1938 campaign was also the last for free-scoring Paraguayan Delfín Benítez Cáceres who was inexplicably allowed to join Racing. Nicknamed *Machetero,* for his ability to slice through defences, the adaptable forward was the first foreigner to hit a century of goals for Boca and continued to find the net after his departure. In hindsight, he was allowed to leave too early.

Aside from the first home game of the season – which Boca lost to River, 2-1 – the club played all their home games at Ferro's ground whilst having their own new stadium constructed. Boca finished sixth in 1939, 16 points behind Independiente who were crowned champions once again. With the departure of Cherro and Benítez Cáceres, Boca were lacking a real goalscorer and not one member of the squad managed to break the double-figure barrier. The team scored, on average, just 1.9 goals per game, a far cry from when the side were clocking up centuries of goals in pursuit of glory.

The end of the season saw the departure of another beloved star, who had come to define Boca in the 1930s. Varallo retired aged 29 due to a knee injury after years of thrashing the heavy footballs of the day, his ferocious power earning him the nickname, *Cañoncito*. The forward was second only to Cherro in terms of goals scored for Boca, and the highest scorer in the professional era until his record was surpassed by Martín Palermo. He coached the club's youth teams for a few years after hanging up his boots and in 1994 Varallo received a FIFA Order of Merit award. When he died aged 100, in August 2010, he was the last surviving player from the first World Cup, in 1930.

In 1936 Alexander Watson Hutton, the father of Argentine football, died and was laid to rest in the British Cemetery in Chacarita, passing away just as the game he had helped build was taking root. Between September 1936 and April 1938 there wasn't a single goalless draw in the Argentine top flight and the attacking football on display drew large crowds to the stadiums. The expansion of the Subte, Buenos Aires' underground metro system, allowed *porteños* to travel across the city with greater ease; increased coverage from radio and the printed press shone a brighter spotlight on Argentine football. Despite the hangover from the Great Depression, the 1930 military coup, and the so-called *Década Infame* that followed, the sport thrived.

Guillermo Schoua helped to explain: 'Argentine football went through a major popular expansion, although the economic conditions for a lot of the clubs, and the country itself, weren't great. Being such a massive activity, which was accessible to people from every social class, it was able to grow with great enthusiasm.'

After moving into the professional era, football proved to be recession-proof and, for many, acted as a release from the harsh realities of daily life. The government, well aware of this growing phenomenon's ability to act as an opium for the masses, backed football clubs in the form of soft loans, which were used to construct durable concrete stadiums, many of which still stand today. The money coming into football changed everything: the sport ceased to be a hobby and became a job.

The dawn of professionalism created a gulf between the so-called Big Five and the rest, and it would take 36 years in the new era for a team to break their hegemony and win an Argentine title. The *Cinco Grandes* were able to offer bigger salaries due to their larger income from attendances, and the extended coverage of the sport in the media spread the news of their exploits nationwide. River earned their nickname, *Los Millonarios*, during this era not just for the move to the plush suburbs, but also for splashing the cash on expensive acquisitions such as Bernabé Ferreyra who joined in 1932 for a world-record fee. In 1937 the Big Five solidified their power when it was declared that the clubs with the most *socios*, money, and length of time in the top flight would have more sway with the AFA. An uneven ecosystem emerged: the clubs from the interior were at the bottom of the food chain whereas the big clubs from Buenos Aires were the kings of the jungle.

Boca, who had 25,000 *socios* by the mid-30s, picked up where they had left off in the amateur era by winning three of the first five professional titles. However, as the decade came to a close the club had gone four years without a league championship, was lodging with Ferro, and was shorn of stars following the departure of several key figures behind the success of the 1930s.

In 1940 Boca flexed their muscles and signed three players – Jaime Sarlanga, Bernardo Gandulla, and Raúl Emeal – from Ferro Carril Oeste. The arrival of the trio, part of a fearsome forward line known as *La Pandilla* (The Gang), showed the power of the *grandes* who were able to pluck the best players from the *equipos chicos* (smaller teams) seemingly at will. Despite the new signings Boca garnered just 11 points from the first available 16.

In late May 1940, they moved into their new stadium. The increasing popularity of football in Argentina had rendered the old wooden stadia unfit for purpose during the 1930s. Cash from gate receipts was king and it was therefore vital that Boca developed a ground that could cope with the growing demand of fans wanting to see Argentina's most popular club. It was also vital for Boca to keep pace with rivals River Plate, who inaugurated their stadium, El Monumental, two years earlier.

The first stone was laid for what would become Boca's home on 18 February 1938, under the presidency of Dr Camilo Cichero. The construction of the new stadium was facilitated by President of the Nation Agustín Pedro Justo, who had taken office in February 1932 and who, as a confirmed fan of Boca Juniors, provided the club with a favourable AR$1.6m loan which allowed construction to begin.

The brains behind the design of Boca's new stadium came from the architecture studio headed by Slovenian Viktor Sulcic, Raúl Bes, and José Luís Delpini, who had already built the iconic Mercado de Abasto earlier in the decade. Twenty-six steps were to take players from the changing rooms in the depths of the stadium, meaning the first thing they would see when ascending to the pitch were the heavens above. The design was formed by the lack of space in the neighbourhood, and with the stands rising almost vertically out of the ground and stacked on top of each other, the stadium acquired the nickname *La Bombonera* (The Chocolate Box). The claustrophobic nature of the stadium would directly influence the club's traditional style of play, which is built around hard work and sacrifice.

The stadium was opened on 25 May 1940, for a 2-0 friendly win against fellow *grande* San Lorenzo. Just hours after the match, Juan Brichetto, one of the key figures in the club's early years, passed away.

After a couple of years on the road during the construction process, Boca were finally home. In the first official match, Newell's Old Boys were easily dispatched 2-0, the new home providing a boost after an uninspiring start to the season. Boca won all of their remaining 12 home fixtures, scoring 40 goals in the process. The scintillating run included a 3-1 victory over River, a win that sent Boca to the top of the league. The final table underlined Boca's dominance over the rest of the field: runners-up Independiente were eight points behind. Sarlanga, in his debut season, was the club's top scorer with 24 goals. Juan Alberto Estrada proved a solid presence in goal and formed part of the best defence in the league which conceded just 1.06 per game.

For Guillermo Schoua, the new stadium was crucial not only in terms of the 1940 championship but also in the club's development: 'La Bombonera was, and is, one of the key pillars of *Boquense* identity and is a temple of world football. It was essential in 1940 and Boca won all of their home games after the inauguration. It has been the scene of many great feats over the years, creating memories and strong feelings for the fans.'

Boca won two and drew two of the first four fixtures of 1941, and in matchday five defeated Banfield in a 4-3 thriller. Aside from a multitude of goals, the fixture saw the debut of Carlos *Lucho* Sosa. Having arrived from Atlanta in exchange for AR$25,000 – three players also went the other way and a friendly was arranged between the buying and selling club – Sosa would go on to cement his reputation as one of Argentina's greatest-ever right-halves in his decade at Boca.

The technician was adept at defending resolutely and, going forward, started many attacks and crossed with pinpoint accuracy for his colleagues to score. A fighting spirit characterised many of the teams of the 1940s but the naturally elegant Sosa proved to be one of the exceptions to this rule. The classy Sosa would develop a wonderful understanding with a youngster from the club's famed youth ranks, Mario Boyé, who made his debut in a 2-1 victory away to Independiente. The match was settled by a Sarlanga double and ended a four-match streak without a victory.

Ultimately, however, Boca were unable to retain their title and finished fourth, ceding domestic supremacy to rivals River Plate. In the penultimate fixture of the campaign, *Los Millonarios* destroyed Boca 5-1, with three of the goalscorers that day – Ángel Labruna, José Manuel Moreno, and Adolfo Pedernera – forming the core of a side that would famously become known as *La Máquina*.

The 1942 season proved to be another of transition as Boca finished fifth, despite recording a mammoth 11-1 win over Tigre, who were later relegated, in front of a rain-drenched crowd at La Bombonera. River sealed their second consecutive title at the home of Boca in the third-to-last match of the campaign, forcing the home fans to endure the ignominy of their rivals performing a lap of honour in front of their eyes. At one point Boca were leading the match 2-1 but, with closest challengers San Lorenzo losing, Pedernera's 81st-minute equaliser effectively sealed the title for River.

Proving the fallibility of River's machine, Boca regained the title in 1943. River drew first blood in the race for the championship, beating Boca 3-1 at El Monumental in May, a defeat which Boca avenged four months later in the return fixture. Félix Loustau opened the scoring for River in La Bombonera after just 12 minutes before Severino Varela drew the sides level with one of the most famous goals in the history of the rivalry.

Varela flung himself at a Sosa free kick to inexplicably head the ball into the back of the net just as it appeared it would go out of play. Such was the absurdity of the goal, which left the River defence dumbfounded, *Crónica* dubbed it the *golazo del misterio* (mystery goal). Varela scored his second of the game on 48 minutes and sealed a crucial victory which sent Boca to the top of the table and set up wild celebrations.

Varela, a Uruguayan forward who distinctively played sporting a white beret, was almost 30 when he joined the club from Peñarol, with whom he had already won four league titles. Due to his age, many prematurely predicted that he wouldn't have the physical capabilities, yet his 46 goals in three seasons proved the doubters wrong. Living almost a double life, Varela retained his day job in his native Montevideo, returning to Uruguay by boat on a Sunday evening after games and working during the week before returning to wow the Boca faithful at the weekend.

Legend has it that the club offered Varela a blank cheque in 1945 in an attempt to retain his services but he refused, humbly admitting that his body hurt too much after matches and that he didn't want to defraud anyone. The Uruguayan solidified his legendary status primarily due to his stellar performances against River and, such was his affection for the club, he even offered to play for free during the institutional problems of 1949.

Going into the last day of the 1943 season, Boca led the table by one point and only Ferro stood in their way. After 79 minutes, with Boca goalless and River winning, the two superpowers were tied on points. Step forward Jaime Sarlanga. The league's most potent marksman gave Boca the lead following an assist from Varela, before confirming the victory, and the championship, on 85 minutes.

Boca became *bicampeón* once again in 1944, retaining their title after another pulsating battle with their great rivals. The architect of the back-to-back success was Alfredo Garasini, a man who would bleed blue-and-gold if he were cut in half. In 12 years as a player, Garasini selflessly represented Boca in pretty much every position on the pitch. As a manager, he built his side around a solid defence – at the heart of which was goalkeeper Claudio Vacca – which gave a platform for a fearsome attacking force. Garasini died in 1950 whilst still employed by the club, literally giving his life for Boca.

In what was becoming somewhat of a duopoly, Boca and River went head to head once again in 1945. The first meeting, at El Monumental, saw the home side record a 1-0 victory with Boca performing well despite missing key performers such as Sosa, Lazzatti and Sarlanga. Going into the return fixture, Boca found themselves four points behind their rivals with just six to play for, needing to win at La Bombonera to keep their hopes alive. A brace from top scorer Boyé, nicknamed *El Atómico,* helped *Los Xeneizes* to an emphatic 4-1 victory. In early August, during the final year of World War II, the United States dropped nuclear bombs which decimated the Japanese cities of Hiroshima and Nagasaki and the sobriquet was a nod to Boyé's power and potency with his head and, in particular, his right foot.

Boca were unable to capitalise on their morale-boosting win, following it up with a 2-0 defeat away to Rosario Central and a 2-2 draw with Atlanta at La Bombonera. The title ultimately went to the men from Nuñez. Boca finished second in both of the following two seasons, firstly to San Lorenzo and then to River Plate once again.

Boca started the 1948 season in dreadful form, winning just two of the first ten fixtures. The side was deprived of one of its best players from recent years, Ernesto Lazzatti. The central-midfielder, who left after 13 years, had formed an excellent trio with Sosa and Natalio *El Leoncito* Pescia, who made his debut in 1942.

Lazzatti played maturely as a youngster yet retained his physical attributes in the latter stages of his career, and made 379 official appearances for Boca. Having won five league titles with the club, he joined Danubio, unwilling to represent an Argentine rival, although his departure wasn't befitting of his trajectory with the club. The board decided not to renew his contract, citing a chronic knee injury, although this was refuted by the doctor who performed the surgery. Lazzatti played on for two years in Uruguay without problems.

Two years earlier, in June 1946, Juan Domingo Perón, who came to prominence in the coup d'état of 1943, had been democratically elected as the president of Argentina. On the ticket of the Partido Laborista (Labour Party), Perón galvanised the working class through his policies. Although footballers were professional by the time his tenure at the Casa Rosada began, they still sought better conditions including higher wages and freedom of movement.

In mid-1948 a strike was called by Futbolistas Argentinos Agremiados (FAA), a players' union founded in November 1944. In Colombia, meanwhile, a professional league, operating independently of FIFA's rules and regulations, was born. The teams were able to pluck players from around the continent without paying transfer fees and, as a result, were able to offer exorbitant salaries. In what amounted to a huge talent drain, more than 60 players left the Argentine league and headed north to the so-called Gateway of South America.

Perón's arrival on the political scene, and the subsequent strike, had a direct and profound impact on Argentine football, and Boca Juniors. 'It was very serious for Argentine football in general as, from that moment, the game's important figures went abroad and the fans stopped going to the stadiums,' explained Guillermo Schoua. 'For Boca, the change of players generated many problems; the 1949 campaign left the club genuinely on the verge of relegation for the only time in its history.'

As the strike rumbled on, most teams fielded youngsters, foreigners, and players crossing the picket line. Throughout the 1948 season Boca used almost 40 players in 30 fixtures. Julio Luis Benavídez's men finished eighth out of 15 teams, their worst classification of the professional era thus far. It was about to get much worse.

Boca were forced to contest the 1949 championship without several key players who had formed the backbone of the side for years: Mario Boyé, the club's leading scorer for four consecutive seasons, played just four games before heading to Genoa, ironically Boca's spiritual home; Jaime Sarlanga departed after almost a decade and 200 goals in the *azul y oro*; and the hardworking Pío Sixto Corcuera also left before the competitive football got underway.

Renato Cesarini, who had both played for and managed River Plate, started the season in the La Bombonera hot seat. His side won just three of the first 17 games in a season that didn't start until late April, a delay caused by the strike. Within weeks Cesarini was gone, replaced by Franz Platko.

In mid-November, the relegation-threatened Boca recorded a morale-boosting 2-0 victory over River at La Bombonera, yet followed it up with four successive defeats.

Going into the last game of the season, Huracán propped up the table with 24 points. Boca had 25, with both Tigre and Lanús on 26 points. With their fate in their own hands, Boca hosted Lanús on the final day, also knowing that defeat, and quite possibly even a draw, would result in relegation to the second division. It was a must-win game, and *Los Xeneizes* duly responded, crushing the visitors 5-1 to avoid the drop by the skin of their teeth.

As the union and football authorities fought on, more players headed to Colombia. By 1951 there were 133 Argentine players in Colombia, a huge number which massively diluted the quality of the domestic league. The 'El Dorado' era declined in the mid-1950s after FIFA and the Colombian league reached an agreement after a long stand-off. Subsequently, many Argentine players headed home.

Thirty-seven players, many of whom struggled to perform with the weight of expectation of playing for Argentina's biggest club, were used by the two managers during 1949. Youngsters were thrown to the wolves when more experienced players were low on confidence. Racing won their first title for 24 years. For Guillermo Schoua, it was the worst year in the first 50 years of the club's history. 'In the early years there were bad campaigns, of course, but that is expected when a club is growing little by little,' he began. 'By the 1940s the club was fully consolidated, its greatness and popularity undisputable. However, the strike, and various institutional problems, generated these complicated seasons towards the end of the decade.'

The first 20 years of the professional game saw great development, but also suffering. Against the backdrop of the Great Depression, and later World War II, Argentine football thrived and Boca cemented their position as the biggest club in the country. Six league titles were won either side of the opening of the stadium on Calle Brandsen that would become home. However, the lows of 1948 and 1949 were fresh in the memory and, going into the following decade, Boca had gone almost six years without a title, desperately needing to bounce back from the worst season in the club's history.

Chapter Three

The 1950s

AFTER THE terrible end to the 1940s, the only way was up as Boca entered a new decade hoping for a fresh start. Remarkably, a year after almost suffering relegation, *Los Xeneizes* finished second in the 1950 table, albeit eight points behind Racing, who retained their title. Halfway through the season, the club said goodbye to a retiring legend: José Manuel Marante. After a rapid rise through the youth ranks, the defender made his debut as far back as 1934 and won eight titles – including five league championships – in his 16 years at the club.

In 1951 Boca finished sixth, despite having the third-best defence which conceded just one more than Racing, who won their third consecutive championship. The issue was at the other end of the pitch: only three teams scored fewer goals than Boca over the 32-game schedule. River were crowned champions in 1952. A poor Boca side, once again hamstrung by an inability to find the back of the net despite a solid defence, finished tenth in the table.

The performance in 1953 represented a slight improvement as Boca moved up to seventh in the final standings. The highlight of an otherwise mediocre campaign came in round 12, with a thrilling 3-2 victory over eventual champions River Plate at El Monumental. With just seven minutes remaining, River led 2-1, although it could have been more had the agile Julio Elías Musimessi not saved a 38th-minute penalty. The Chaco native, who acquired the nickname *Arquero Cantor* (Singing Goalkeeper) due to his performances on the radio, signed from Newell's after almost a decade with the Rosario outfit. Within the space of four late minutes, goals from Juan Carlos Navarro and Roberto Rolando gave Jorge Orth's men a memorable victory.

Despite closing in on a decade without a league title, the popularity of the club showed no sign of abating. A campaign to increase the number of *socios* was initiated, with the numbers swelling from 30,000 to 44,000. To accommodate the demand, an extra tier was added to the stadium; floodlights were introduced to facilitate night matches.

The expanded capacity of the new-look La Bombonera generated increased levels of gate receipts and provided Boca with a spending power which belied their current performance on the pitch. It allowed the club to sign Eliseo Mouriño from Banfield for AR$1.2m, a record transfer fee for Argentine football. At the time many observers were surprised that such a vast sum was outlaid on a player known more for his defensive, rather than offensive, qualities, yet it was necessary as Boca had been unable to replace Ernesto Lazzatti since his departure in 1948.

Lazzatti, who played more than 500 games in the *azul y oro* and was part of the last title-winning squad in 1944, returned for his second spell as manager. The former number five had previously guided Boca to a second-place finish in 1950 and was now hoping to go one better. Lazzatti's side won 12 of their first 16 games, one of the four reverses a 1-0 home defeat to River.

In round 17 Boca suffered another defeat, 3-1 at Independiente. It was a forgettable result for the side from La Boca yet proved to be a landmark as the most attended match in Argentine football history: 62,000 tickets were sold but it was thought that more than 80,000 were squeezed into the Avellaneda outfit's La Doble Visera stadium. This year was also the peak for average attendances which stood at just over 15,000, up from 10,221 in 1941 and 6,552 in 1931, the first year of professionalism. The construction of concrete stadiums, much safer than their wooden predecessors, facilitated the larger crowds as more people were seeking out leisure activities such as football.

In the third-to-last fixture, Boca were soundly beaten 3-0 in El Monumental, River completing a league double over their rivals. Yet in the very next game, Lazzatti's men put the derby disappointment firmly behind them. Tigre visited La Bombonera in the penultimate round, with 29,300 expectant *Bosteros* in attendance. Minutes before the half-time break Miguel Ángel Baiocco scored the only goal of the game and when English referee Harry Hartles blew his whistle for the final time Boca were champions once again.

Lazzatti, the player, had been a key figure in the 1944 championship and now, as a manager, led the club to the league title after ten years of anguish. His side conceded an average of just 0.87 goals per game and scored 60 in 30 fixtures. Lazzatti was an excellent man-manager and the players fought tooth and nail for him.

The final fixture of the season, away to Gimnasia in La Plata, was a real exhibition of attacking football, the Boca players enjoying being let off the leash now that the title was in the bag. Four of the goals in the 7-1 destruction were scored by José Borello, who had signed for the club in 1951 but had just returned following a loan spell at Chacarita. The man from Bahía Blanca, who came through at local club Olimpo, bagged 19 in the campaign and was the league's leading marksman. The good-looking number nine could prise open stubborn defences and was renowned for his strong shots and powerful headers. Borello's goals were crucial in Boca topping the final league table, four points ahead of nearest rivals Independiente.

Lazzatti left the club at the end of 1954, deciding not to renew his contract after a fallout with Alberto J. Armando. The new president wanted to put a stamp on his reign by signing costly players but Lazzatti deemed them unnecessary. The man who replaced Lazzatti in the dugout was yet another former player – Jaime Sarlanga – who had scored 129 official goals for the club in the previous decade, although he failed to enjoy the same success as a manager and only lasted 30 games.

Despite being the club's 50th anniversary, there was little to celebrate in the *cincuentenario* year. River won the league, finishing eight points ahead of third-place Boca, and were able to rub salt into the wounds with a 2-1 victory at La Bombonera in the penultimate round of the championship.

Mario Fortunato returned to the dugout once again in 1956, 26 years after he had started his first managerial stint which had gleaned four league titles. In round 17 of the championship River visited La Bombonera, and Fortunato handed a debut to 19-year-old youth-team product Antonio Ubaldo Rattín. The towering 6ft 3in defensive-midfielder was tasked with man-marking River legend Ángel Labruna, who was still dangerous despite his advancing years. Rattín kept Labruna quiet and received a standing ovation from the crowd as Boca won 2-1. River, however, had the last laugh and won the title, finishing two points ahead of Lanús and three clear of Fortunato's men.

At the season's end, Natalio Pescia, a symbol of the club who straddled two eras and fought valiantly for every ball in his 15 years wearing the famous blue-and-gold shirt, retired. In winning the 1943 and 1944 championships Pescia formed a midfield trio with Lazzatti and Carlos Sosa; in 1954 he remained a constant, captaining the team whilst combining superbly with Mouriño and Juan Francisco Lombardo. The one-club man departed with 500 games under his belt, and a section of the stand behind one of the goals is now named in his honour.

Boca finished fourth in 1957 and watched River secure their third title in a row. If goalscoring was an issue in 1957 it certainly wasn't the case the following season: in the 1958 championship Boca scored 70 goals in 30 games, one more than eventual champions Racing. Ángel Osvaldo Nardiello, signed from Newell's two years earlier, was the top scorer with 21 goals in 29 appearances. José Borello, another player who was no stranger to finding the back of the net, ended his association with Boca at the end of the season.

In 1959 Boca recorded a memorable double over River, destroying their rivals 5-1 at La Bombonera and coming back from two goals down to win 3-2 at El Monumental. The two victories were the high points of a season in which Boca finished eighth, nine points off the basement, and 15 behind champions San Lorenzo.

As the club entered the 1960s Alberto Armando returned as president, following his 18-month stint in the mid-1950s. The 49-year-old from Santa Fe had his first spell cut short when Perón – to whom Armando dedicated the 1954 title – was overthrown in a military coup in late 1955, the second of six Argentina would suffer in the 20th century. Armando's second spell as president would produce much success and longevity.

The Armando regime invested heavily to bolster the playing squad. Silvio Marzolini and Antonio Roma arrived from Ferro and Brazilian Paulo Valentim from Botafogo.

The latter signing, plus a Peruvian and two Uruguayans, was part of the *Fútbol Espectáculo* campaign to bring fans back to the stadiums following Argentina's disastrous showing at the 1958 World Cup that did so much to damage the reputation of the country's football. It was deemed that exotic foreign signings would reinvigorate the league.

With former player Carlos Sosa in the dugout, Boca kicked off the 1960 season with a 2-1 win in La Plata over Estudiantes. After three consecutive goalless stalemates in May, Boca and Huracán shared a 2-2 draw at La Bombonera, Valentim scoring his first goal in the *azul y oro*. The Brazilian had come to the attention of Boca playing alongside Pelé at the 1959 South American Championships, in which he scored five goals in as many games.

A 3-1 reverse away to Rosario Central in round 12 proved to be Eliseo Mouriño's last appearance for the club. The midfielder, who was converted into a defender in the autumn of his career, played the game with a clean and gentlemanly spirit. The one league title he won with Boca, in 1954, contradicted his talents and, tragically, he died in a plane crash less than a year after departing La Bombonera. Boca ultimately finished fifth in 1960 as Independiente lifted the title.

An inconsistent 1961 saw Boca finish fifth once again as Racing won the championship to ensure the title remained in Avellaneda. Vicente Feola, who had overseen Brazil's triumph at the 1958 World Cup, was hired by Armando and led his troops to some memorable victories in *clásicos* against Independiente, San Lorenzo and River, playing an adventurous 4-2-4 formation. Yet these results were juxtaposed against inexplicable defeats, most notably a 1-0 home loss to bottom club Los Andes, and his team finished in fifth position.

Feola lasted just one season but laid the foundation for his successor to build on. José D'Amico, who was the club's fitness coach under the Brazilian and managed the team on a caretaker basis in 1960 following Carlos Sosa's departure, stepped into the breach. Carmelo Simeone and Norberto Menéndez, acquired from Vélez and Huracán respectively, were amongst eight new signings.

D'Amico's side were unbeaten after 13 games before succumbing to defeat at El Monumental. Valentim put Boca ahead but River scored three second-half goals to take the points. Boca bounced back well, losing just two of the next 13 in the lead-up to the return fixture against River, the two rivals neck and neck through the campaign.

The historic rematch at La Bombonera, the penultimate fixture of the championship, boiled down to two penalty kicks. After 14 minutes Valentim stepped up to face Amadeo Carrizo. The legendary River goalkeeper, who passed away in March 2020, dived to his left, with the Brazilian forward slamming his penalty into the opposite bottom corner. Advantage Boca.

With just ten minutes remaining, River were awarded a penalty of their own. Delém, who joined *Los Millonarios* from Vasco da Gama in 1961, was hoping to emulate his compatriot by scoring from 12 yards in the very same goal at the Aristóbulo del Valle end of the stadium. River's Brazilian forward put the ball in the same corner as Valentim yet Roma guessed correctly, taking a few steps off his line before diving heroically to his right and pushing the penalty wide.

Roma's team-mates rushed towards him, the match-winning save celebrated on the pitch and in the stands as enthusiastically as any goal would be. The emotional victory, on a hot and sticky summer night in Buenos Aires, gave Boca a vital two-point lead over their rivals going into the final fixture. The pitch invasion showed how much importance the fans gave to the result.

Estudiantes were brushed aside 4-0 at La Bombonera, Valentim scoring the only goal of the first half to give Boca the lead going into the break. Just after the restart Menéndez doubled the lead before Héctor Pueblas made it three. After 78 minutes Valentim – Boca's leading scorer for the third consecutive year – grabbed his second, his 19th of the season, to complete the scoring and wrap up the title for Boca.

Marzolini and Alberto González were two of just three players – the other being Brazilian Orlando Pecanha de Carvalho – to feature in all 28 fixtures of the championship, the duo developing an excellent understanding down Boca's left-hand side. With his blond hair and blue eyes, Marzolini was one of the first heartthrobs of Argentine football and became one of its finest full-backs. González, signed from Atlanta, played wide but tended to drift inside, allowing Marzolini to bomb forward, overlap, and exploit the space, which he did time and again to great effect.

The much-welcomed 1962 title triumph ended Boca's eight-year drought and was just the second domestic championship in 18 seasons. Despite the lack of relative success during this period, an inordinate number of idols wrote their history with the club, and the following season would create even more, as Boca ventured into the uncharted waters of the Copa Libertadores for the very first time.

Chapter Four

The Swinging 60s – The Birth of the Copa Libertadores

AT THE dawn of the 1960s, foreign competition was hardly an alien concept. In November 1872 Scotland had hosted England in what is regarded as the first-ever official international football match and, in 1901, Argentina faced Uruguay in the first international to be held outside the British Isles. FIFA, world football's governing body, was founded in 1904 and, during the same year, Southampton FC embarked on a tour of Argentina and Uruguay.

In 1904 the Argentine and Uruguayan winners of each country's respective Copa Competencia also faced off for the first time. The first edition of the Copa Aldao, another competition which pitted Argentina and Uruguay's best against one another, kicked off in 1913. The first final was postponed due to rain and the silverware was only lifted for the first time, by Nacional, in 1916. Racing won the next two editions before Nacional defeated Boca Juniors in both 1919 and 1920. From thereon in the cup, for a variety of reasons, was scheduled irregularly.

On 28 December 1940 Boca Juniors faced Nacional. Raúl Emeal gave Boca the lead in the Estadio Centenario after 19 minutes but the Uruguayans equalised just before half-time. Boca took the lead once again on 82 minutes through Bernardo Gandulla and looked set to escape Montevideo with a classic victory until García completed his double to make it 2-2.

The Argentine contingent claimed that the equaliser came outside the allotted 90 minutes and protested to the referee, who expelled forward Pedro Suárez as well as coach Enrique Sobral. Boca promptly left the field in protest and the match was abandoned. In the aftermath Nacional were declared victors and awarded the trophy but, following an agreement between the Argentine and Uruguayan federations, the decision was revoked and the match was effectively expunged from the records.

In February and March 1948, the Chilean capital, Santiago, hosted the Campeonato Sudamericano de Campeones. The tournament, the brainchild of Colo Colo director Robinson Álvarez Marín, was facilitated by Luis Valenzuela, the Chilean president of Conmebol, South American football's governing body. The competition, the first of its kind in South America, featured the crème de la crème from Argentina, Bolivia, Brazil, Chile, Ecuador, Peru, and Uruguay. Although the round-robin format deprived fans of a definitive final, in Vasco da Gama there was at least a nominal champion of South American football for the very first time.

Developments across the Atlantic would also have a significant impact on the future of South American football. In June 1954 in Basel, Switzerland, European football's governing body UEFA was formed. In April of the following year, the nascent organisation founded the European Champion Clubs' Cup, with its maiden tournament kicking off in September 1955. The success of the tournament, later rebranded as the Champions League, helped pave the way for the birth of the Copa Libertadores.

UEFA's secretary-general, Frenchman Henri Delauney, wrote to the head of Conmebol, Brazilian professor José Ramos de Freitas, in 1958 to enquire about setting up a game between the best sides from each continent. With the sport traditionally stronger in Europe and South America than elsewhere, the Intercontinental Cup would unofficially crown a club world champion. Ramos de Freitas subsequently visited Paraguay, Uruguay, Argentina, and Chile, to discuss the future of the South American game with the idea of a continental competition, the winner of which would compete for the Intercontinental Cup, high on the agenda.

On 30 July 1959 the confederation convened a congress in the Venezuelan capital, Caracas, and, after extensive discussions, the new idea was passed by an overwhelming 8-1 margin. It was later decided that the competition would be named in honour of the men – such as Simón Bolívar, José de San Martín, Manuel Belgrano, and Bernardo O'Higgins – that liberated South America from the chains of the Spanish Empire during the wars of independence in the late 18th and early 19th centuries. The inaugural competition featured the champions from seven nations: Argentina, Bolivia, Brazil, Chile, Colombia, Paraguay, and Uruguay.

Thanks to the establishment of the Copa Libertadores, Boca's 1962 domestic league title didn't just represent local bragging rights and put an end to an eight-year drought, it also provided an opportunity for the club to compete on a continental level for the very first time. After overcoming Paraguay's Olimpia, runners-up in 1960, and Universidad de Chile in the group stage, Boca were drawn against the formidable Peñarol, who had featured in the first three finals of the embryonic tournament and lifted the trophy in 1960 and 1961, in the semi-final. On 7 August Boca won 2-1 in Montevideo with both goals coming from Paulo Valentim. Ten days later Boca won the second leg 1-0 through José Sanfilippo – whose signing from San Lorenzo was a real statement of intent – progressing 3-1 on aggregate.

Boca's opponents in the final were defending champions Santos, the outfit who had popularised the Copa Libertadores. The side, from the port city approximately one hour from São Paulo, included a young man called Edson Arantes do Nascimento. The forward, better known as Pelé, had introduced himself to a global audience as a precocious teenager at the 1958 World Cup in Sweden, where he helped Brazil win their first Jules Rimet trophy. 'Santos were one of the best teams in history, with records of all kinds in the State Championship, on a national level, and all over the world where they would play friendlies due to the presence of their star man, Pelé,' explained Guillermo Schoua.

The Santos side of the early 1960s was 'extremely revered', according to Tim Vickery, yet it was far from a one-man team. 'Pelé joined a club that were São Paulo state champions and in 1963 he's surrounded by great players, some of the giants of Brazilian football history,' stated the English journalist, who has been based in Rio de Janeiro for over 25 years. 'Gilmar in goal is a legend and there is no doubt that, until Cláudio Taffarel emerged, he was the greatest goalkeeper that Brazil had produced,' added Vickery. 'Mauro was the captain when Brazil won the World Cup in 1962 and was a magnificent player, up there with the best centre-backs the country has produced. Zito was a box-to-box midfielder who helped Brazil win the 1962 World Cup Final with a vital goal that he started in his penalty box and finished in the opposing six-yard box.'

On the 4 September Boca travelled to Rio de Janeiro for their date with the *Alvinegro da Vila*. Santos's stadium, approximately 500km away, was relatively small so the club tended to relocate to the Maracanã for high-profile games despite the distance. 'Santos were a great team that transcended the localism of Brazilian football and they became nationally loved. It doesn't often happen, but it happened because Santos were a national treasure,' explained Vickery.

Playing an open 4-2-4 formation, Santos demonstrated their capability by taking a 3-0 lead with less than half an hour played of the first leg, shell-shocking Boca with a Coutinho brace and one from Lima. Rather than folding in front of a 100,000-strong crowd, Boca stubbornly dug their heels in, with two strikes from Sanfilippo giving the scoreline an air of respectability and providing the Argentine champions a lifeline ahead of the second leg. The first of his two strikes came just before half-time, the striker drilling the ball low with his left foot; the second came on 89 minutes after a one-two with Ángel Clemente Rojas. Affectionately known by the diminutive of his surname, Rojitas, the young forward only debuted for the club three months before the final but over time would cement a legacy as one of the club's most beloved sons.

A week later the two sides met at La Bombonera for the second leg, where a goalless first half poised the tie perfectly going into the final 45 minutes. Just two minutes of the second half had elapsed when Sanfilippo scored his seventh in as many Copa Libertadores appearances to level the tie on aggregate. It was an easy finish for the prolific marksman after the Brazilian defence had failed to deal with a cross from the right-hand side.

Santos, wearing their famous all-white kit, were able to find another gear, equalising shortly after through Coutinho. A terrible goal kick fell at the feet of Dorval who fed Pelé who, in turn, laid the ball on a platter for the goalscorer.

'Pelé's strike partner Coutinho is not particularly remembered outside Brazil,' explained Vickery. 'The two were physically very similar and exchanged passes at high speed. They gave shows week in, week out and were a magnificent partnership for years.'

The magisterial Pelé then sealed the tie himself after 82 minutes and Santos were champions of South America for the second year running. 'The last goal in La Bombonera is one of the great moments of Pelé's career,' added Vickery. 'It's probably the most decisive goal that he scored in a big final.' The Brazilians proved that they were more than just attractive on the eye. The tough pitch was expected to disrupt their free-flowing football and suit Boca's more attritional style, yet this proved not to be the case. Santos had to be brave in the intimidating cauldron created by the Boca fans, and Pelé in particular came in for a rough ride in the form of a string of hefty challenges which weren't atypical of clashes between Argentine and Brazilian sides.

The men from Calle Brandsen were the first Argentine side to truly take the competition seriously. Being so close to lifting the Copa Libertadores trophy gave Boca a taste of glory that the club was unable to shake and would become a particular obsession of president Alberto Armando throughout his two decade tenure. 'Armando saw that the competition could raise Boca's profile to a global level,' explained Guillermo Schoua. 'With the TV coverage, playing across South America against other big clubs, and the possibility of playing against European sides in the Intercontinental Cup, it was an attractive idea. And, in years to come, he would be proven right.'

In 1963 Boca's continental exploits took all of the club's attention and the squad were unable to cope on more than one front. As a result, the league campaign played second fiddle and the club finished fourth in the domestic championship.

A 2-1 win in El Monumental, in the penultimate round of fixtures, scuppered River's title aspirations and handed Independiente the title on a silver platter.

After a season focusing on the Copa Libertadores, Boca, now managed by former River forward Aristóbulo Deambrossi, concentrated fully on the domestic championship in 1964. With a solid foundation, which conceded just 15 goals in 30 games, the league title returned to La Bombonera. At the heart of the defence was goalkeeper Antonio Roma, who at one point during the season went more than 700 minutes without conceding. In June and July, he kept six consecutive clean sheets; in August and September, he embarked on another run which lasted seven matches. Roma's assured air, which instilled confidence in the defenders, was a key feature of a backline that was hell-bent on not being breached.

Boca's coronation came in the penultimate fixture of the schedule when River visited La Bombonera. Going into the game *Los Millonarios* knew a victory would put a spanner in the works and open the door for Independiente. Luis Artime looked to spoil Boca's party, opening the scoring with just 11 minutes gone, but after 66 minutes Norberto Menéndez brought Boca level, earning a point that was enough to seal the title and pave the way for celebrations.

Valentim, who was the top scorer in the championship triumphs of 1962 and 1964, headed back to his home country of Brazil, joining São Paulo. The forward had scored 71 goals in 111 competitive matches for Boca, with ten of those coming in just seven clashes against River. After experiencing financial problems in later years, Valentim died, aged just 50.

In 1963 the visionary Armando purchased six hectares of land in San Justo for AR$13m. Outside the city limits, approximately 30km from La Bombonera, what would become known as La Candela was a space for the players to concentrate in the build-up to games, shut off from the outside world and free from distractions. But it was in 1964 that Boca's ambitious president was given the green light to begin his most audacious project yet: Ciudad Deportiva (Sport City).

President of the Nation Arturo Illia, who took office in 1963, was entranced by Armando. Seeing the benefit to the city of the facility he had in mind, Argentina's Congress passed Law 16,575, gifting Boca the land and setting a ten-year deadline to complete the project. The idea was to create a series of man-made islands on the banks of the Río de la Plata, 3km from La Bombonera. The planned 40-hectare complex was to feature restaurants, a drive-in cinema, camping areas, swimming pools, and tennis courts. A place of leisure, culture, and entertainment for the city's inhabitants.

The centrepiece of the project was a mammoth 140,000-capacity stadium, which would also spearhead Argentina's World Cup bid for the 1978 tournament. La Bombonera was full to the brim and it was impossible to expand the stadium to allow more fans to watch the popular club and extract further income from gate receipts. A new arena was, therefore, seen by Armando as vital in allowing the club to continue growing and competing at the top level.

Boca retained the title in 1965, becoming champions of Argentina for the third time in four years, and back-to-back champions for the third time in their history. However, *Los Xeneizes* had started the season slowly, registering just five wins in the first 14 games in the lead-up to the season's first *Superclásico* on 4 July. Boca won 2-1 at El Monumental with goals from Ayres Moraes Albuquerque and youth-system graduate Oscar Pianetti.

The two rivals faced off once again in the third-to-last round of the season, with River ahead of Boca in the table going into the game. Artime grabbed an early goal for River and once again Boca showed great character to bounce back. The quick and agile Pianetti crucially struck first for *Los Xeneizes*, equalising with a *golazo* from outside the area to leave Carrizo with no chance. With River down to ten men following the expulsion of Juan Carlos Lallana, Menéndez won the game for Boca with a classy finish after 87 minutes.

Boca leapfrogged the men from Nuñez in the table, and subsequently drew 1-1 away at San Lorenzo before beating Atlanta at La Bombonera, thanks in no small part to a Pianetti double, on the final day of the season. Néstor *Pipo* Rossi, another former River man, was Boca's head coach and the architect of the success. Menéndez, who won league titles with River in the 1950s, completed a unique record of having won three championships with both of Argentina's biggest clubs.

A dominant Racing lost just once en route to winning the championship in 1966, finishing 13 points ahead of Boca in the process. The men from Brandsen 805 went six games without a win in July and August, significantly affected by the loss of key figures who had been selected for the Argentina World Cup squad. Antonio Roma, Silvio Marzolini, Carmelo Simeone, Antonio Rattín, Rojas, and Alberto González were all part of the group that eventually succumbed to defeat by hosts England at the quarter-final stage. Continental competition also diluted Boca's strength in 1966: the club were eliminated from the Copa Libertadores in the second phase, finishing third in the group behind River Plate and Independiente.

At the end of the 1966 season, Ernesto Grillo retired after six years and three league titles. Grillo scored a famous goal for Argentina against England on 14 May 1953, a day that is now designated as *Día del Futbolista* in Argentina in his honour. Grillo came through Independiente's youth system and played more than 200 games for the Avellaneda outfit before winning the Serie A title with Milan in 1959. After retiring, Grillo worked with Boca's youth teams.

The Metropolitano and Nacional championships were born in 1967, the new short-form tournaments replacing the year-long format. With dissatisfaction growing under the rule of Juan Carlos Onganía, who came to power in a military coup, it was hoped that the new format would assist in quelling dissent in the interior, as well as creating a less Buenos Aires-centric sport. The Metro was for clubs directly affiliated to the AFA, effectively a championship for teams from the capital and the wider Buenos Aires province. The Nacional was for the Buenos Aires sides plus the best teams from the interior provinces.

A frustrating Boca were underwhelming in both tournaments, finishing fourth in the Metro and eighth in the Nacional. Breaking the 36-year hegemony of the *Cinco Grandes,* Estudiantes de La Plata won the Metro, their first title of the professional era, under the guidance of Osvaldo Zubeldía, who had spent a season as a player with Boca in the late 50s and, as a manager, would become synonymous with *anti-fútbol.*

The 1968 Metro was a terrible campaign for Boca, without multiple league winners Carmelo Simeone and Norberto Menéndez who had left the club. Once again under the tutelage of José D'Amico, who had led them to the 1962 title, Boca finished fifth, scoring just 15 goals in 22 games, the same haul as bottom club Platense. Any action on the field would, however, pale into insignificance in light of events that came following a 0-0 draw at River Plate on 23 June.

The Tragedy of Puerta 12, Argentina's worst football disaster, unfolded as Boca fans headed down El Monumental's steep stairs to the dimly lit and narrow exits following the final whistle. Seventy-one fans were crushed and suffocated to death, with hundreds injured. Rattín was driving home following the match when he heard the tragic news on the radio, and immediately spun his car around and sped to Hospital Pirovano, 3km from the stadium. The humble giant wanted to give blood but was unable to donate due to fatigue, having played for 90 minutes.

In the aftermath of the disaster, investigations failed to apportion any blame. 'There are different versions of what happened,' began Guillermo Schoua. 'Some suggest that the police were repressing the Boca fans who were singing the Peronist March, which had been banned by the Onganía regime. Others suggest that the River employees had failed to open the doors and turnstiles properly. Maybe it was a combination of several things. River didn't take responsibility, nor did the AFA. The police even less so. The investigation was left in limbo.'

Boca finished joint fourth in a hotly contested 1968 Nacional championship, just one point away from the top three teams. Boca had by far the meanest defence in the league but goalscoring was once again a problem. At least some pride had been restored, something the side could take into the following season. Boca won Zona A in the 1969 Metro before being eliminated by River in the semi-final after a goalless draw, an arbitrary and controversial ruling allowing River to progress having found the net more times during the group phase. Boca's defence was once again formidable, conceding an average of 0.5 goals per game; Roma set a record that would stand for many years, shutting out rival forwards for more than 782 minutes.

Twenty-four days after Boca exited the Metro tournament, the club competed in the inaugural Copa Argentina Final. The competition was introduced by the AFA, inspired by domestic cup competitions in Europe, such as England's

FA Cup, to further spread the game beyond the borders of Buenos Aires. Boca eliminated Atlético Tucumán in the first round, before cruising past Sarmiento (Santiago del Estero) 7-3 on aggregate in the second. The return leg marked the debut of the Uruguayan Orlando Medina, a central-midfielder with great vision. Chacarita and Medina's former club Colón, were knocked out in the quarter-final and semi-final respectively. Boca beat Atlanta 3-2 over two legs in the final which was played at the home of San Lorenzo. All of Boca's goals – scored by youth-team product Ramón Ponce, Norberto Madurga, and Ignacio Peña – came in the first meeting and just six months into the job for Alfredo Di Stéfano.

As a player, Di Stéfano had won two league titles with River in the 1940s but it was with Real Madrid where he had truly excelled, winning 15 major trophies in just over a decade. As a manager, he was a relative novice yet the Copa Argentina was a great start to his new career. His team took the cup form into the 1969 Nacional, losing just one of the first 16 fixtures. Boca travelled to El Monumental on the final day of the campaign two points ahead of their opponents River, who needed to win to force a title-deciding play-off.

In front of 33,000 fans, Boca raced into a two-goal lead after 35 minutes. Madurga, enjoying his greatest 90 minutes in a Boca shirt, scored both goals. *Muñeco,* who got his break in the team due to the absence of the injured Rattín, broke from midfield and headed a through-ball past the onrushing José Pérez who was miles out of his goal, before finishing into the empty net. The second came from another excellent deep run followed by a neat finish from the edge of the box. The accomplished passer of a ball proved himself equally adept at finishing, gaining a modicum of revenge on the club that had rejected him at the age of 13 due to his physique.

River hit back through Oscar Más after 38 minutes and went into half-time with renewed vigour. After 67 minutes the home side equalised through Víctor Marchetti and were just one goal away from forcing a play-off. The blue-and-gold defence stood firm; there were no more goals and Boca were champions.

Di Stéfano's adventurous 4-2-4 formation bucked the negative trend of the day and was also atypical in style for Boca, who for decades had built their sides on blood, sweat, and tears. The ecstatic champions performed a *vuelta olímpica* (lap of honour) around El Monumental, applauded by large swathes of River fans. The embittered staff at El Monumental had other ideas, however, turning on the water sprinklers to drench their rivals yet the spirit of the champions couldn't be dampened. Peruvian Julio Meléndez was a key figure in the offensive side, often displaying his exquisite talent and balletic movement; the touch, tricky quick feet, and *gambetas* (dribbles) of Rojas were a major draw in enticing people to the stadium.

Following success in the 1969 Nacional, Di Stéfano headed back to Spain to manage Valencia and was replaced with José María Silvero. The 38-year-old from Corrientes was kick-starting his managerial career with the club for whom he had made over 100 competitive appearances and won three league titles.

Boca finished fourth in the 1970 Metropolitano and, during this campaign, Silvero only selected Antonio Rattín on five occasions. The 33-year-old, one of the world's best defensive-midfielders in his prime, had dropped back into defence in the autumn of his career and now, after 15 years in the first team, the one-club man decided to hang up his boots. Rattín, who captained the club for many years, represented Boca in almost 400 official games, won three league titles and the Copa Argentina in 1969. The courageous man-mountain led by example, providing a commanding voice and a presence that encouraged others and raised team spirit. Despite his imposing physique, he could play. His statue was inaugurated in the club museum in July 2015.

With the Copa Libertadores campaign out of the way – Boca were eliminated in the second phase – Silvero's men were able to concentrate fully on the Nacional in the second half of 1970. Boca finished joint top of the Zona B group, beating Chacarita 2-0 in a one-off semi-final at Racing's ground, thanks to a Jorge Coch brace, to progress to the final.

Two days before Christmas, Boca and Rosario Central faced off in El Monumental. Ángel Landucci gave the *rosarinos* the lead after 40 minutes, giving Central a slender advantage going into the break. With the minutes ebbing away, man of the match Rojas scored from close range to force extra time. With 108 minutes on the clock, Coch sent a header back across young Peruvian goalkeeper Ramón Quiroga and into the net to win the title for Boca. It was the second successive year that Boca were able to enjoy a lap of honour around the home of their great rivals.

* * *

The first three decades of the Argentine professional game had seen increasing crowds watching free-flowing, carefree, attractive football. The early golden period, which became known as *La Nuestra* (Our Way, or Our Thing), came crashing down on 15 June 1958. One year after scoring 25 goals in six games on the way to winning the 1957 South American Championship, Argentina – including Boca players Juan Francisco Lombardo, Julio Musimessi, Federico Edwards, and Eliseo Mouriño – travelled to Sweden for the World Cup, high on confidence.

Approaching the final game of the World Cup's group phase, Argentina knew that victory over a winless Czechoslovakia in Helsingborg would send them through to the quarter-final. The unexpected 6-1 massacre that Guillermo Stábile's side suffered produced a seismic shift that would negatively shape the next phase of the Argentine game's history, with beauty and artistic endeavour replaced by cynicism and brutality. Dawn had broken, but it was a dark, new day in Argentina's football history.

The professionalisation of Argentina's club game in the early 1930s increased the importance of the local game in the eyes of the nation's football supporters. The exciting, new, national championship, and a lack of international football, created a bubble in which Argentine football evolved in its own way. Goals dried up across the Argentine domestic game in the 1960s as not losing became more important than winning. Between 1936 and 1938 there wasn't a solitary goalless draw in Argentina's top flight yet during one matchday on 21 July 1963, just nine goals were scored in the day's seven matches. The 1967 championship produced a record low of 1.94 goals per game.

Fans became apathetic to a sport that they had previously adored; crowds declined by between 25 and 40 per cent from their peak in 1954. In the 1960s more families were acquiring cars and television sets and therefore had alternative entertainment sources. With more choice, Argentines were less prepared to pay for an inferior product.

The Intercontinental Cup clashes between the finest clubs from Europe and South America produced a litany of powder-keg moments during the 1960s. The deciding clash of the 1967 version between Racing and Celtic took place in the Uruguayan capital and became infamously known as the Battle of Montevideo. Zubeldía's Estudiantes participated in the next three versions of the competition, creating such a level of controversy that throughout the 1970s several European champions refused to participate. Boca weren't exempt from such violent and problematic encounters and the 1971 Copa Libertadores produced the ugliest and most notorious on-pitch battle in the club's history.

Boca's triumph in the 1970 Nacional gave them another crack at continental glory. Silvero's charges started the group stage strongly enough, beating Rosario Central 2-1 at La Bombonera. However, a trip to Lima, featuring two games in four days in the Peruvian capital, saw Boca fail to score, registering a 2-0 defeat to Sporting Cristal and a goalless draw with Universitario. With only one team per group progressing, the visit of Sporting Cristal on 17 March took on heightened importance.

Cristal selected the same XI as in the first clash, hoping history would repeat itself and they would once again take maximum points off the Argentine side. The Peruvians took the lead after 17 minutes, silencing the 60,000-strong crowd, but Boca soon hit back with two quick-fire goals of their own through Coch and Rojas. In the 69th minute, Cristal hit back to make it 2-2 and with the clock ticking the intensity of the action multiplied with each passing minute. The crowd became increasingly hostile as the momentum swung back and forth with both sides pushing forward in search of a winner.

In the game's dying embers Boca launched another attack and Roberto Rogel found himself on the turf in the Peruvian's penalty area. The home side were incensed when Uruguayan referee Alejandro Otero, convinced that the Boca man had fallen of his own accord, dismissed their penalty appeal. In response, Rubén Suñé hacked down Cristal's Alfredo Quesada in the next passage of play out of sheer frustration. The blue touchpaper had been lit and all hell broke loose. Suñé attacked Alberto Gallardo with a corner flag; Gallardo responded by launching a flying kick to the head of his assailant, opening a bloody wound that required seven stitches. Boca's captain, like a man possessed, needed several policemen to subdue him and the image of his bleeding head later adorned the cover of classic monthly Argentine sports magazine *El Gráfico*.

Nineteen players were dismissed and the only three to escape Otero's wrath were the two goalkeepers – Rubén Sánchez and Sporting Cristal's Luis Rubiños – along with Boca's Julio Meléndez. The Peruvian refused to take part in the battle against his countrymen and later left the pitch in tears. Ironically one of the players of the match, Cristal's Ramón Mifflin, was dismissed despite having stayed fairly neutral in the brawl, and Boca goalkeeper Sánchez escaped punishment despite being at the forefront of the trouble. Whilst the rest of the officials escaped to the relative sanctuary of the dressing room, the referee – a policeman in his day job – remained in the heat of the battle in the volatile Bombonera.

Barring those receiving medical treatment, the culprits of the evening's shenanigans were sent to a police station three blocks away from La Bombonera on Calle Pinzón, with many forced to spend the night there in close quarters. Those involved were given 30-day jail sentences which were later quashed after some back-door diplomacy. Many were also given lengthy bans, ranging from one year to 18 months, by South American football's governing body, but these were rescinded on 1 May, allowing the players to continue plying their trade. The incident was huge news in both countries and, seen as the aggressors, Boca were ejected from the competition. Armando publicly voiced his disgust at his players' role in the hostilities of the *Bombonerazo* of 1971.

With the backdrop of the Copa Libertadores shame dominating the early rounds, Boca finished eighth in the Metropolitano championship, one point closer to bottom club Platense than they were to champions Independiente.

Boca fared much better in the Nacional tournament, under Chilean coach Fernando Riera, finishing third in Zona B and only missing out on progression to the semi-final on goal difference. Rosario Central were the eventual champions, the first side from the interior to win an AFA-organised competition.

Halfway through the Nacional, in November, a players' strike disrupted two rounds of the tournament. Nearly all of the teams fielded youngsters in the absence of star men and this opened the door for 18-year-old Roberto Mouzo to make his first-team debut. Rather than being a stop-gap, Mouzo would go on to break the club's all-time appearances record.

Towards the end of the Nacional campaign, Boca faced River on the neutral territory of Racing's El Cilindro. Despite fielding a strong XI, Boca fell 3-1 to River's youngsters. Replacing Nicolás Novello after an hour was Ángel Clemente Rojas, playing his last 30 minutes in a blue-and-gold shirt. The unconventional Rojitas bucked the trend of the era, playing football when *anti-fútbol* ruled. The winner of four league titles, and the 1969 Copa Argentina, was adored by the terraces and is widely considered as one of the club's top three idols. Rojitas was capable of doing marvellous things with a ball, the *quiebre de cintura* (broken hip) his speciality. Upon leaving, Rojas ironically headed to Peru, joining Deportivo Municipal, rivals to Sporting Cristal in the capital city of Lima. Yet he will never be forgotten by the Boca faithful and, like Rattín, has a statue in the club museum. Perhaps Rojas belonged in a different era, one where beautiful football was more celebrated; perhaps he stood out, and is therefore idolised to such an extent, exactly because he excelled during the years of *anti-fútbol.*

Including the 1970 Nacional, the decade produced five league titles as well as the inaugural Copa Argentina, and introduced idols such as Ruben Suñé, Madurga, Ponce,

Medina, and Menéndez, protagonists in much of Boca's glory. Yet a decade into Armando's reign as president the club had yet to achieve what he most craved: Copa Libertadores glory.

Chapter Five

La Nuestra 2.0 – The Lorenzo Era

BOCA STARTED the 1972 Metropolitano in fine form, winning five of the first six games and scoring 21 goals in the process. The scintillating start included a 5-0 win at Ferro and a 7-1 thrashing of Estudiantes in La Plata. The 4-0 destruction of River at El Monumental – with a brace apiece from Ramón Ponce and Hugo Curioni – was the biggest away win in *Superclásico* history. The previous year the AFA had introduced goal difference in an attempt to create more attacking teams. If Boca's early results were anything to go by, the initiative had certainly worked.

After the historic result, Boca went into freefall, winning just one of the next seven games. The next clash with River came in round 20, the two sides drawing 2-2 after Boca had led twice through Curioni and youth-team product Osvaldo Potente. Antonio Roma was culpable for both of River's goals, the giant goalkeeper making his third and final competitive appearance of the campaign and, more significantly, his last as the custodian of Boca's number one jersey.

By the time the legend hung up his gloves, he had completed more than 500 matches for Boca, including friendlies, conceding an average of just 0.92 goals per game. He kept goal in campaigns which gleaned six major honours, and broke individual records for time without conceding a goal. His gloves would be large ones to fill. Boca won just five of the remaining 14 games to finish ninth in a campaign that had promised so much at the outset.

Boca won the Zona B group in the 1972 Nacional with relative ease, losing just once in 13 to set up a semi-final clash with River at the home of Vélez. River breathed a sigh of relief when Curioni missed a 13th-minute penalty but Roberto Rogel spared his team-mate's blushes, giving Boca the lead after half an hour. River then hit back three times in 22 minutes either side of the break. A late Curioni goal gave Boca hope but it was River who progressed to the final, where they lost to San Lorenzo.

Ahead of the 1973 Metropolitano there was much change on Calle Brandsen. Rogelio Domínguez, who had crafted good sides at Chacarita and San Lorenzo, replaced José Varacka, ending his poor six-month stint. Domínguez, a former goalkeeper who won two European Cups with Real Madrid, dispensed with the services of key figures Rubén Suñé and Silvio Marzolini who had been at the forefront of a players' strike in 1971. Ageing blond full-back Marzolini, who amassed 400 official appearances in 12 years and remained loyal to the cause during his peak despite overtures from European clubs, retired. Suñé, still only 25, joined Huracán. Vicente Pernía, a feisty 23-year-old right-back, arrived from Estudiantes.

Boca opened the campaign with a 2-1 defeat to River, Curioni's opener cancelled out by two late strikes in El Monumental. Five straight wins followed, allowing Boca to keep up with early pace-setters Huracán, themselves unbeaten. After a hangover that had lasted more than 15 years since the debacle in Sweden in 1958, there were signs that the glorious attacking football of old was returning to Argentina.

Huracán coach César Luis Menotti, a 44-year-old from Rosario who had formed part of Boca's title-winning side in 1965, assembled one of Argentine football's greatest ever sides, featuring attacking luminaries such as René Houseman, 1973 Footballer of the Year Miguel Ángel Brindisi, Carlos Babington, and former Boca men Omar Larrosa and *Chapa* Suñé.

Menotti's first defeat came at the hands of River and when Boca and Huracán met in round 16 they went toe to toe in a feast of attacking football at La Bombonera. Domínguez's charges established an 11th-minute lead through a Potente header. Larrosa, a member of Boca's 1970 Nacional title-winning team, brought the men from Parque Patricios level with a penalty three minutes later. Boca had the chance to regain the lead before half-time with a penalty of their own but Curioni's kick was saved by Héctor Roganti. Potente restored Boca's advantage on the hour with a diving header from a yard out, before Curioni atoned for his spot-kick miss by making it 3-1. Potente completed his hat-trick in the 81st minute to record a memorable 4-1 win that took Boca to within four points of their vanquished opponents.

Three days later Boca welcomed River to La Bombonera, thrashing their rivals in a seven-goal thriller. The first half was a cagey affair with Carlos Guerini's penalty cancelling out River's opener. The game came to life in the second half and Boca scored four goals without reply in the space of 29 minutes, the first time one of the two clubs had put so many goals past the other in one half. River grabbed an 89th-minute consolation.

On the final day of the season, Boca travelled across town to Huracán's Estadio Tomás Adolfo Ducó, famed for its art deco tower. The two sides played out a 2-2 draw but, in reality, the result was irrelevant: Menotti's men won the league with a four-point cushion over second-place Boca. The modest Huracán picked up their first professional title and in doing so proved that exciting, adventurous football could win titles, contradicting the prevailing mindset which had dominated much of the last 15 years. Winning and beautiful football were no longer mutually exclusive concepts. Menotti was rewarded with the national team manager's job, tasked with leading *La Albiceleste* in the home-soil World Cup in 1978.

In the 1973 Nacional Boca finished fifth in their zone, failing to progress to the next round. On the opening day of the 1974 Metropolitano campaign, Boca thrashed River 5-2 at La Bombonera, with four goals coming from Carlos García Cambón. Boca finished second in the first round before coming third in the final phase. Boca won their group in the first phase of the 1974 Nacional before performing terribly in the final phase, only avoiding bottom spot courtesy of goal difference. Ramón Ponce, the winger who had a stellar record of one goal every four games, left for Gimnasia.

In 1975 River Plate won the Metropolitano, their first title in 18 years. Despite boasting the most fearsome attack – 80 goals in 38 games – and going unbeaten for 19 matches between April and July, Boca could only finish third. River completed a double in winning the Nacional title whereas Boca failed to progress past the first phase. The team's poor performance brought the curtain down on Domínguez's three-year reign which had produced excellent offensive football yet, ultimately, no silverware.

Ahead of the 1976 Metropolitano campaign, Armando appointed Juan Carlos Lorenzo as successor to Domínguez.

The fans were fed up with playing well in defeat, and the back-to-back success of River rubbed salt into the wounds. With no title for five years, Lorenzo's task was clear.

Born into a middle-class family in October 1922, *Toto*, a nickname given to him by his mother, had played more than 50 matches for Boca in the mid-1940s. Lorenzo's playing career had also taken him to Spain, France, and Italy, soaking up the wisdom that exposure to distinct footballing cultures bestowed. His first managerial achievement was gaining promotion to Spain's top flight with Mallorca in 1960. Lorenzo, a disciple of compatriot and influential tactician Helenio Herrera, led Argentina at the World Cups in 1962 and 1966 before winning consecutive titles with San Lorenzo in 1972. A solid campaign with Unión preceded his move to La Bombonera.

The pragmatic coach moulded a physical side based on a solid foundation, repeatedly drilling his ideas into the players' heads during training sessions. The squad was strengthened with three pivotal signings from Unión: Rubén Suñé returned after more than three years away from La Bombonera, along with Hugo Gatti and Ernesto Mastrángelo. Gatti was a madcap goalkeeper with a penchant for leaving his 18-yard box to involve himself in the play, decades before the concept of the sweeper-keeper was *de rigeur.* Francisco *Pancho* Sá, a winner of four successive Copa Libertadores titles with Independiente, swapped Avellaneda for La Boca.

Elegant attacking midfielder Jorge *Ruso* Ribolzi joined from Atlanta. 'In 1975 I had the opportunity to go to Rosario Central or River,' recalled Ribolzi. 'One morning, towards the end of the year, I picked up a copy of *Clarín* [the largest daily tabloid newspaper in Argentina] which contained a small story suggesting that Boca were interested in me and days later the transfer was completed. It was a big surprise for me that it all happened so quickly. I felt enormous happiness with the expectations and everything that it means to move to such a big club, and to get to know the world of Boca.'

For Ribolzi the differences between Atlanta and Boca were stark. 'With Atlanta, there wasn't as much responsibility to reach an objective,' stated the man from Ramos Mejía in Buenos Aires province. 'It was a great team that we had at the time but it was a humble club trying to do the best it possibly could. The world of Boca is large, full of demands and responsibility and the fans are all over you.' The 24-year-old had to tweak his style to match his new surroundings. 'I always wanted to run and work hard for my team-mates, and I enjoyed arriving in the box to get close to the goal,' remembered Ribolzi. 'When I went to Boca I was working under a different coach, for a different team with a different idea of how to play the game. My starting position was slightly deeper and I formed part of a famous screen in front of the back four alongside *Chapa* Suñé. But I still had the liberty to get forward.'

In the first eight games of the first phase of the 1976 Metropolitano Boca lost just once, and the defensive statistics were proof of Lorenzo's ability to tighten up at the back: Boca conceded just three goals and kept six clean sheets in the process.

In between Boca's matches against San Telmo and Banfield, the military seized power in a coup, Argentina's sixth in less than 50 years. Three years earlier Héctor Cámpora, an ally of Juan Domingo Perón, had been democratically elected as Argentina's president. Perón returned from exile in Madrid in June 1973 and, two months later, Cámpora's resignation led to fresh elections which Perón duly won. However, his third term in the Casa Rosada was beset by problems from the outset. The president died from natural causes in July 1974 and was succeeded by his wife, Isabelita. Inflation and violence multiplied and the economy became increasingly unstable. Unable to maintain control, the out-of-depth president was ousted with the Junta assuming power in the early hours of 24 March 1976. Over the course of the next seven years, the vile regime disappeared more than 30,000 of its own people in the name of its National Reorganisation Process.

Football, however, continued uninterrupted and Boca lost 1-0 at home to River on 18 April. Lorenzo's side finished fourth in the final table of the first phase, progressing as the top six qualified for the final rounds. In round eight of the final phase Boca drew 1-1 with River and, in the third-to-last match, faced title rivals Huracán at El Monumental. The crucial clash – in which 29-year-old Carlos Veglio, another Lorenzo signing, was the man of the match – was settled by a 20th-minute long-range wonder strike from midfield maestro Jorge *Chino* Benítez, the victory all but rendering Boca champions. Despite the black cloud hanging over Argentine society at least Boca now had something to celebrate. The wait of more than five long years was finally over.

Rather than resting on his laurels, Lorenzo strengthened the squad ahead of the 1976 Nacional campaign, bringing in Mario Zanabria from Newell's. The *enganche*, renowned for his vision and for spraying passes with his left foot, had previously won the league with the Rosario outfit in 1974 and was one of the final pieces of Lorenzo's jigsaw. Zanabria was courted by the biggest clubs in the country but Boca offered more money and sent two players in the other direction as part of the deal.

José Maria Suárez was another addition. The versatile full-back impressed Lorenzo with his excellent anticipation during a friendly when Boca faced Belgrano in Córdoba on a national holiday in August. Three days later the 25-year-old was moving from his native province to Buenos Aires to join the champions. 'The difference between Boca and Belgrano is huge,' stated Suárez. 'Belgrano is a *grande* in the province of Córdoba but Boca is the undisputed biggest club in the country. I had the great luck to play for Boca. When I played for Boca, I was a fan of Boca; when I played for Belgrano, I was a fanatic of Belgrano. So for me, it was tough when the two sides met because, in reality, I loved them both.'

Boca kicked off the campaign with a 1-0 home win over Temperley. The following week, *Colorado* Suárez made his debut in a victory, by the same scoreline, away to Quilmes, a match settled by a Ribolzi header. Seven days later Boca drew 1-1 with River at La Bombonera, a match Suárez remembers vividly: 'Lorenzo was a very strategic coach who knew the details of everything. I would be marking Pedro Alexis González and, in the week leading up to the game, Lorenzo explained to me how to mark the player, what he would do, and what his qualities were. I kept him quiet. I began to win over the fans and they sang my name.'

Three successive wins followed before a trip to Independiente. Morón native Alfredo Oscar Márquez came on as a substitute in the friendly defeat against Belgrano which sealed José Maria Suárez's move to La Bombonera but it was at La Doble Visera, on 17 October 1976, where his competitive debut came. The 18-year-old youth-team graduate featured at every level on his way to becoming a professional, under the tutelage of the likes of Bernardo Gandulla and Ernesto Grillo. 'The central defender José Luis Tesare told me at the table after a meal that Lorenzo had commented to him that there was a young right-back that was doing very well and that he was going to give him some minutes in the Primera,' remembered Márquez. 'That young right-back was me. You can imagine the joy that this news gave me.'

Independiente took the lead after just one minute through Peruvian international Percy Rojas and the score remained the same going into the half-time break. 'In the second half the referee sent off Armando Ovide and we were losing 1-0,' recalled Márquez. 'Lorenzo called me over and asked me if I wanted to go on. He told me he bought me because I'm a *crack* (top-class player) and that my job was to nullify Daniel Bertoni and, if the chance arose, have a shot on goal. I told myself, "If Lorenzo puts me on it's because he has confidence in me and rest assured that I won't let him down." Lorenzo withdrew a striker, Jorge Salas, to put me on when the logical thing to do would have been to leave the team as it was. The first ball I intercepted I was too strong for Bertoni and he had to be attended to by the physio. With Bertoni off the pitch, I was free to join the attack. I hit the ball and scored the goal of my life.' The first and only goal of Márquez's career levelled the score with 17 minutes to go but on 85 minutes Bertoni, now recovered, scored the winning goal to send Boca home empty-handed.

Despite the defeat, the young full-back had impressed sufficiently to replace the suspended Ovide and start the following match – alongside Ribolzi and Suárez – at home to Chacarita. 'Although I had played in La Bombonera many times with the reserves, and knew what the stadium was like with many people, this is a day that I will never forget,' remembered Márquez. 'When you are in the tunnel waiting to enter the pitch the sensation caused by the fans is indescribable and, after, when the fans sing your name it is impossible to explain. During the match you don't hear anything; the shouts from the fans are deafening.' With the score goalless, Márquez was replaced after an hour by Héctor Kees. Chacarita took the lead after 83 minutes but a dramatic late double from Tesare and Mastrángelo gave Boca the points.

After finishing joint-top of their group in the first phase, Boca needed a play-off against Quilmes to reach the quarter-final, Abel Alves and Ovide providing the goals that sent Lorenzo's men to the last eight. Banfield and Huracán were edged out in the knockout phase, leading Boca to a final against River Plate, the first and only time the two superpowers have met in a one-off final to determine a competitive title.

On 22 December, in the heat of a Buenos Aires summer, Boca and River fans headed across the Riachuelo to Racing's El Cilindro for the winner-takes-all clash. River's team contained Ubaldo Fillol, Daniel Passarella, and Leopoldo Luque, all three of whom would go on to lift the World Cup with Argentina just 18 months later.

The almost 70,000 in attendance witnessed a cagey first 70 minutes, a poor spectacle with few clear-cut chances played mainly in the centre of the field. Soon after, Arturo Ithurralde blew his whistle and awarded Boca a free kick after Veglio was fouled by Passarella. Roberto Mouzo and Veglio stood over the ball but, with the green light from the referee, Suñé appeared and struck the ball into the far corner giving Fillol, who had been busy arranging his five team-mates in the wall, no chance. Fillol, one of the best Argentine goalkeepers of all time, later admitted to Suñé that even if he had been fully prepared, he still wouldn't have been able to stop the strike such was its accuracy and ferocity. The goal settled a game that was short on chances and was almost certainly heading to penalty kicks.

Mouzo, who debuted in 1971 but really came to the fore two years later following the sale of Julio Meléndez, who he had idolised, marked Luque out of the game and was crucial in Boca keeping a clean sheet. 'It was a dream to play against River, for the first time in history in a final, knowing that whoever won would be champions,' remembered Jorge Ribolzi, another man who starred in the historic victory. 'It was a unique experience, a unique joy, different to winning the first Copa Libertadores or the first Intercontinental Cup.'

After the final whistle, president Armando ran onto the pitch, hugging players in his business suit. Boca were double champions of 1976, mirroring River's achievement from the previous calendar year. Suñé's strike was the most important goal in *Superclásico* history and perhaps remains so to this day. Not only did it directly decide a final, but it also became shrouded in mystery because all footage of the strike vanished with numerous conspiracy theories attached. For more than 40 years the legend of the *gol fantasma* (ghost goal) was passed from generation to generation via word of mouth, interpreted through black-and-white photographs.

Incredibly, in late 2019, shortly after Suñé's death, a film of the goal surfaced. 'A person approached the club saying he had the footage,' said Guillermo Schoua, who was involved in the process of bringing the film to life. 'The fan filmed the repeat of the match, shown the next day, using an 8mm camera pointed at the television. He had various recordings of Boca goals but hadn't found Suñé's until now. He brought it to us at the club's history department where we projected it and digitised it. The whole process took a few months until we were finally able to make it public.'

After an agreement between the technical staff and the board, Boca more or less abandoned the 1977 Metropolitano to focus on trying to win the Copa Libertadores. They fielded experimental sides in the expanded domestic tournament and, despite using 41 players, Boca still finished a respectable fourth.

Armando, who had been obsessively chasing the Copa Libertadores title for 17 years, offered large bonuses to the players if they could fulfil his dream of lifting the trophy. Boca opened their continental campaign at La Bombonera, beating River Plate 1-0 thanks to a late goal from Mouzo, who converted the rebound after Fillol had saved his penalty. *Los*

Xeneizes, unbeaten in six, topped the group and progressed to the next round. Lorenzo's men won the semi-final group stage at the expense of Deportivo Cali and Libertad to set up the final against Cruzeiro. The Brazilians had defeated River Plate in the 1976 final of South America's premier club competition and wouldn't give up their title lightly.

Boca won the first leg, a fourth-minute Veglio goal separating the sides at La Bombonera. Back in Brazil, at Belo Horizonte's Mineirao, Cruzeiro won the return leg by the same score courtesy of a free kick from Nelinho, a player who Lorenzo had singled out as a danger man before the final. A goalless draw in the deciding game in Montevideo led to a penalty shoot-out, the first time in the competition's history that this method would be used to decide the winner of the trophy. The first nine kicks were all converted successfully, giving Boca a 5-4 lead. Vanderley needed to score to force sudden death yet Gatti saved. Boca were champions of South America for the first time.

A tough defence, which conceded just three goals in 13 and kept ten clean sheets, was the backbone of the success, and the new champions returned to Buenos Aires to a heroes' welcome. The next step was to conquer the world.

After just four games of the 1978 Metropolitano campaign, the South American champions welcomed Borussia Mönchengladbach to La Bombonera for the first leg of the Intercontinental Cup. The Germans were competing in place of European champions Liverpool, who declined to participate. Despite their substitute status, Gladbach's formidable squad contained Berti Vogts, Herbert Wimmer, Rainer Bonhof and goalkeeper Wolfgang Kleff, all of whom had won the 1974 World Cup with West Germany.

Boca took the lead after 16 minutes, after Mastrángelo rounded Kleff and rolled the ball into the empty net. Udo Lattek's men equalised after 24 minutes, before taking the lead five minutes later and silencing the Buenos Aires crowd. At half-time Jorge Ribolzi came off the bench to replace Jorge Benítez. 'The ultimate objective was the Intercontinental Cup,' stated Ribolzi. 'After winning the bi-championship in 1976 and the Copa Libertadores in 1977 it was the icing on the cake. We faced a great side with many players from the West German national team as well as the Danish forward Allan Simonsen who had won the Ballon d'Or in 1977. A great team in an era when German footballers were hard and strong.'

Just five minutes after entering the field, Ribolzi headed in a Daniel Pavón cross to make it 2-2 and give Boca a lifeline ahead of the second leg. 'The draw was very important,' said Ribolzi. 'If we had lost, we would have had to have gone to Germany and won. With the draw, we had more possibilities.' Frustratingly there would be an agonising five-month wait before the return in Germany.

After 15 games, the Metropolitano took a 42-day break for the 1978 World Cup, with Boca holding the lead, one point clear of River. Despite the shadow cast by the military regime, the coach who had led unfancied Huracán to an unexpected title triumph in 1973, Menotti, now conquered the world, as Argentina triumphed whilst playing a brand of football that was diametrically opposed to what came before it in the 1960s, and what was happening in society. With Boca's success, and that of the national team, Argentine football appeared to be emerging from its dark days.

The Metropolitano championship resumed in early July and Boca showed that no momentum had been lost, winning three and drawing one of the first four games after the break. Next came the small matter of travelling to Germany to resolve the Intercontinental Cup. Following the 2-2 draw in La Bombonera many thought Boca were dead and buried. Argentine television didn't screen the second leg, and journalists didn't bother making the trip over to Germany. Even in the absence of away goals, it was thought the Germans would be too strong on home soil. 'Practically nobody gave us a chance because we had to determine the cup in Germany,' remembered José Maria Suárez, who missed the first leg but played the full 90 minutes of the second. 'Nobody believed in us. Nobody.'

The obsessive Lorenzo, however, had other ideas and was convinced Boca would win, a belief he transmitted to his players. The meticulous coach sent a spy to Germany to watch Gladbach's pre-season matches to understand them further. The conclusion was that a fast team would be required to counteract their strengths. In defence, the experienced Sá was left out with Tesare preferred; further up the pitch, three out-and-out forwards were selected.

Boca took the lead after just two minutes from a sublime Darío Felman effort with the outside of his right boot. The forward had joined Boca in 1975, but left for Valencia two years later to link up with compatriot Mario Kempes. However, it was written into his contract when he left for Spain that he could return to Boca to take part in the Intercontinental Cup. The early goal allowed Boca to control the match, and launch counter-attacks whenever *Die Fohlen* dared to venture forward in search of an equaliser. After 33 minutes Mastrángelo controlled a cross from the left and was able to take two touches before finishing. And just four minutes later Carlos Salinas – the attacking midfielder from Tucumán who had won two league titles with River in 1975 – made it three for Boca.

In just one half of football, the Argentines had completely blitzed their German rivals and in the second 45 minutes, Boca took the sting out of the game entirely. The miracle result meant that Argentina now boasted world champions in both club and international football. The gracious

German fans applauded as Lorenzo's heroes performed a lap of honour. 'For us, it was a tremendous joy to be the first Intercontinental Cup champions in the history of Boca,' remembered Suárez fondly. Ribolzi, whose goal in the first leg was crucial in the tie, missed the encounter in Germany as he was recovering from an injury. 'I was on the bench but in reality it was one of the greatest nights in Boca's history,' recalled Ruso.

Shortly after the Intercontinental Cup triumph, Ribolzi left after winning four titles with the club in less than three years. 'I left Boca due to differences with Lorenzo,' stated the attacking midfielder who had been one of the pillars of Toto's successful sides. 'I was still young and in my best moment but we had our differences. I asked Armando to transfer me and I went to Deportivo La Coruña. I had a beautiful experience in Spain but I didn't adapt to the climate and it was very difficult. Belgrano were interested so I went there, and it was much closer to Buenos Aires than Spain.' Ribolzi returned to Boca at the end of 1979 and, although he formed part of the 1981 title-winning squad, his second spell there wasn't as successful as the first due to injuries and the vastly changed landscape at the club. After leaving Boca again, he returned to Atlanta, then went to Colombia where he had the pleasure of playing with Carlos Valderrama, and then to Ferro de General Pico. In 2005 he returned to La Bombonera in an altogether different capacity.

On 22 September 1978 Boca lost 3-1 at home (although the fixture was played in Atlanta's stadium) to San Lorenzo in the Metropolitano, and it was the last 45 minutes for Alfredo Oscar Márquez in a Boca shirt. 'On the advice of Lorenzo I went to Tigre in 1979 with goalkeeper Héctor Pistone and we won the second division. Once a week we would both return to train at La Candela under Toto's supervision,' remembered the full-back. After three years with Tigre, Márquez represented Deportivo Español, Lanús, Arsenal, and Defensores de Villa Ramallo before ending his professional career with El Porvenir.

Despite his career in the blue-and-gold not quite panning out how he would have liked, Márquez feels great pride at having represented such a club during its first golden era. 'It's a beautiful thing to be a professional footballer, even more so at a club like Boca Juniors,' recalled the man from Morón. 'Many doors are opened for you. You don't have to queue at banks, people give you gifts, you are invited on TV and radio shows, and recognised in the street. It was a great source of pride to belong to the world's biggest club.' Now, aged 62, Márquez still keeps himself in shape and plays with other ex-Boca players.

Boca went toe to toe with Quilmes in the last few months of the 1978 Metropolitano campaign. Managed by José Yudica, the Rosario native who had spent two years at Boca between 1959 and 1961, the unfashionable outfit finished one point ahead of Boca to lift their first title of the professional era. Lorenzo used 41 players over the course of the tournament as the squad was rotated to prioritise the international competitions and, in that context, the second-place finish was admirable.

The 1978 Nacional was another domestic competition sacrificed in order to focus on the Copa Libertadores. As holders, Boca were given a bye to the semi-final group phase where they were drawn with River Plate and Atlético Mineiro. Boca eased through, drawing with River at La Bombonera before beating the Brazilians home and away. In the return in El Monumental, Boca beat River 2-0 with goals from Mastrángelo and Salinas and the frustrated home side ended the game with nine men. Under Ángel Labruna – one of Argentine football's most potent forwards – River were feared for their offensive prowess yet failed to breach Boca's backline in many of the decisive derbies of the era.

Deportivo Cali, foes from the previous year, awaited in the final. Cali, coached by future World Cup winner Carlos Bilardo, were the first Colombian side to reach the Copa Libertadores final. Bilardo had already taken Estudiantes to the final in 1971 and therefore had previous, pertinent, experience in the competition. The debutants held Boca 0-0 in the first leg at the Estadio Olímpico Pascual Guerrero.

Boca overwhelmed their less experienced opponents in the return leg at La Bombonera, dominating the match to run out 4-0 winners. Hugo Perotti's first-half goal was augmented by three in the space of 26 second-half minutes from Mastrángelo, Salinas, and another from Perotti. The unbeaten Boca were once again rulers of the continent yet were denied the chance to defend the Intercontinental Cup after European champions Liverpool once again refused to take part, as did beaten finalists Club Brugge. For Francisco Sá it was the second Copa Libertadores triumph with Boca, and his sixth overall, making him the most decorated individual in the history of the competition.

Despite the success achieved so far in his three years at the helm – two domestic championships, two Copas Libertadores, and one Intercontinental Cup – Lorenzo announced his resignation at the end of 1978 due to a dispute with the club's directors. The finances were also in disarray, set against the backdrop of a dwindling national economy. The space on the front of Gatti's shirt was sold to Jet, an electronic video game company. This was the first advertisement of its kind and it heralded a new era in which the shirt was no longer a proud representation of the club's colours. Instead, players would increasingly become walking billboards.

Lorenzo ultimately retracted his resignation and the club pressed ahead with plans for 1979. The Metropolitano was once again pushed to the back of the priority list as Boca focused on retaining the Copa Libertadores, where they were given another bye to the semi-final stage and were grouped with Independiente and Peñarol. Boca and their compatriots both gained five points and had to play-off, a de facto one-off semi-final to see who would progress to the final to face Paraguay's Olimpia.

Boca and Independiente squared off at El Monumental and after 84 minutes the game had yet to produce a goal. The reds from Avellaneda looked to have the upper hand when Sá was dismissed against his former club leaving Boca with a numerical disadvantage with extra time looming. With seconds remaining on the clock after more than two hours had elapsed, Mastrángelo pounced to send Boca through to the final, their third in as many years. It was yet another crucial goal for the prolific right-sided forward from Santa Fe.

The first leg in Asunción was disastrous for Boca, Luis Cubilla's Olimpia taking a 2-0 lead within 27 minutes. After conceding the first early goal, Lorenzo's side were forced, uncharacteristically, to come out of their shell, rather than sitting back with the aim of bagging an away draw. The Paraguayans seized on this and were able to score that crucial second goal and hold on to their advantage.

Boca were unable to produce a rousing comeback and turn the tie around in the second leg at La Bombonera. After just two minutes both sides were reduced to ten men, Suñé and Roberto Paredes given their marching orders by Uruguayan referee Daniel Cardellino. After 69 minutes another double red card – including Jorge Benítez for Boca – saw the last 20 minutes played out as a nine-a-side affair. Despite the game's stretched nature, Boca were unable to find the breakthrough and, with Olimpia's goalkeeper in inspired form, the quest to become continental *tricampeón* had failed.

Boca performed poorly in the 1979 Nacional as River did the double once again, winning both of the championships in the calendar year. On the final day of the season, Boca drew 0-0 away to San Lorenzo, who were playing the last game in their iconic Gasómetro home. Also saying goodbye was Juan Carlos Lorenzo after four unforgettable years. The departing coach had presided over the most glorious epoch of Boca's history thus far and never had the club been so successful in such a short period of time.

Márquez, Ribolzi, and Suárez all agreed that Lorenzo was ahead of his time. 'He looked after all of the details,' began Ribolzi. 'He was a hardworking coach, with a good eye for a player, and had a lot of conviction as to what he wanted. He told us in the very first week when we were reunited ahead of the season that we simply had to win each and every time we stepped foot on the pitch.' His experience was also key, according to Suárez: 'Lorenzo brought a lot of new ideas with him, from Europe and the national team. A lot to do with training and match preparation. He changed the structure of Boca Juniors and Argentine football as a whole.' His eye for detail was a vital part of his armoury. 'He was an impressive strategist,' according to Márquez. 'He observed our rivals and we knew the qualities and defects of each team which made it easier to play them. He also had an excellent fitness coach, Jorge Castelli, one of the best I ever had.'

Antonio Rattín was hired to replace Lorenzo but was somewhat hamstrung from the start. The former midfielder inherited an ageing squad on the wrong side of its peak, and the club lacked the finances to overhaul the playing staff. The chaos showed in the league finishes as Boca performed poorly in both the Metropolitano and Nacional standings. The end of 1980 saw big changes across all areas of the club and, after much success, it was clear that the cycle was over.

Rattín's short reign was ended, and he left along with his technical staff and around 60 per cent of the squad, many of whom had taken the club to unimaginable heights in the latter half of the 1970s – players such as Rubén Suñé. *Chapa* won eight major titles with Boca over two spells and was rewarded for his service when, in December 2016, to coincide with the 40th anniversary of his historic goal against River, a statue of him was unveiled to proudly stand in the club museum. The bronze, life-size statue depicts the player with a serious, concentrating face, standing straight with his arms folded, and wearing the captain's armband. Suñé, a lifelong fan of the club, struggled with depression after retiring from football, a period of suffering which culminated in a suicide attempt in 1984. After falling from the seventh floor of a building in which he lived in Pompeya, he suffered injuries to his limbs and internal organs. Luckily, Suñé showed the same steel he had displayed during his playing career to recover from the life-threatening injuries, returning to work with Boca's *inferiores* before passing away in June 2019.

Another protagonist from Lorenzo's glory days, José María Suárez, remained at the club until May 1982, making the 1981 Metropolitano his fifth major honour won there. 'When I left, I actually had a contract for another year but Lorenzo had left,' remembered *Colo*. 'Rattín, Cap, and various other coaches had come and gone because the club wasn't in great shape and was suffering from economic problems. I wanted to see out my contract but didn't see eye to eye with the incumbent coach.' After 208 games in all competitions in the *azul y oro*, Suárez played for Nueva Chicago, Huracán and Racing but has never forgotten the time spent at Boca. 'When Boca bought me, it was like touching the sky with my hands because for me it's a place where every player wants to be,' said Suárez. 'It was great to win these titles with such a grand institution. When I left Boca my football career was over. What can you do after leaving Boca? Which club is going to be bigger or better than Boca? None.'

Armando's two-decade stint also ended in 1980, with Martín Noel and a new *Comisión Directiva* replacing him. The outgoing president had turned winning the Copa Libertadores into a personal obsession and was able to realise his dream in 1977 after a 17-year wait. The visionary died in December 1988 and in 2000 the stadium was officially renamed the Estadio Alberto J. Armando in his honour. However, at the start of the 1980s, the club's finances were in dire straits. The club needed a lift, and it would come in the form of a new signing, an exciting young player that would go on to become one of the best ever to grace the game.

Chapter Six

Maradona and the 1981 Metropolitano

IF FOOTBALL in Argentina did blossom in the slums, as written by famed Uruguayan writer Eduardo Galeano, then the quintessential embodiment of this concept came in the form of Diego Armando Maradona. The poster boy of the *potrero*, wasteland areas where many honed their footballing craft, was born in October 1960 in the unforgiving Villa Fiorito neighbourhood, 15km from Downtown Buenos. The dusty, uneven surfaces forced players to adapt, to do whatever it took to win, even if it meant tricking your opponents. The two faces of *potrero* football were evident in the quarter-final of the 1986 World Cup in Mexico. Maradona deceived the referee with the famous 'Hand of God' goal, proving he would do anything to win, yet minutes later displayed brilliant dribbling and close control skills to score one of the greatest World Cup goals of all time.

Long before he lifted the World Cup trophy in the Estadio Azteca, a young Maradona rose through the famed youth ranks of Argentinos Juniors, debuting for the first team in October 1976, ten days shy of his 16th birthday. Such was his impact with *El Bicho*, the club from La Paternal would later rename their stadium in his honour. In 1979, one year after César Luis Menotti led *La Albiceleste* to World Cup glory on home soil, Maradona, now scoring freely at club level, destroyed the field at the FIFA World Youth Championship showing that he was in a different stratosphere to his age-group peers.

Maradona introduced himself to Boca fans, in earnest, in September 1980 when he put four goals past Hugo Gatti as Argentinos ran out 5-3 winners before receiving a round of applause. The two adversaries would later go on to become team-mates and great friends. It was inevitable that Maradona would ultimately outgrow the club that gave him his start in professional football. At just 20 years old, Maradona had already amassed 24 senior international caps, scoring 11 goals in the process. The phenomenon had scored 116 goals in 166 appearances over five years in La Paternal and, despite his tender age, was already considered one of global football's brightest lights.

Despite the individual brilliance he displayed with Argentinos Juniors, Maradona won nothing; his generation-defining talent needed a platform. When they signed him on an 18-month loan agreement, Boca paid Maradona's parent club US$4m, inherited US$1.1m of Argentinos' debt, and sent six players the other way as part of the deal. There was an option to make the transfer permanent for a further US$4m. Boca's bank balance was almost empty but the costly signing of Maradona was a case of speculating to accumulate. After a period of low attendances, his presence brought fans back to La Bombonera and created a buzz not seen since the glory days under Lorenzo.

River Plate also showed strong interest in signing the precocious youngster – offering him a contract on a par with their highest earner, accomplished goalkeeper Ubaldo Fillol –

but he chose to follow his heart instead of his wallet to fulfil a dream. Like when he joined unfashionable Napoli years later, Maradona wanted to be Boca's saviour and throughout his career thrived as a rebellious man-of-the-people. It would, however, be too romantic to suggest that he was playing solely for the love of the sport. Including sponsorships, his earnings were said to have topped US$2m per year.

Maradona arrived at La Bombonera nursing a thigh injury that restricted him to, according to his calculations, 60 per cent of his usual capacity. However, he was still able to crown his competitive home debut with a brace of penalties in a 4-1 win over Talleres that opened the 1981 Metropolitano championship. The number ten turned creator for Boca's second goal which was scored by fellow debutant Miguel Ángel Brindisi, the former Huracán legend with whom he struck up a wonderfully fruitful partnership. Brindisi, nominally playing alongside Maradona at the tip of a 4-2-2-2 formation, added the third.

The 30-year-old forward, whose acquisition cost the club US$300,000, was intelligent and technically sound and acted as a perfect foil for Maradona. A former national team-mate of new coach Silvio Marzolini, a club legend from the 1960s, Brindisi had been taken to his first Boca match by his father at the age of seven. As a youngster, he had idolised the Brazilian forward Paulo Valentim

Instituto were the visitors to La Bombonera on matchday two. Maradona scored another double, although it wasn't enough to earn maximum points, with the home side having to settle for a 2-2 draw. One of his goals came from the penalty spot, but his first goal from open play showed a glimpse of his genius. The youngster performed a *sombrero*, flicking the ball over the head of the defender, before putting it through Carlos Munutti's legs in the Instituto goal with his weaker right foot.

The thigh injury that had plagued Maradona since his arrival forced him to sit out the next five games. In his absence Boca coped remarkably well, clocking up five successive wins against Huracán, Platense, Sarmiento, Unión, and San Lorenzo. Brindisi shouldered the goal-scoring burden, notching five in as many games. Diego returned as Newell's Old Boys visited La Bombonera on matchday eight. The *rosarino* outfit headed home with a point after a 2-2 draw in which Maradona scored another from the penalty spot. His proficiency from 12 yards and ability to keep calm under pressure belied his age. Next, a 2-0 win away to Independiente, with another goal courtesy of Maradona's left foot, meant that Boca were going into the first *Superclásico* of the season unbeaten.

River were also in fine form heading into the crunch clash, and between them the two rivals were unbeaten in 18 matches. Rain of biblical proportions inundated La Bombonera's turf on the evening of Friday 10 April and would continue throughout the 90 minutes. The first half failed to produce any moments of brilliance and was more synonymous with violence. Maradona himself was booked after just four minutes. River were reduced to ten men after 23 minutes when Reinaldo Merlo was dismissed for punching Brindisi in the stomach but the numbers were evened up two minutes later when Osvaldo Escudero was sent off for raising his fists.

After 55 minutes Boca drew first blood and Maradona was instrumental in Brindisi's goal. Five minutes after breaking the deadlock, the number nine doubled his tally, coolly slotting the ball past Fillol. On 67 minutes, completing a whirlwind 12-minute spell in which Boca simply blew away their visitors, Maradona sealed the victory and, in the process, created one of the most cherished moments in the history of the rivalry. *El Pibe de Oro* controlled a cross from the right-hand side before deceiving Fillol, dropping his shoulder to leave the goalkeeper red-faced and on his backside, before slotting the ball home from close range despite the best last-ditch efforts of the River defence. The celebration was pure joy. Maradona slid to the corner flag on his knees and soaked up the adulation of the adoring crowd.

Whilst Maradona rightly took the plaudits for his match-winning performance and unforgettable goal, the architect of the strike deserves a huge amount of credit for his role in the build-up. Unheralded full-back Carlos *Cacho* Córdoba picked up the ball deep on the left before driving diagonally across the pitch and centring a pass to his more celebrated team-mate. 'I think that is perhaps the one night that Boca fans will never forget,' remembered Córdoba fondly. 'Firstly, for the result. Secondly, because Diego was there. Thirdly, because the River players were on the floor with every goal we scored. And fourthly, because of the rain and the fact that the pitch was a complete mud bath, exactly how the Boca fans like it. It was an unforgettable night. At this point we felt like we were going to be champions.'

The native of Moreno, in Buenos Aires province, made his debut for Boca's first team as a 19-year-old in March 1978 after coming through the club's youth ranks. 'It all began the day before the match when the coach, Juan Carlos Lorenzo, gathered me and three other players who played the same position, in the canteen at La Candela,' explained Córdoba. 'The coach asked us how we would feel if one of us were selected to play against Estudiantes, in La Plata. My answer was I felt confident enough that I could even eat the grass [referring to a South American superstition that eating grass when entering the field brings luck]. Lorenzo must've liked what I said because I started the game and we had the good fortune of winning 1-0.'

The left-back's home debut in the top flight came the following Sunday against Independiente. 'Never in my life have I felt so relaxed and sure of myself as I did on that day. I felt great physically and mentally and, although I was a Boca fan and had waited for this moment, I didn't feel any nerves or pressure,' recalled Córdoba. 'My coaches, who were almost like father figures, simplified everything and prepared me for this moment. La Bombonera was full and I felt the support of the fans as we made our way from the tunnel to the pitch. I'm a *Bostero* since birth and to defend the colours of my club gave me an immense happiness that I'm not able to put into words.'

Córdoba's breakthrough came in 1980: 'I had been working hard for three years, alternating between the first team and the youth teams. Juan Carlos Lorenzo left and in came Antonio Rattín as the new coach. We weren't having a great season so Rattín gave me the opportunity to play regularly. From this moment, until the day I left, I was a starter. Injuries aside, I always had the luck to be starter under every coach Boca had. They all gave me the number three shirt.'

Immediately after the tense derby match in which Córdoba's assist for Maradona's timeless goal gave Boca a memorable win, their coach suffered a heart attack and was rushed to the hospital where he later underwent bypass surgery. Marzolini reportedly smoked upwards of 60 cigarettes a day, a habit which raised his cholesterol and exacerbated his physical demise. Mentally, the pressure cooker of the Boca hot seat must have also played a role.

With Marzolini convalescing and therefore absent from the dugout, Boca's first defeat of the season came in the very next game. The 1-0 loss away to Vélez Sarsfield was followed by two successive wins that got the season back on track. Colón were then brushed aside 3-0 at La Bombonera, Maradona jinking past several defenders before firing a low shot from the edge of the box.

The following game saw Boca make the short journey to face Ferro Carril Oeste, with whom they shared a goalless draw. Ferro's coach, Carlos Griguol, who won the 1973 Nacional with Rosario Central, had the unpretentious outfit organised and working hard. In 1982 and 1984 Griguol would lead Ferro to their only two championships which showed that, despite their modest history, they were serious rivals for the 1981 title.

Another Maradona penalty helped Boca defeat Rosario Central 3-2 in their next outing. Despite opening up a five-point lead at the top of the table, inconsistency continued to plague a talented squad which had yet to truly click. Only two points from the next three games were collected and suddenly the feeling around the club was that there was a long way to go before the finishing line was crossed. However, three successive victories followed. Huracán were defeated 3-2 at La Bombonera, Platense were thrashed 4-0 away from home courtesy of two Maradona goals, and Sarmiento were beaten 2-1 at La Bombonera.

Boca lost 2-0 to Unión in Santa Fe. The hapless San Lorenzo were the next visitors to Calle Brandsen, and were on the other end of a 4-0 thrashing. Maradona found himself on the scoresheet, bending a low free kick around the wall and into the net. For San Lorenzo the result was characteristic of a dreadful season which saw them suffer the humiliation of becoming the first *grande* to be relegated from the top flight.

Maradona, who Córdoba describes as a 'phenomenon, as a person and team-mate', was in full swing now, yet the on-field relationship between the player and his team-mates took some time to develop. 'Diego was always seen in a good light by his team-mates but the problem at the start was on the pitch. We'd see that he'd be always marked by two or three opponents and therefore didn't give him the ball. One day Diego spoke to a few of us and told us not to fear giving him the ball even if he had five marking him, because he would always evade them. From then we started doing that and the rest is history.'

Boca then won 2-0 away at Newell's. The versatile Roberto Passucci wasn't always a starting player throughout his time at Boca, but was guaranteed to carry out his coach's instructions to the letter. Ahead of the Newell's clash Maradona recommended to Marzolini that Passucci's attributes were perfectly suited to the occasion. The coach handed Passucci the number 11 shirt and the decision was vindicated: Passucci scored his only goal of the season in the match.

Unsatisfactory results then returned with a sequence of four draws. Diego found the net in the first three of those stalemates, against Independiente, River Plate, and Vélez. The fourth draw of the run was 2-2 against Maradona's old club, Argentinos Juniors, with the first goal coming after four minutes from the left boot of Carlos Córdoba, who unleashed a stunning half-volley into the top corner from 25 yards, his only goal of the season. As a result of the draw, Ferro drew level on points with Boca at the top of the table and it proved to be the straw that broke the camel's back for the hardcore fans.

On Saturday, 18 July, the night before the following fixture at home to Estudiantes, Boca's squad were customarily holed up at La Candela. A large number of Boca's *barra brava*, led by the fearsome José *El Abuelo* Barritta, showed up to voice their displeasure and issue a stark warning that an immediate improvement in form was required. It is alleged that the telephone wires were cut, preventing anyone alerting the authorities or anyone else in the outside world.

Córdoba remembers the night vividly: 'It was a tense moment, especially because they had firearms. If they didn't have guns it would have still been a problem because there were so many of them, but the guns could have created an even bigger mess. Prominent players such as Jorge Ribolzi and Francisco Sá crazily went to the front to try to speak, but the *barra* didn't want a discussion. They simply said what they wanted to say and left.' Boca's star player also learned a lesson that night. 'I think, on this night, Maradona realised just how big Boca was,' explained Córdoba.

The energy-sapping friendlies, which Boca were playing alongside the Metropolitano schedule, stopped following the night at La Candela. With the focus fully on the domestic championship, Gatti returned to the starting line-up for the first time in over four months as Marzolini's men notched a 1-0 win over the visitors from La Plata thanks to Hugo Perotti's 38th-minute goal. Colón were defeated 2-0 on their patch the following week, but it was far from routine. The home side withdrew from the match after 78 minutes, following their second red card of the game, in protest at the referee's decisions. The points were Boca's, nicely setting up a crunch clash with title rivals Ferro.

The stubborn Ferro, one point behind Boca going into the game, frustrated an expectant La Bombonera, yet also managed to craft openings of their own. Man-of-the-match Gatti was called into action several times and the tense affair was settled by a single goal which was created by Maradona and scored by Perotti. In the penultimate game Boca lost 1-0 away at Rosario Central with the usually dependable Maradona smashing a penalty off the crossbar. Ferro also slipped up, held at home 3-3 by Huracán, taking the title down to the wire.

Boca knew that if they avoided defeat on the final day at home to Racing they would be crowned champions for the first time in five years. Maradona put the disappointment of the previous week behind him, slamming home a penalty before half-time to notch his 17th goal of the season, form which earned him the Argentine Footballer of the Year accolade for the third successive season. Racing drew themselves level with a late goal in a feisty game which saw the referee brandish five red cards, including one for Carlos Córdoba, whose expulsion was due to frustration with a knee injury he had been carrying as opposed to anything sinister. Abel Gnecco blew his whistle to signal full time and the fact that Boca, wearing the iconic Adidas home strip, were officially the 1981 Metropolitano champions.

Córdoba, the only player to start all of Boca's league games that season, waxes lyrical about the youthful 1981 side and feels that it is often overlooked when discussions turn to Boca's greatest-ever teams: 'I think the 1981 Boca was one of the best sides in the club's history, and I'll tell you why. Many people don't know, and journalists never wrote about it, but most of the starting XI were 21 or younger. Of the regular starters in this team only Roberto Mouzo, Carlos Rodríguez, Jorge Benítez and Brindisi were older.'

Mouzo, who had given the captain's armband to Maradona at the request of Marzolini, was never the most technically gifted, yet made up for it with unerring persistence. His athleticism and will to win ensured he stayed in the team for more than a decade, spanning the managerial reigns of Rogelio Domínguez, Juan Carlos Lorenzo, Marzolini, and many more.

Just before the Metropolitano triumph, the peso was devalued and Argentina's economy continued to freefall. Boca defaulted on the next instalment of their loan agreement with Argentinos and, three weeks after being declared champions, the club's assets were frozen. The fans hoped the title would kick-start a new era but the club was broke and before long the title-winning squad began to fall apart. 'We would have made history with that team had we been able to keep it together, but the economic situation made that impossible,' lamented Córdoba. 'Diego, Brindisi, Benítez, Marcelo Trobbiani, Carlos Morete, Escudero, Vicente Pernía, Ribolzi, Sá and many more left the club within a year or two. It was such a young team, and this is something that you don't always see at Boca.'

There would be no back-to-back success in the 1981 Nacional as Boca were eliminated by Vélez in the quarter-final. Boca led 2-1 after the first meeting in La Bombonera, yet they would have to travel to Liniers without the suspended Maradona, one of six players red-carded in the first leg. For *El Diego*, it would prove to be the last competitive game of his first spell in the blue-and-gold shirt. Vélez took advantage of the missing talisman to win the return 3-1 and progress to the final four. Boca's exhausted players were simultaneously participating in numerous money-spinning friendlies during the Nacional campaign, a schedule designed to help pay for Maradona's transfer. The series took the club to Mexico, Spain, France, Italy, Brazil, Peru, Ecuador and even the Ivory Coast.

Silvio Marzolini was fired and replaced with Vladislao Cap. The dawn of the 80s had promised much yet less than two years into the decade the honeymoon period was well and truly over. Boca took on an even more ludicrous run of friendlies in January 1982, taking in Los Angeles, Hong Kong, Kuala Lumpur, Japan, Mexico and Guatemala. The ill-prepared players performed poorly in the 1982 Nacional, switched to the first half of the year and kicking off in mid-February, failing to progress past the first phase. Maradona missed the campaign as he had already joined up with the national team ahead of the 1982 World Cup, Menotti calling the squad up early to aid preparation. Following the tournament, in July, Maradona completed a long-expected transfer to FC Barcelona for more than US$7m.

The Metropolitano championship, which kicked off in July 1982, was named in honour of the Argentine Sovereignty of Las Malvinas (known as The Falkland Islands in the English-speaking world). In April 1982, midway through the Nacional, Argentina's flailing military junta rolled the dice one last time, attempting to retain some sense of legitimacy amidst a broken economy and plummeting levels of popularity, by launching an invasion to reclaim the British overseas territory. Just 73 days later Argentine forces surrendered after a resounding defeat and the demise of the regime paved the way for democratic elections which took place in October 1983. Despite the club's economic woes, the Maradona-less team, coached by Carmelo Faraone, performed admirably, finishing third as Carlos Bilardo's Estudiantes claimed the title.

Boca finished rock bottom of their group in the first phase of the 1982 Copa Libertadores and exited the 1983 Nacional at the quarter-final stage. The seventh-place finish in the 1983 Metropolitano masked the truth: in terms of points Boca were closer to the bottom than the top and conceded ten more goals than basement club Racing de Córdoba. This campaign saw the introduction of the controversial *promedios* system, in which relegation is worked out on a team's average performance over three seasons. Following the recent relegation of San Lorenzo, it was deemed bad for business, and a blow to the prestige of the Argentine top flight, to see one of the most prominent teams drop out. The measure was meant to offer the biggest clubs an extra layer of protection but the irony was that in 1983 the system led to the relegation of Racing, although it did conveniently save River Plate, who finished second-bottom of the table.

There was no improvement for Boca in 1984. Institutional problems that had been brewing for years were finally coming home to roost, on and off the field of play, and chaos ensued. The coffers of the debt-riddled club were empty, and competitive games continued to be intertwined with distracting friendlies aimed at bringing in cash to stave off bankruptcy. The introduction of the club's first shirt sponsor – los vinos Maravilla – didn't raise the required funds. Boca played many games during this period away from La Bombonera and it wasn't the same without their spiritual home. The company hired by the club to perform vital rebuilding work went unpaid and effectively downed tools halfway through the process, forcing the local council to close the arena, deeming it unsafe.

The most striking example of how far the club had fallen came on matchday 15 of the Metropolitano championship. On 8 July 1984 Boca lost 2-1 at home to Atlanta in what became known as the 'evening of the faded shirts'. Before the game Boca lost the coin toss and were forced to wear an alternative kit yet, due to financial constraints, the club didn't have one. Instead, the players wore white T-shirts and drew the numbers on the back with a marker pen. After a short while the ink began to run on the shirts due to the players' sweat as well as the winter drizzle. At half-time Boca reverted to their traditional kit. The side that faced Atlanta was made up of reserves, and throughout the Metropolitano the club used a staggering 55 players.

A month before the watershed clash with Atlanta, the club's most prominent players staged a strike after non-payment of wages. Backed by the FAA union, and the Ministry of Labour, the stars requested freedom from their contracts. Players fought amongst themselves, and also rallied against the directors. Domingo Corigliano, who had only become president in December 1983, was forced to resign soon after taking office after breaking promises made following his election victory.

Numerous players left during this period, including Hugo Alves, Jorge Vázquez, Juan Sotelo and José Berta. Roberto Mouzo, the one-time club captain who has made more appearances for Boca than any other player in the club's history, including 29 *Superclásicos*, bid farewell to the club. Oscar Ruggeri, World Cup winner in 1986, and Ricardo Gareca both drew ire from Boca fans in joining arch-rivals River Plate. In this era it was common for players to remain at one club for their entire career. Contracts of professional players under the age of 23 were renewed automatically with a 20 per cent increase in salary yet Ruggeri and Gareca, as two of the club's key players, demanded a rise above and beyond the standard 20 per cent.

Carlos Córdoba was another player caught up in the unfortunate events of 1984, another who would soon leave the club: 'Leaving took a lot of time and energy, and having to leave left me hurt and with a pain in my soul. Boca was, is and always will be my home and I never wanted to leave, but the things that happened, happened. I gave 100 per cent for 12 years of my life, and Boca not only gave me my name in football, but made me a man in life.' *Cacho*'s path soon took him to the United States, where he still lives with his family today, and he now coaches a professional team in Milwaukee, Wisconsin.

The 1980s started brightly with the appointment of Marzolini as manager and the acquisition of Maradona, both of which helped Boca to the 1981 Metro. Yet the capturing of the title for the first time in five years only masked problems that had been brewing since the end of the previous decade and the final days of the Armando administration. After a disastrous first half of the 1980s there was a genuine chance of Boca going bankrupt and it would take the arrival of a new president to save the club.

Chapter Seven

Alegre and the 1992 Apertura

IN THE mid-1980s Boca were in the worst position of their storied history and, without exaggeration, in grave danger of disappearing altogether. On 6 January 1985 Antonio Alegre assumed the presidency of the club and began the monumental task of turning around the ship during a time of real crisis.

The bricklayer-turned-entrepreneur came from a humble background, born in Buenos Aires to Lebanese immigrants in August 1924. Alongside his running mate, banking executive Carlos Heller, Alegre would revive the club's fortunes over the next decade. To ensure the much-loved institution survived in the first instance, the new president pumped his own money into the chaos-stricken club. Alegre mortgaged his personal assets to raise US$250,000, loaned the club a further US$800,000 and settled 153 lawsuits.

Alegre hired Alfredo Di Stéfano, the architect of the fondly remembered 1969 league and cup double, as coach ahead of the 1985 Nacional campaign. The club signed three players that would go on to win the World Cup in Mexico 18 months later: José Luis Brown, who would score in the final against West Germany, came from Estudiantes; Julio Olarticoechea and left-footed attacking midfielder Carlos Tapia came from River as part of the deal that took Oscar Ruggeri and Ricardo Gareca to El Monumental. Unlike Ruggeri and Gareca, and the majority of players who have crossed the bitter divide, Olarticoechea would forever remain popular with both sets of fans. Boca also signed fierce offensive left-back Enrique Hrabina from San Lorenzo and forward Alfredo Graciani from Atlanta. Despite the new faces, Boca won their group before being eliminated by Vélez.

The 1985 Nacional signalled the end of the Metropolitano and Nacional tournament format after almost 20 years. In their place, a long-form championship, designed to run alongside the European calendar, was adopted. The first clash of the 1985/86 season between Boca and River came in round 17, on 27 October 1985. River were 1-0 to the good in El Monumental when, after 73 minutes, Roberto Passucci was red-carded, one of 16 he would receive whilst wearing the blue-and-gold shirt. His offence was a two-footed, knee-high tackle on former team-mate Ruggeri. As Passucci left the pitch the Boca faithful sang his name – *Passuuuuuuucci, Passuuuuuuucci* – as he touched the crest on his shirt, solidifying his status as a fan favourite.

Ruggeri, however, had the last laugh. The return fixture took place on 6 April 1986, exactly four weeks after a rampant River had sealed the title. Despite being down to ten men for the last 25 minutes of the match River, managed by future Boca boss Héctor Veira, won 2-0 with a brace from Norberto Alonso. The mischievous champions, who ultimately finished 15 points ahead of fifth-place Boca, performed a lap of honour around the La Bombonera pitch and were showered with projectiles from the stands.

In between April and June, whilst Diego Maradona was leading Argentina to World Cup glory in Mexico, Boca won a mini-tournament, the Liguilla, to determine which other teams would qualify for the upcoming Copa Libertadores. Boca, back in the continent's top competition, finished third in their group and failed to progress to the knockout rounds. River, who had been almost relegated from the Argentine top flight just three years earlier, bagged their first-ever Copa Libertadores title.

Boca started the 1986/87 campaign in poor fashion, the Copa Libertadores proving an unwelcome distraction in the first couple of months of the new season. On 21 December Boca were trounced 3-0 by Ferro and, in the wake of the defeat, Mario Zanabria resigned after winning just 23 points in as many games. The combative Passucci followed him out of the exit door, signing for Talleres after six years and 191 appearances. Although Passucci won just one title in Boca colours – the 1981 Metro – he was idolised for his loyalty and sacrifice, putting the team first during an incredibly difficult era. As with many of his peers, he returned to work for the club in 2012.

Zanabria's replacement in the dugout was none other than César Luis Menotti. Argentina's World Cup-winning coach from 1978 had an immediate impact, winning seven games on the bounce. In the final 15 games, Boca won as many points as they had in the first 23 under Zanabria, going top of the table after the 34th round. But just two points from the last three games ended their title hopes. Rosario Central finished three points ahead of Menotti's men and completed a unique double, having won the Primera B and been promoted to the top flight just the season before. For Boca, it was an acceptable campaign despite the lack of star quality in the side, the major highlight being the acquisition of Jorge Comas who scored 19 goals in 33 games after signing from Vélez.

After losing the second leg of the Liguilla final to Independiente, Boca failed to qualify for the Copa

Libertadores. Surprisingly, Menotti resigned, citing health and personal problems. Yet just days later the coach popped up in Madrid, signing on to manage Atlético, before returning to Argentina to take charge of River Plate.

Looking to retain the Menotti style, Alegre hired one of his former assistants to lead Boca into the 1987/88 season. Roberto Saporiti lasted just five games, one of which saw his side fall 6-0 away to Racing. Juan Carlos Lorenzo, at the time the club's most successful coach, returned to the hot seat but, suffering health problems, he was gone by December. José Omar Pastoriza, who won five major honours with Independiente, became Boca's third coach of the season in January and steered the club to a lowly 12th-place finish. Newell's, with former Boca player José Yudica in charge, won the league after finishing runners-up for two consecutive seasons, ensuring that the title stayed in Rosario.

Ahead of the 1988/89 season, Pastoriza made several key signings. Carlos Tapia returned for his second spell at the club after a short stint with Brest, and elegant defender Juan Simón joined him in signing from the French league after five years. Despite earning well during his spell in France, 28-year-old Simón had been out of sight, out of mind of the national team coach and wanted to cement his place in the squad for Italia 90, which he duly did, in no small part thanks to his courage and impeccable timing in the tackle. Colombian goalkeeper Carlos Navarro Montoya signed from Vélez; elegant midfielder Claudio Marangoni, who had a spell with Sunderland in the English Second Division, joined from Independiente where he had won the Copa Libertadores and Intercontinental Cup under Pastoriza.

Deportivo Armenio were the guests at La Bombonera on the first day of the season, taking a surprise lead after 34 minutes. The visitors' striker had been put through on Gatti's goal and the eccentric goalkeeper completely misjudged the path of the ball, allowing Sergio Maciel an easy finish. Boca lost the game 1-0 and for 44-year-old Gatti, it was the end of the road. The crowd-pleasing stopper, who saved 26 penalties throughout his career, had guarded Boca's goal for 417 official appearances over 12 years. Between his signing, in 1976, and 1981, the trailblazer won six titles, yet in the last seven years won nothing. For Gatti, at Boca, it was a distinct career of two halves.

The following week, with Navarro Montoya in goal, Boca atoned for the opening day defeat by beating River 2-0 at El Monumental. When the two sides met again in February 1989, they shared a 0-0 draw at La Bombonera. Thanks to a bizarre new rule from the AFA, introduced for this season and then rightfully scrapped, draws went to penalty kicks, with a bonus point awarded to the victor. In this instance River were the beneficiaries, winning 4-3 on spot-kicks. Boca finished ahead of their rivals in the 1988/89 table yet eight points behind champions Independiente.

Conmebol brought the 1989 Copa Libertadores forward so Boca, second in the table at Christmas 1988, qualified. After winning the group Boca were knocked out at the last-16 stage by Olimpia. A dramatic late comeback in the second leg had given Boca a 5-3 win and made it 5-5 on aggregate, but the Paraguayans progressed on penalty kicks. In the post-season Liguilla, Boca were trounced 4-0 by San Lorenzo, a result that led to the departure of Pastoriza. He was replaced by Carlos Aimar, a former assistant to Carlos Griguol.

Ahead of the 1989/90 season, the squad incorporated José Daniel Ponce, a midfielder who had partnered Miguel Ángel Russo at Estudiantes as the La Plata outfit won back-to-back titles in 1982/83 under the guidance of Carlos Bilardo. Another midfielder, 25-year-old Blas Giunta, was repatriated to Argentina after a season in Spain with Murcia.

Aimar's side amassed just 19 points from the first 18 games of the new domestic campaign, with all eyes on the Supercopa Libertadores. In the second version of the tournament, created by Conmebol to honour previous winners of the Copa Libertadores, Boca beat Racing and Grêmio to set up a final versus Independiente. With goalless draws in each of the two legs, the match went to penalty kicks at the end of the second leg at La Doble Visera. The first seven efforts were all successfully converted before Luis Fabián Artime, son of the great goalscorer of the 1960s, stepped up to face Navarro Montoya. *Mono*, diving to his left, pushed the effort on to the post, giving Blas Giunta the chance to make it 5-3 and seal the cup for Boca.

Giunta, the ultimate exponent of the *huevos* (literally translated as eggs but referring to courage) mentality so admired at Boca, carefully spotted the ball before lashing home. The away fans erupted, and Boca celebrated their first title since the 1981 Metropolitano. After such a difficult decade, which saw a major drought of trophies as the club nearly went out of existence, the Supercopa Libertadores was a welcome tonic.

The second half of the 1989/90 league campaign, with the Supercopa in the bag, saw much improvement from Aimar's side, with just one defeat in the first eight games after Christmas. In March 1990 another chance for a trophy presented itself. The Recopa Sudamericana was another new creation of South American football's governing body, pitting the Copa Libertadores champions, Atlético Nacional, against the holders of the Supercopa Libertadores, Boca. For the Colombians, with strong links to Pablo Escobar and the Medellín Cartel, the Copa Libertadores triumph of 1989 was their first continental trophy.

The Recopa, originally scheduled over two legs, was converted into a one-off match due to security concerns in

Colombia and, instead, took place in Miami's Orange Bowl stadium. After 38 minutes Diego Latorre, the supremely gifted 20-year-old youth-team graduate, rounded René Higuita before finishing from 18 yards. It had taken Boca more than eight years to win a title, and now Aimar had bagged two trophies in the space of four glorious months.

Boca ultimately finished third in the league table, ten points behind champions River Plate. Once again, the Liguilla provided a back door to the Copa Libertadores and Aimar's side bested Independiente over two legs to win the mini-tournament and qualify for the upcoming continental competition.

Following Italia 90, where Maradona and Argentina reached the final only to lose to West Germany, the domestic championship was split into two – the Apertura and Clausura – with the winners of each to meet to declare the overall champion of the season. The Apertura started brightly enough for *Los Xeneizes*, with four straight wins and a draw leading into the first *Superclásico* of the season in September 1990. A 2-0 defeat at El Monumental seemed to send the side into a downward spiral.

Aimar signed his death warrant in the following match, a 2-1 home defeat to Rosario Central, by leaving out the popular veteran Marangoni. The fans were livid with the decision and made their disgust known publicly. The anger swirling around the stadium was exacerbated by a red card for the temperamental Giunta – one of 14 he would be shown in the *azul y oro* – and a late winner for the visitors. A 1-0 loss away to Newell's on 7 December signalled the end of Aimar, who tendered his resignation.

The penultimate fixture of the Apertura saw San Lorenzo visit La Bombonera on Friday, 14 December, with Osvaldo Potente in caretaker charge of the side. San Lorenzo took the lead after four minutes but, at half-time, the match was suspended because of a tragic incident. Boca fan Saturnino Cabrera, a 37-year-old father of three, was struck by a three-metre-long metal pipe, ripped out of the bathrooms, and thrown from the visiting fans' enclosure situated above, killing him instantly. Throughout the next couple of decades, Argentine football would become almost synonymous with fan violence; the *barras bravas* became increasingly intertwined with the clubs they purported to support.

Boca finished eighth in the Apertura. The winners of the tournament, Newell's, would await the Clausura victors to determine the definitive champions of the 1990/91 season. Uruguayan coach Óscar Washington Tabárez was installed as Boca manager ahead of the Clausura portion of the season, and came with considerable pedigree. *El Maestro,* a former teacher in his homeland, had taken Peñarol to the Copa Libertadores title in 1987 and led his national side at the 1990 World Cup in Italy. He would have to face his first season without Marangoni, who retired in pre-season, aged 37.

Boca went unbeaten in the first five games of the Clausura, then defeated River at La Bombonera through a long-range strike from Latorre. Five days later Tabárez's men qualified from a tight Copa Libertadores group. Corinthians and Flamengo were knocked out by Boca, completing a Brazilian double, before Colo Colo ended the run at the semi-final stage. The second leg against the Chileans, in Santiago's Estadio Monumental, produced an on-pitch battle which echoed Boca's clash with Sporting Cristal 20 years earlier. The home side were 3-1 to the good after 82 minutes when a brawl erupted, featuring players, staff, and even photojournalists. Navarro Montoya was bitten by a police dog and Giunta was dismissed by the referee along with Colo Colo's Patricio Yáñez.

The league fixture following the Copa Libertadores heartbreak saw Boca trounce Racing 6-1 at La Bombonera. Latorre grabbed two of the goals but the star of the show was his strike partner, Gabriel Batistuta, who scored a hat-trick in what was his breakthrough season. The fearsome duo featured in all 19 of the Clausura's rounds, bagging 20 goals between them. Boca finished five points clear at the top of the final Clausura table, ending the schedule unbeaten having conceded just six goals, and setting up a title decider against Apertura winners Newell's. *Los Xeneizes*, crucially, were without Latorre and Batistuta, who had both been selected for Argentina's Copa América squad.

At Rosario Central's Gigante de Arroyito stadium, Newell's, managed by Marcelo Bielsa, took the first leg honours with a slender 1-0 victory. Two days later, on the other side of the Andes, Batistuta bagged a brace as Argentina brushed Venezuela aside 3-0 in the Chilean capital. It was a reminder of exactly what Boca were missing. In the return at La Bombonera, Gerardo Reinoso, brought in on loan purely for this two-legged affair, scored the only goal of regulation time, finishing from 12 yards. Both sides saw a player dismissed in extra time: Cristian Domizzi for Newell's, and Simón for Boca.

The resulting penalty kicks took place on a bed of ticker tape. Newell's number one Norberto Scoponi saved efforts from Graciani and Claudio Rodríguez; Giunta converted his kick before Walter Pico missed to hand Newell's the title. It was a ridiculous administrative error to schedule a game of such importance at a time when the star performers were away on international duty. It was a mistake that wasn't repeated: following the debacle the Apertura and Clausura were treated as individual tournaments, with the victor in each awarded a championship.

Tabárez had breathed new life into the club, but they would have to dust themselves down and regroup without Batistuta. After his breakthrough campaign, and stellar international performances – his six goals contributed to Argentina's Copa América success – the powerful forward was whisked off to Europe by Fiorentina, where he became a club legend synonymous with Serie A's glory years.

In an attempt to replace the firepower provided by Batistuta, Tabárez recruited 30-year-old Paraguayan striker Roberto Cabañas from Olympique Lyonnais. The charismatic firebrand, who played each game as if it were a final and celebrated his goals with a trademark cartwheel, proved a welcome addition, scoring seven in ten games. Cabañas had come to prominence at the 1979 World Youth Cup and, aged 19, joined the New York Cosmos and played alongside luminaries such as Franz Beckenbauer and Johan Neeskens.

Boca scored just 22 goals, 11 fewer than champions River who finished a comfortable seven points ahead to lift the title. An astonishing run of seven successive draws midway through the campaign highlighted the problem of Tabárez's side: its lack of ability to create chances and break down stubborn defences.

In December 1991 Boca dipped back into French football for another acquisition, this time bringing Alberto *Beto* Márcico back to Argentina after he had been plying his trade in Toulouse. The 31-year-old *enganche* was born just nine blocks away from La Bombonera but failed a trial with the club as a youngster. The mulleted number ten, who had been idolised by a young Carlos Tevez, won two titles with Ferro under Grigoul in the early 80s. His route to the Boca first team was rather circuitous but it would prove shrewd business and better late than never.

Much to the chagrin of former president Alberto Armando, the Alegre regime sold the Ciudad Deportiva in 1992 for US$21m. The sale of 'Sport City', which had been a millstone around the club's neck for the best part of 30 years, was the endpoint of a project that was never really born. Armando later admitted that his biggest mistake was predicting that the new complex, including a 140,000-capacity stadium, would open at exactly 11am on 25 May 1975. After being given the green light to commence the project by the Argentine government in 1964, economic instability and inflation, which caused costs to spiral, and political instability – military coups in 1966 and 1976 undermined government support – were key factors which precipitated the end of the grandest of grand plans.

La Candela, another Armando innovation, had stopped being used in 1991. For more than 20 years, the *concentración* at this venue was a ritual for Boca players, but the club wanted to move closer to La Bombonera. The land was eventually sold in 2005.

Finding the back of the net was once again an issue in the 1992 Clausura. Despite scoring just 20 goals in 19 games, two fewer than in the previous campaign, Boca finished three points behind Bielsa's Newell's in fourth place. The club had now gone an unthinkable 11 years without a domestic championship and the most recent triumph, driven by a young Diego Maradona in 1981, seemed like a lifetime ago. An extra trophy was, however, added to the cabinet in May. The Copa Master, featuring the four winners of the Supercopa Libertadores, saw Boca beat Olimpia then Cruzeiro en route to lifting the inaugural cup.

Continuing to prune and cultivate the personnel, Boca's Uruguayan coach added flame-haired full-back Carlos Mac Allister, forward Sergio *Manteca* Martínez, and Carlos Tapia – returning for his fourth and final spell – to his squad ahead of the 1992 Apertura. In the first three games of the campaign, two away goalless draws bookended a

2-0 home victory over Belgrano. Displaying his agility and positional intelligence, Cabañas opened the scoring with a diving header after 16 minutes; José Luis Villarreal, the exquisite midfielder signed from Belgrano by Saporiti back in 1987, doubled the advantage against his former club from the penalty spot before half-time.

Four straight wins were then recorded. A goalless draw with Ferro was followed by a 1-0 win over Argentinos Juniors. The *Superclásico* then took place at La Bombonera on 11 October 1992. Uruguayan striker Martínez proved to be the match-winner, finishing from close range after a Villarreal free kick fell to his feet in the box, before whipping off his shirt and scaling the fence behind the goal. Navarro Montoya's contribution was just as vital at the other end, his second-half penalty save from Hernán Díaz helping to seal maximum points. The Colombian goalkeeper was in the midst of a run which saw him keep eight consecutive clean sheets, setting a club record of 825 minutes without conceding.

The side, which had been so efficient in the first 14 fixtures, had a wobble in late November and early December, picking up just one point from three games, allowing River to maintain hopes of pipping their rivals to the post. Boca played Platense in the penultimate fixture, at Independiente's ground, racing into a 2-0 lead after 22 minutes with Martínez and Cabañas grabbing one apiece. Platense pulled one back from the penalty spot on 82 minutes, potentially setting up a nervous ending, but a third Boca goal just a minute later helped to settle the nerves. Luis Medero, a month shy of his 20th birthday and only deputising for the injured Simón, etched his name into Boca folklore. The youngster picked the ball up in his half, went past five opposition players, and then put it in the top corner from 18 yards. The victory, however, came at a cost:

Martínez went off injured after 25 minutes and would miss the final game through injury.

The title race went down to the wire. Boca knew that a point would be enough to seal the championship on the last Sunday of the season, 20 December 1992, yet doubts were raised when, after just 19 minutes, San Martín de Tucumán took the lead via a scruffy Ricardo Solbes goal. Boca's defence looked in vain for an offside, but the linesman kept his flag pointed to the floor.

The hero for the home side was as unexpected as Medero in the previous game. In a team full of grizzled veterans two youngsters proved invaluable. This time it was the turn of 21-year-old midfielder Claudio Benetti, making his first and only appearance of the campaign. Early in the second half, just as night was falling, Benetti picked up the ball 40 yards from goal and, showing maturity beyond his years, took the game by the scruff of the neck. He drove at the defence and drilled the ball across the goalkeeper and into the bottom corner from inside the penalty box before doing his best Spiderman impression in scaling the fence behind the goal. Hundreds of cameramen seemed to appear out of nowhere to capture the iconic moment. In that instant, everyone in La Bombonera knew the title was Boca's.

As the seconds ticked away Boca's defence played keep-ball as the ecstatic fans sang *Dale Campeón*. The longest title drought in the club's history was over; the relief was evident in the wild celebrations following the final whistle.

The honeymoon period didn't last long. Villarreal left for Atlético Madrid before joining River Plate shortly after. He kissed the River badge after scoring against Independiente, and he would never be forgiven by the Boca fans that once adored him for his role in the memorable title triumph. Despite acquiring internationals Alberto Acosta and Alejandro Mancuso, recently returned from Ecuador with the rest of the victorious Copa América squad, Boca suffered a hangover of almighty proportions.

Heading into the *Superclásico,* Tabárez's men had won just three of the first nine games. Giunta was missing for Boca, suspended after a red card against Ferro. In a show of *huevos* that he would become renowned for, Giunta parked his car ten blocks away and walked to the stadium, undeterred, surrounded by River fans.

The eventful match at El Monumental saw Boca take the lead through Martínez after eight minutes, heading in a corner from close range. On the hour Tapia played in Acosta who slid the ball under the advancing keeper to double the lead. Four minutes later both sides were reduced to ten men: the red cards were shown to Díaz, who had missed a penalty against Boca the previous October, and Cabañas, one of five he would receive in the blue-and-gold shirt. On 72 minutes Tapia, against his former club, saw red but Boca hung on for the points.

Boca took just one point from the next two games, and it was the end of the road for Tabárez. With poor results and a divided dressing room replete with internal strife, the Uruguayan announced his resignation. In his two-year spell, *El Maestro* had lifted the Copa Master but, more importantly, ended the 11-year wait for a domestic title.

Osvaldo Potente took the reins on a caretaker basis, overseeing three draws whilst the board searched for a successor to Tabárez. Jorge Carlos Habegger, the Argentine who had won league titles in Bolivia and Ecuador, was the chosen one and led the side in the final four games. A seventh-place finish represented a poor defence of the title the club worked so hard to achieve.

Soon after his appointment, Habegger was given an opportunity to lead Boca to another international title. Another new competition was organised by Conmebol, to feature the holders of their numerous competitions. Boca qualified as holders of the Copa Master and did a Brazilian double over Atlético Mineiro and São Paulo to lift the inaugural trophy. Another short-lived tournament ultimately ceased to exist but it represents another star on Boca's crest and gave Habegger some early goodwill. He would need it.

Ahead of the 1993 Apertura, Cabañas and Giunta, two iconic members of the 1992 title triumph, were sold to Barcelona SC (Ecuador) and Toluca (Mexico) respectively. Such bold decisions would have to be backed up with success on the field.

Habegger's men won just four of the first nine fixtures, including a 1-0 win at El Monumental. However, a home defeat to Belgrano by the same scoreline sealed his fate and Habegger was sacked. Enrique Hrabina, the son of Czechoslovakian immigrants, who had retired in 1991 after six years at Boca, oversaw a 1-1 draw at Rosario Central. For the following fixture, a 2-0 home win over Newell's, the new coach was in place. Despite the inauspicious circumstances that surrounded his 1987 exit, Menotti was back.

The team's fortunes improved massively under the World Cup-winning coach, losing just once in eight games. The highlight of the run was undoubtedly a 6-0 drubbing of Racing at home, with Martínez, once again Boca's top scorer in the championship, completing a 34-minute hat-trick either side of half-time. To this day the resounding victory is the biggest in a derby in the 80-year history of La Bombonera. The impressive run wasn't enough for the title, but the fourth-place finish, two points back from champions River, restored a semblance of respectability.

The momentum gained towards the end of the 1993 Apertura couldn't be maintained upon resumption of football in early 1994. Simón, not fancied by Menotti, retired aged 33, and *El Flaco*'s signings failed to have the desired effect.

Boca crashed out of the Copa Libertadores at the first hurdle, finishing rock bottom of the group. The 1994 Clausura, which rumbled on until the end of August after a break for the World Cup in the USA, wasn't much better: a mediocre Boca finished seventh and scored just 25 goals in 19 matches.

Once again Menotti's signings failed to ignite a spark and another flat campaign followed. Cabañas was brought back towards the end of the year but only played a handful of games before returning to his homeland with Libertad. When the Paraguayan striker died of cardiac arrest in 2017, aged just 55, he was buried in a Boca shirt, displaying the connection he was able to make with the club despite his relatively short stay.

In the third-to-last fixture of the 1994 Apertura Boca were comfortably beaten 3-0 by River at La Bombonera. Menotti departed following that humiliation and Hrabina once again stepped into the breach on a caretaker basis to see out a season in which Boca finished 13th and their great rivals won the title without losing a single game.

If the return of Menotti failed to bring success, it didn't stop the club's administration hiring another ex-coach to take them into the 1995 Clausura. A legend as a player, and the man who led the club to the 1981 title, Silvio Marzolini was back. Curiously, Boca signed a Cameroonian striker, Alphonse Tchami, from Danish club Odense BK. His stay at La Bombonera bore mixed results, although he did score in a 4-2 win at El Monumental. The team improved under Marzolini, finishing fourth; San Lorenzo notched their first title in 21 years.

Just six months remained in the Alegre era, an administration that quite literally saved Boca, rendering the president the second most popular in the club's history behind Armando in the eyes of most aficionados. During his decade-long tenure, the club won four international titles but, more importantly, ended a seemingly interminable 11-year wait for domestic supremacy, a triumph that remains one of the best-loved in the club's history. Soon Alegre would be replaced by a young, hungry president who would bring much success to the club. Before that, though, one of the club's favourite sons was about to come home after a long and winding road.

Chapter Eight

Maradona and the President

ALTHOUGH JUST over 13 years had passed since Maradona had crossed the Atlantic for the bright lights of European football, he had experienced enough to last a lifetime. The scars of excess, soaring highs and unimaginable lows had left their mark; the carefree 21-year-old with the thick mop of curly black hair was now a portly veteran.

It was during a troubled two-year spell with FC Barcelona that Maradona first dabbled with cocaine, yet it was in Naples – ironically where he simultaneously cemented his position as the undisputed best player on the planet – where he descended into the depths of mental and physical hell. After his time in Southern Italy, Maradona briefly represented Sevilla and Newell's Old Boys before two short and unsuccessful spells in management.

Four World Cups had passed since Maradona left Boca, the joy of dominating the field and lifting the trophy in 1986 atoning for a poor individual and team performance in 1982; the heart-breaking final defeat in 1990 paling in comparison to the failed drug test and acrimonious exit at USA 1994.

In 1995 an unmissable opportunity presented itself to Maradona: a return home to Boca, where it was hoped he could rekindle his form of old for one final and glorious encore. 'There was a lot of excitement when it was rumoured that Maradona would sign for the club in 1995,' remembered 38-year-old freelance journalist and lifelong Boca fan Leandro Cordobez. 'The best player in history, before the emergence of Messi, came to play at our club, again. They were turbulent times at the club and things hadn't gone well since the title win in 1992. There were internal problems and the squad was constantly renovated. The arrival of Maradona was a boost for everyone.'

Víctor Fucci of Somos Boca, an independent multimedia site, shared similar sentiments: 'The return of Maradona was a balm for the soul. It awoke a collective madness that I haven't seen on any other occasion. There were T-shirts with his photo on, new members joining the club, graffiti on the streets, and young boys with their hair dyed like Diego.'

Financing the deal of such a star, despite his stock not being as high as it once was, was problematic for the club. Sponsorships and a sequence of money-spinning friendlies helped pay his salary and the contract was heavily weighted in terms of appearances and performance. The player trained hard in anticipation of the expiration of the 15-month ban handed down to him by FIFA in August 1994 after the World Cup.

A phone call with manager Silvio Marzolini – who had also been in charge during Maradona's first spell – cleared the air between the pair. 'It was clear that it wasn't the Maradona of 1981 or 1986,' stated Cordobez. 'The news was now dominated more with his off the field activities than his football. But it was Maradona. Argentineans have the belief, irrational or not, that with Maradona anything is possible. We hoped he could put the club back on top after so

La Boca's busy port in 1895, ten years before the club's foundation.

Pedro Calomino, one of the club's first idols, won eight honours in the amateur era

Francisco Pancho *Varallo and Roberto Cherro, who scored more than 400 official goals between them in the 20s and 30s.*

Sosa, Lazzatti, and Pescia: a formidable midfield trio in the 1940s.

Facing Pelé's Santos in the 1963 Copa Libertadores Final.

Silvio Marzolini, the blond-haired heart-throb who was a mainstay of the 1960s, on the front cover of El Gráfico. *He also led the side to the 1981 Metropolitano title.*

Diego Maradona in full flow, wearing the famous Adidas kit in 1981.

The prodigal son returns. Maradona makes his second debut in October 1995.

Martín Palermo scores the iconic gol de las muletas *against River Plate in 2000*

Street football in La Boca.

Carlos Bianchi attends a press conference in Yokohama prior to the 2003 Intercontinental Cup clash against Milan.

Carlos Tevez celebrates scoring against River Plate in 2004, shortly before receiving a red card for an incendiary gesture.

Alfio Coco *Basile, who led the team to five titles in 425 days, pictured in 2006.*

Riquelme's crowning moment against Grêmio in the 2007 Copa Libertadores Final

Riquelme wheels away after scoring a stunning free kick in his last Superclásico.

The Twelfth Man. Boca's colourful and boisterous fans.

Guillermo Barros Schelotto with the 2017/18 Superliga Argentina trophy.

Tevez solidifies his status as a club idol, scoring the winning goal to seal the 2019/20 Superliga Argentina before celebrating with fans.

La Bombonera, a temple of world football.

many setbacks. We had a good team already and Maradona was the icing on the cake.'

Finally, on Sunday, 7 October, Maradona walked out on to the La Bombonera turf to make his second debut for the club of his heart. Boca defeated Colón 1-0 and Maradona – sporting the iconic blond stripe in his hair – was selected by the drug testers immediately after the game. The side were still unbeaten after seven rounds of the season had elapsed – three wins and four draws – and were genuinely in the hunt for the 1995 Apertura title.

The following week Maradona scored his first goal for Boca since late 1981, ironically against his former club Argentinos Juniors. At the home of Vélez Sarsfield, Maradona settled the game with a free kick from the edge of the box and, respecting the club that gave him his start in professional football, declined to celebrate. With five games remaining, the unbeaten Boca were six points clear and odds-on to win the title and seal a dream return for Maradona. However, two goalless draws followed, leaving the door ajar for fellow challengers to make an unwelcome entrance.

On 3 December, the third-to-last fixture, fellow *grande* Racing visited La Bombonera and left with maximum points following an inexplicable 6-4 loss for Boca in what should have been a routine home win. The six goals conceded in 90 minutes equalled the number Boca had leaked in the previous 16 league matches; three of the goals against Racing were conceded during a disastrous 15-minute spell in what amounted to a major implosion. Implemented at the start of the season in all FIFA-affiliated championships, victories were now rewarded with three points instead of two in order to promote attacking football. This was exactly the kind of gung-ho, no-holds-barred action that the world's governing body was looking for.

The defeat all but ended stuttering Boca's chances and a rampant Vélez, who won their final five fixtures, ended up winning the title comfortably. In the final round Maradona scored from the penalty spot at La Bombonera as Boca shared a 2-2 draw with Deportivo Español, resigning them to fourth place in the championship. With the title already out of reach, unhappy fans stayed away, resulting in a lower than usual attendance. Marzolini paid with his job. 'The team was never everything that it should have been,' lamented Cordobez. 'Many of the victories were down to individual brilliance rather than solid performances from a well-oiled machine.'

On the day of the ill-fated goal-fest against Racing, Boca members hit the polling booths to vote for the club's next president. In the stands that day, before the on-pitch chaos ensued, much of the talk revolved around who would win the election and, as a result, who the winner would appoint as head coach. Change was in the air.

The successful candidate was the highly ambitious Mauricio Macri, who had been born in February 1959, one of four siblings raised in comfortable middle-class surroundings in Tandil, Buenos Aires province. The civil engineering graduate spent periods studying economics and finance at home and abroad, including stints at the prestigious Columbia University in New York City and the Wharton School of the University of Pennsylvania.

Upon finishing his studies, Macri worked in the construction and automotive industries and by the time the 36-year-old favourite was elected as Boca president he was one of the richest men in the country. During his election campaign, the moustachioed Macri used classic political strategies, spending heavily on propaganda and maintaining a massive presence in the media. He enlisted support from Boca's *barra brava* as well as much-loved former players such as Antonio Rattín, Roberto Mouzo and Ernesto Mastrángelo, who visited more than 2,500 homes whilst on the election trail.

The new president had his work cut out in stemming the club's latest financial crisis in the wake of the recession that hit Argentina in late 1994. With Carlos Menem in the Casa Rosada, neoliberalism reigned and Macri sought to apply this model to Boca Juniors. The new president, who understood business on a global scale, intended to make Boca an international brand. The local, working-class club from La Boca, which in many ways hadn't altered since the meeting on the park bench in Plaza Solís in 1905, would change irrevocably under Macri's mandate. 'Macri was a rich and successful businessman who represented fashionable values in our country at the time: fierce neoliberalism,' stated Leandro Cordobez. 'He promised money that Boca didn't have, and good management. Curiously he won the election the day Boca lost 6-4 to Racing and effectively lost the championship. Symbolically, I don't think this is a coincidence. Under Macri, Boca enjoyed unprecedented sporting success but we are still trying to recover some of the pillars of our identity.'

No stone was left unturned in a full root-and-branch review of every facet of the club. A dedicated marketing department was created; advertising and commercial deals were signed. Boca teamed up with American sportswear giant Nike, changing the kit design slightly (whilst maintaining the classic vertical golden stripe atop a blue background) every year, purely as a money-making exercise.

From a football perspective, Macri's first key task was to appoint a new manager to take charge of first-team affairs following the sacking of Marzolini. The pragmatic Carlos Bilardo, who had led Argentina to World Cup glory in 1986, was a popular choice with many fans, yet this proved problematic for the club's biggest star. Maradona and *El Doctor* had clashed during their time together at Sevilla, and Maradona's opposition to his appointment put him on a collision course with Macri. Maradona threatened to leave but ultimately decided to stay for the sake of his adoring fans. It was perhaps unsurprising that Maradona and the president clashed so soon as the two were born at diametrically opposed ends of the political and financial spectrum.

Despite the simmering animosity, Boca kicked off the Bilardo era in fine fashion in March 1996, triumphing on the opening day of the Clausura campaign by beating Gimnasia y Esgrima de Jujuy 4-0 at home, Maradona starting the party by scoring from the penalty spot after just three minutes. Boca were unbeaten after five games but then, in round six, the issues began in Rosario. In the space of 14 first-half minutes Maradona missed a spot-kick and pulled a muscle, an injury which ruled him out for several weeks, Fernando Gamboa was sent off for Boca, and Hérnan Franco scored what would prove to be the decisive goal for Newell's Old Boys.

In Maradona's absence, Boca picked up just one point from a possible nine and suffered a shameful 6-0 mauling at La Bombonera by Gimnasia, Guillermo Barros Schelotto bagging a hat-trick. Alberto *Beto* Márcico, one of the heroes of the 1992 title-winning team who was considered surplus to requirements by Bilardo, scored from the penalty spot. Márcico, aged 35, had lost 6kg in order to make the move to Gimnasia and work under Carlos Griguol. After converting his penalty, the former Boca favourite refused to celebrate and asked the fans for forgiveness. He retired in 1998 and returned to Boca in 2002 as part of Oscar Tabárez's backroom team.

Awkwardly for Macri, the crushing defeat to Gimnasia happened on the day of the inauguration of the new executive boxes, the first of their kind in Argentina, on Calle Del

Valle Iberlucea. This was part of a programme intended to modernise La Bombonera and increase matchday revenue.

Maradona returned in a comfortable 4-1 win over his former club Argentinos Juniors which returned Boca to winning ways, but it also came with a price: another muscle injury which sidelined Maradona once again. He was back in round 12 as Boca hosted Belgrano at La Bombonera. After 46 minutes Maradona missed yet another penalty but defiantly hit back in the closing moments of the game, sealing the victory and showing flashes of his old genius in spotting the goalkeeper off his line and exquisitely flicking the ball into the net with the outside of his left foot.

In the following game Boca were downed 5-1 at Vélez. Claudio Caniggia gave *Los Xeneizes* the lead after 15 minutes, heading in from close range. The forward had come through the youth ranks at River Plate, debuting in 1985, yet left aged 21 and spent seven years in Europe. Caniggia was more synonymous with the national team rather than a particular club, and, at Maradona's request, signed for Boca in mid-1995.

Despite Caniggia's early goal, Boca's afternoon swiftly began to unravel. By half-time Bilardo's men were down to nine following the expulsions of Néstor Fabbri and Maradona. So vociferous was Maradona's reaction to his own red card he almost passed out, his behaviour so wild he was picked for the post-match drug test once again. Vélez scored five without reply and, to compound matters, Boca were reduced to eight men following the late dismissal of flame-haired full-back Carlos Mac Allister.

Maradona served his suspension as Boca beat Banfield 3-2 at home, returning in a 1-0 win at Rosario Central, although he missed another penalty. He repeated the trick in the following game but it didn't affect the team: Boca trounced River 4-1 at La Bombonera.

Following the *Superclásico* victory, Boca headed to China in July for two friendly matches in three days. Twenty-four days later the team resumed the league campaign with a 1-0 defeat at Racing's El Cilindro. Maradona missed his fifth penalty in succession, a short-tournament record and unthinkable given the aplomb with which the carefree youngster had dispatched penalties during his first spell at the club. Boca were all but ruled out of the title race and an under-pressure Maradona wept in the changing rooms after the game.

In the penultimate game of the season Boca suffered a 2-1 home defeat to Estudiantes – both of the away side's goals coming from Martín Palermo – and ultimately finished fifth in the table. Bilardo was of the opinion that the tour of China killed the team's momentum with only one point from nine available won following the trip to the Far East. Maradona decided to take a break – to enter a drug rehabilitation programme and recuperate – and wouldn't pull on the Boca shirt for another 12 months. Caniggia, Boca's top scorer in the Clausura with ten goals, also decided to take time out.

It was hoped that the break would do Maradona good, physically and mentally. 'It was a chaotic time and Diego was moving far away from what a professional footballer should be,' stated Cordobez. 'His injuries and streak of missed penalties illustrate this perfectly but, despite his terrible relationship with the club's leadership, he was never cut off because his presence still benefitted the club in some way.' Time out of the spotlight was also necessary for the star. 'At this time Boca wasn't an ideal place for him to recuperate,' recalled Cordobez. 'The media pressure around the club was already notable. The arrival of the first dedicated sports newspaper [*Olé*] and 24-hour news channels constantly made him the centre of attention. Everything was unstable with constant rumours. The people that loved Diego understood that his health was the priority. We were sad that we would be without him but hoped that he could definitively solve his problems.'

In Maradona's absence, Boca performed poorly over the course of the next two short championships. Ahead of the 1996 Apertura, Bilardo completely renovated the squad, with many key figures leaving and almost a dozen coming in, including a return for Diego Latorre after time in Spain and Italy. Another signing was Julio César Toresani from Colón. In his first game, a 3-2 victory over Estudiantes at the stadium of Vélez, Toresani was booed initially by the Boca fans due to his previous association with River and an old bust-up with Maradona which had been played out in the media. The right-sided midfielder played 16 of the 19 games, scoring five goals, and showed great determination to win the affection of the Boca faithful.

Halfway through the campaign, Boca lost 1-0 at home to César Luis Menotti's Independiente and, in the aftermath of the defeat, Carlos Navarro Montoya publicly declared himself to be a *Menottista*. One of Argentine football's greatest debates has centred on the seemingly opposing philosophies of their two World Cup-winning coaches, Bilardo and Menotti. By siding against his current coach his days were numbered. The goalkeeper, Argentina's Footballer of the Year in 1994, played three more games to make it 400 competitive outings in the Boca goal before being replaced by Sandro Guzmán. The Colombian, now a naturalised Argentine, joined Spain's Extremadura before enjoying a nomadic career in Chile, Brazil, Uruguay, and several other clubs in Argentina.

Bilardo himself left the club in December 1996 with two games of the season remaining, which were overseen by Francisco Sá. Following so many ins and outs in the transfer market, there was an alarming lack of cohesion in the squad and the tenth-place finish was a testament to that. At one point Bilardo had the likes of Maradona, Caniggia, Juan Sebastián Verón, and Kily González at his disposal but, like his ideological rival Menotti, failed to add any stars to Boca's crest.

Blas Giunta, now 34, also left the club signalling the end of his second spell. Nurtured at San Lorenzo but with Boca DNA running through his veins, Giunta made 189 official appearances for the club and returned in 1995 to play under Marzolini. However, he was used infrequently by Bilardo and departed when Héctor Veira arrived at the club as the new manager.

Boca finished ninth in the 1997 Clausura under the tutelage of *Bambino*, who had led River Plate to the Argentine title, Copa Libertadores and Intercontinental Cup a decade earlier. The mid-table finish came despite the goals of Sergio Martínez, who finished as the side's top scorer with 15 before leaving for Deportivo La Coruña. The one bright spark of the campaign was the return of Maradona. Diego appeared just once, late in the season – the 3-2 home victory over Racing – and it was assumed that, with all of his troubles behind him, he would be ready and raring to go in time for the following campaign. Caniggia also returned, signing an 18-month contract, yet a suspension and injuries restricted him to just five appearances in the 1997 Apertura.

The club enjoyed a great start to the campaign, picking up seven points from the first available nine. Maradona scored two goals in those three games, firstly from the penalty spot in a 4-2 win over Argentinos Juniors. Unlike the last goal he had scored against his former club, where his reaction had been rather muted, Maradona celebrated wildly, doing a forward roll before jumping on the fencing that surrounds La Bombonera's pitch. It was a reaction that was pure relief, a release of months of sheer frustration.

The second of his two goals that season came in the very next home game, and once again from the penalty spot, in a

2-1 win over Newell's. It was his 35th and final goal in the *azul y oro*. On 25 October 1997 Boca travelled to El Monumental, picking up a 2-1 victory. Maradona was replaced at half-time by Juan Román Riquelme and it signified the last 45 minutes of his professional career. A drug sample Maradona had given after the recent Argentinos Juniors game tested positive for cocaine. Once again Maradona protested his innocence but, exhausted from the constant speculation, negative press and intrusion into his family life, decided to hang up his boots for good on 30 October 1997, his 37th birthday.

For Leandro Cordobez, Maradona's second spell at the club was a sweet and sour experience. 'The return of the prodigal son filled the fans with hope and euphoria which will forever live in the memory,' began the freelance journalist. 'Technically it wasn't a success because we lost a championship and failed to win anything but it was very special for a generation of fans who idolised him yet didn't get to see him in a Boca shirt previously. Of course, the presence of Maradona is explosive and full of highs and lows, but what stays with me is a packed stadium, unconditional love and the last snippets of a stunning player.'

As if often the case with talented Argentine footballers, due to the economic imbalance between South America and Europe, Maradona had been spirited away from Boca Juniors and his home country before he was able to mature as a man or fully realise his potential as a player. When he returned to La Bombonera 13 years later he was a broken man, chewed up by the unforgiving brutality of years at the top-level of club and international football. Who knows how things may have turned out had he been given the opportunity to develop at home, although his generational gift precluded that from happening. On the other hand, perhaps somehow, someway, he was always destined to fall into the abyss.

The zenith of Maradona's time in a Boca shirt came when he was just a fresh-faced, innocent 20-year-old, without the scars of addiction, and the 1981 Metropolitano would prove to be his only honour with the club he dreamed about playing for as a young boy in Villa Fiorito. It may have not worked out the way he or the fans wanted it to but he can take solace in the fact that he got to live his dream and lift a title with his beloved Boca. 'The relationship between Maradona and the Boca fans began before he even played for the club,' stated Víctor Fucci. 'When his arrival at the club [in 1981] was confirmed, it started a revolution that remains until the present day. It goes beyond the one title that he won with the club. It's a love at first sight which isn't easily forgotten.'

The team finished the 1997 Apertura strongly, winning six in nine following Maradona's retirement, and finishing second, just one point behind champions River Plate. With just one defeat all season, and freed from the circus the club had become with the presence of Maradona, the club could look to the future with hope.

Going into the 1998 Clausura there was a real feel-good factor around the club, boosted by the arrival of Rodolfo Cardoso, who had spent several years in the Bundesliga, and Colombian Mauricio Serna. Although Boca beat River 3-2 at La Bombonera, it was one of only three home wins in a disappointing season that saw Boca finish sixth, 17 points off the summit.

The end of the campaign saw further personnel churn including the exit of manager Veira and several players that had formed the backbone of the side over the last few years. Two and a half years into the Macri regime and the president had yet to taste success or enjoy any kind of consistency. The impending appointment of Carlos Bianchi would soon change everything and new heroes would emerge from the shadow cast by the legacy of Maradona.

Chapter Nine

The Viceroy and the Magician

IN JULY 1998 Mauricio Macri pulled off a masterstroke in securing Carlos Bianchi for the position of head coach, two months after negotiations had begun in a Madrid hotel. Six years had passed since the last league title, the 1992 Apertura under Óscar Tabárez, and the man affectionately known as *El Virrey* was charged with returning Boca to the top table of Argentine football. Bianchi was Macri's third appointment – after Carlos Bilardo and Héctor Veira – and one the president had to get right to maintain his credibility.

Bianchi was a prolific striker during a playing career which saw a seven-year stay in France bookended by two spells with Vélez Sarsfield. Whilst he plundered numerous individual awards, he only won one team title: the 1968 Nacional. It was, however, on the other side of the white lines where Bianchi truly excelled. Then 44 years old, Bianchi returned to Vélez as head coach in 1993, embarking on a whirlwind period in which the club from Liniers won the 1993 Clausura, and Copa Libertadores and Intercontinental Cup double in 1994. Two more domestic titles followed.

Despite a short and unfruitful stint in Italy managing Roma, Bianchi's track record with relatively unfashionable Vélez was enough to convince Macri that he was the man to propel Boca to similar success. Change was needed after a lacklustre campaign in the 1998 Clausura which saw the fancied Boca finish a lowly sixth, 17 points off the summit, and Veira was ousted. There was a considerable turnover of players, with Peruvian Nolberto Solano, Diego Latorre, Néstor Fabbri, and the unreliable Claudio Caniggia all ending their time at La Bombonera.

Bianchi replaced the departed players with Antonio Barijho from Huracán, the Peruvian José Pereda from Universitario, and Hugo Ibarra from Colón de Santa Fe. José Basualdo returned for his second spell with Boca and was already familiar to Bianchi from their time together at Vélez. The most important relationship the new coach would cultivate was with a 20-year-old youngster who, in what seems to have been divinely preordained, was born on the eve of Argentina's 1978 World Cup triumph. After joining from Argentinos Juniors, following a path trodden by Maradona, Juan Román Riquelme was handed his debut by Bilardo in November 1996 in a 2-0 home win over Unión, five months after his 18th birthday.

The highest-profile of his 42 competitive appearances before the arrival of Bianchi came on 25 October 1997 when, wearing the 20 shirt, he replaced Diego Maradona at half-time in El Monumental in his last-ever game as a professional footballer. Although he was one of many to be saddled with the 'new Maradona' tag, few could have predicted that the lanky and languid *enganche* would go on to surpass *El Diego* as the club's biggest idol in the eyes of many *Xeneizes*.

Although Riquelme struck up an excellent bond with Bianchi, the chances are that he would have risen to the top regardless. 'Bianchi brought out a lot from Riquelme, but many other coaches did later in his career: Miguel Ángel Russo at Boca (2007) and José Pekerman with the national team (2004–2006) are the best examples,' stated Buenos Aires-based journalist and member of the Boca in English podcast and Twitter team, Francisco Aure. 'Riquelme was a world-class player.'

Víctor Fucci, journalist and part of the Somos Boca team, believes that Riquelme was already on his way to the top but that Bianchi was nevertheless important to his progression: 'Riquelme had already demonstrated his ability with Bilardo and Veira. So much so that on his debut he was one of the players of the match and the fans recognised this by giving him a standing ovation. On his debut no less. Without doubt, the arrival of Bianchi gave Riquelme the prominence and the freedom necessary to exploit 100 per cent of his quality.'

Diego Tomasi, the author of *El Caño Mas Bello Del Mundo*, believes that Bianchi's confidence in the mercurial youngster was crucial. 'Riquelme debuted under Bilardo, and later was coached by Veira, and with both he had brilliant matches without ever finding his ideal position,' began Tomasi. 'Due to his natural tendencies and knowledge of the game he was able to stand out anyway but it was not until the arrival of Bianchi that he took centre stage. Bianchi took a series of brave and risky decisions, playing Riquelme in his favourite position, making him a starting player, handing him the coveted number ten jersey and making him responsible for deciding how Boca would play. Román became a world star thanks to those decisions.'

Riquelme's style was atypical of the prominent approach of the day. 'It is often said that the typical style of Boca is more about effort than aesthetic beauty and although it may be true that *garra* is highly valued, two of the greatest idols in the club's history are the hugely talented Ángel Clemente Rojas and Diego Maradona,' stated Tomasi, whose book describes the football philosophy of Riquelme. 'When Riquelme debuted in 1996 the team had become a symbol of effort, fight, and *huevos*. Across Argentina managers of the day preferred players who would run, who would put their bodies on the line. In this context, Riquelme emerged, at the largest and most complicated club in the country no less, with a style all of his own. From his debut to his last game in 1996, he played the game in the same way, with the absolute certainty that football is better, more enjoyable, and more effective if you pass the ball cleanly to a team-mate.'

Bianchi wasn't as charismatic as many of the men to have sat in the Boca dugout, yet he was still able to impose his methods on the squad and fill the group with confidence. 'He was excellent at motivating players, no matter if it was a new signing or a young lad from the reserves,' stated Francisco Aure. 'Bianchi brought out 150 per cent from each one.' Bianchi preferred not to overcomplicate instructions. In possession, the team was expected to form a compact block and recover the ball as quickly as possible. They were whipped into superb physical shape which allowed them to play 90 minutes with the same intensity from start to finish. The coach instilled a culture of heightened professionalism in the dressing room and, over time, weeded out characters that didn't fit into his mould. 'Bianchi, from his time at Vélez, showed traits of being an austere coach who was able to form great teams with players who didn't need to have grand reputations to be able to carry out his ideas and conquer what seemed impossible in theory,' stated Víctor Fucci.

Ironically the Bianchi era kicked off with a 1-0 home loss to former club Vélez in the Copa Mercosur, a tournament featuring the biggest teams from Argentina, Brazil, Uruguay, Chile, and Paraguay. Boca recovered from that defeat and made it to the quarter-final where they were eliminated by Palmeiras. The cup was hardly a priority and this was evidenced in Bianchi's team selections; what everyone associated with the club craved was a domestic championship.

Boca won two and drew two of the first four games of the 1998 Apertura, before trouncing Huracán 6-2 at La Bombonera with a wonderful display of creative, attacking football. Martín Palermo scored two, one from the penalty spot, and Guillermo Barros Schelotto also grabbed a goal. Bianchi created a solid defensive base – conceding less than a goal per game in the Apertura – which allowed Riquelme to flourish and supply the bullets for Palermo and Barros Schelotto who developed a fruitful, yet unlikely, partnership.

The pair grew up in La Plata and were sworn enemies as young players, emerging on either side of the cross-city divide, but would become close friends off the pitch after excelling together on the grass. Palermo, who arrived from cash-strapped Estudiantes, debuted on 3 September 1997 and his acquisition would prove to represent excellent business. Eleven days later, Guillermo Barros Schelotto launched his Boca career after joining the club from Gimnasia alongside his twin, Gustavo, a dependable central-midfielder who never quite hit the same heights as his brother in a blue-and-gold shirt. The 25-year-old forward scored the winner on his debut versus Newell's yet, with Veira in charge, he played second fiddle to Caniggia and Maradona. The twin was another player who thrived under the tutelage of Bianchi.

In round 12 Bianchi's side faced River for the first time, going into the game top of the league with a six-point cushion. A goalless draw was secured, thanks in no small part to Óscar Córdoba who repelled a 43rd-minute penalty from Marcelo Gallardo.

On matchday 15 Talleres were the visitors to La Bombonera and Boca were still in pole position in the championship, maintaining their healthy lead over Gimnasia. Guillermo Barros Schelotto scored a *golazo* within 60 seconds but it looked like Boca would have to settle for a draw when Talleres equalised on 83 minutes. Displaying all the hallmarks of champions, Bianchi's side persisted and were rewarded with a last-gasp winner. Palermo, sporting his iconic blond fringe, scored from close range. Bedlam ensued in the stands, the players and coaching staff embraced on the touchline, and a shirtless Maradona celebrated wildly in his executive box. With just four games to go the late strike felt like a watershed moment.

The following week Talleres beat Gimnasia 2-1 in Córdoba whilst Boca won 3-2 away to Rosario Central with another late goal from Palermo, underlying his aerial prowess with a diving header from a Mauricio Serna pass. The Colombian international arrived at the start of 1998 and, with Racing also interested in acquiring his services, the presence of countrymen Córdoba and Jorge Bermúdez at La Bombonera proved crucial. *Chicho* didn't hit the ground running at Boca. The retired Maradona, now just a fan of the club, criticised the purchase on the radio before apologising the next day and offering his full support to the 30-year-old midfielder. Serna also had to contend with Boca having filled their quota of foreign players but he persevered and his excellence, in part, was a factor in the club selling Solano to Newcastle United.

In the next round, a home defeat to Lanús all but ruled Gimnasia out of the title race. The result of Boca's match – a 0-0 draw against Independiente – was irrelevant: the championship was celebrated with the players performing a lap of honour on La Bombonera's turf.

Boca ultimately finished nine points ahead of Gimnasia, and 23 clear of River, and were champions for the first time under Macri's presidency. Bianchi's faith in Riquelme was repaid in droves, and Palermo finished as the tournament's top scorer with an astonishing 20 goals in 19 games in an era when even a goal every other game was still considered a healthy strike rate for a forward. Bianchi finally allowed himself to use the word 'champion', avoiding it throughout the title race so as to not tempt fate. Rather than resting on his laurels, however, the players were afforded the Monday off after the season's final match before returning to training on Tuesday morning.

Without the complication of a continental competition to provide a distraction, the objective for the first part of 1999 was clear: win the Clausura and become back-to-back champions. The campaign didn't kick off until 7 March, the opening day delayed due to an FAA strike over unpaid wages, yet it didn't disrupt the momentum of Bianchi's men. Unbeaten in the first 11 games, Boca then beat River 2-1 at La Bombonera with goals from Jorge Bermúdez – who was sent off 20 minutes later – and, of course, Palermo.

In round 16 another Bermúdez goal proved the difference in a narrow home win over Rosario Central. The victory stretched Boca's unbeaten run to 40, setting a professional-era record for the longest stretch without defeat in Argentine football. Just four days later, the record-breakers were handed a heavy loss, sinking to a 4-0 defeat away to Independiente, yet River's defeat on the same day handed the title to Boca with two games to spare.

The *bicampeones* finished seven points ahead of their fiercest rivals and conceded just 11 goals in 19 games. Riquelme, Palermo, and Guillermo Barros Schelotto scored almost 70 per cent of Boca's league goals between them, the attacking trident underlying their importance to Bianchi's well-oiled machine.

Bianchi's side started the 1999 Apertura in strong fashion, losing just one of the first ten. A 2-0 defeat at El Monumental in round 11, with goals from Pablo Aimar and Juan Pablo Ángel, proved costly. Although an injury-hampered Boca remained unbeaten in the final eight fixtures, the title went to the men from Nuñez by a margin of three points.

Although Boca had failed to become *tricampeón* for the first time in their history there was much to be excited about. In 18 months it was possible to count the league defeats suffered under Bianchi's reign on one hand, and the prolific Palermo, the 1998 South American Footballer of the Year, was still scoring at a rate of just under one goal per game. There was a real feeling that something special was building at La Bombonera and the quiet end to 1999 was merely the calm before the storm.

Chapter Ten

2000

HAVING WON the 1998 Apertura and the 1999 Clausura, Boca's primary focus in the first six months of the new millennium was the Copa Libertadores. Carlos Bianchi had restored the club to a position of domestic dominance and now, for the first time in six years, the next challenge was to take his blue-and-gold revolution across South America. There would be more hurdles to overcome than in previous years, as Conmebol introduced a new expanded format featuring 32 teams.

Boca's start to the campaign, however, was less than auspicious. An opening day defeat to Bolivia's Club Blooming in Santa Cruz was symptomatic of the patchy continental form that saw Boca pick up just four points from the opening three group-stage fixtures. However, three wins from the final three matches saw Boca comfortably top the group with a four-point cushion.

In the last 16, Boca travelled to Quito to face Nacional, returning to Buenos Aires having secured a credible 0-0 draw at high altitude. The floodgates opened after just two minutes of the second leg in La Bombonera. A Hugo

Ibarra cross from the right-hand side was flicked on and landed at the grateful feet of Juan Román Riquelme, who controlled it sublimely with his left foot before opening up his body and, using the defender as a shield, passing the ball across the helpless goalkeeper with his right boot. Alfredo Moreno doubled the home side's lead after just ten minutes, although the Ecuadorians pulled one back just two minutes later.

After 22 minutes Riquelme was once again instrumental in restoring Boca's two-goal lead, slipping the ball through to Gustavo Barros Schelotto who drilled it across the goalkeeper and in off the post from just inside the 18-yard box. Five minutes later it was 4-1. Riquelme instigated a short-corner routine before whipping in a cross that was glanced in by the head of Rodolfo Arruabarrena. The rout was completed three minutes before the half-time interval when another Riquelme assist, this time directly from a corner, found the head of Jorge Bermúdez who powerfully directed the ball into the net from the penalty spot. Nacional pulled two goals back in the second half but they were nothing more than a consolation, a token souvenir from a night in Buenos Aires that they would much rather forget.

Boca's reward was a mammoth quarter-final clash with River Plate, with the first leg at El Monumental on 17 May 2000. The home side opened the scoring after 15 minutes, future Aston Villa star Juan Pablo Ángel lashing the ball home from eight yards after fellow Colombian and Boca custodian Óscar Córdoba had misjudged a cross. On the half-hour mark, Boca were awarded a free kick on the right-hand corner of River's 18-yard box. Rather than lifting the ball over the wall and to the goalkeeper's right, Riquelme called Roberto Bonano's bluff and aimed for the opposite corner, wrong-footing Bonano who could only watch the ball nestle in the goal.

Javier Saviola made it 2-1 to River just before half-time, driving at the heart of Boca's defence before unleashing an unstoppable shot from more than 20 yards, leaving Córdoba no chance. Boca would have to turn around a one-goal deficit in the second leg and rested several players in a routine league win over Rosario Central to ensure that key performers were fresh for the deciding clash.

The first hour of the second leg, on a cold night, was a cagey affair, and the onus was on Boca to attack. A Riquelme cross led to a mix-up in the River defence, reminiscent of the goal Boca conceded in the first leg, allowing Marcelo Delgado to break the deadlock and level the tie on aggregate. With no away-goal rule in place, the game opened up as both sides now needed to score a winner to progress to the last four.

After 74 minutes Bianchi made the first of two substitutions, both of which would have a profound effect on the outcome of the match. First to enter the field was Sebastián Battaglia, who replaced Gustavo Barros Schelotto. Ten minutes after joining the fray Battaglia burst into the box only to be felled recklessly. It was a clear penalty that Riquelme dispatched with typical aplomb.

Boca were now ahead in the tie, stretching the game even further as River tried to force their way back in. Riquelme's confidence was sky high and, two minutes after his effortless penalty, the maestro produced a moment of magic. The unfortunate victim was Colombian central defender Mario Yepes, who enjoyed a stellar career that included over 100 international caps as well as spells in France and Italy. Julio Marchant clipped the ball down the right-hand side in the direction of Riquelme, who controlled it close to the halfway line. Feeling the breath of the wildly out of position Yepes on the back of his neck, Riquelme ran his foot over the ball before dragging it back through the Colombian's legs, spinning off to his left to collect it on the other side. The 22-year-old number ten toyed with a further four defenders and when the ball finally went out of play the matador received rapturous applause from the delighted crowd who had witnessed one of the greatest nutmegs of all time.

River's task became a gargantuan one when an 86th-minute red card for Gustavo Lombardi reduced them to ten men. There was still time for Boca to further rub salt in the wounds of their great rival. Martín Palermo came on for Moreno after 77 minutes even though his presence in the matchday squad was deemed almost impossible in the days leading up to the game. Palermo had been missing for six months after tearing the anterior cruciate ligament of his right knee 193 days earlier in a match against Colón in November 1999, an injury which scuppered a mooted move to Italian giants Lazio. With mind games in full swing, River coach Américo Gallego had laughed off suggestions that Palermo would have any involvement, joking that if *El Titán* featured for Boca that he might haul Enzo Francescoli out of retirement.

With the clock ticking down, Riquelme picked up the ball on the left-hand side, continuing to torment River's exhausted and beleaguered defenders before feeding Battaglia. The tenacious midfielder once again penetrated the 18-yard box, cutting the ball back to Palermo. The striker was given all the time in the world and was thus able to perform almost a 360-degree turn, as if it were in slow motion, before finishing neatly with his left foot. Comically, the goal became known as the *gol de las muletas* (the goal of the crutches) due to Palermo's physical condition. Whilst the strike may not have been the most aesthetically pleasing of his 236 in a Boca shirt, it was arguably the most memorable. In a pattern that the popular forward would repeat numerous times during his career, Palermo had once again shown great resolve to overcome adversity.

With the eyes of the media firmly fixed on him, the resurrected Palermo was visibly moved as he left the pitch at the end and shared an emotional embrace with the doctor who performed the career-saving surgery on his knee. On the night, Boca had a better attitude and fully deserved the victory. River's plan – to defend their lead from the first leg – backfired, isolating their talented attacking trident of Pablo Aimar, Saviola and Ángel. Fans remained in the stadium for more than 15 minutes following the final whistle, spilling into the streets of La Boca and turning the neighbourhood into a party zone. It was the perfect night. 'The nutmeg of Riquelme, and Palermo's third goal, were the final link, the defining thrust to lift them both on to the podium of the most important players in Boca's history,' stated Sebastián Sellaro, journalist and member of the Somos Boca team.

Boca flew out of the traps in the first leg of the semi-final against Mexican giants Club América, running up a cricket score in front of their adoring home crowd. Arruabarrena scored the first goal after just eight minutes with a neat finish following an ingenious back-heel from Antonio Barijho. Four minutes later the provider turned goalscorer, Barijho doubling Boca's lead from close range, turning in Delgado's cross. With less than half an hour on the clock, Marchant made it 3-0. Just six minutes after the restart Barijho grabbed his second of the night. Club América scored what appeared to be a consolation on 78 minutes but the goal would more than complicate the second leg in the iconic Estadio Azteca.

Club América gave Boca a taste of their own medicine in the return leg at the high altitude of Mexico's capital city. After 81 minutes *Las Águilas* were leading 3-0 on the night, blowing Boca's seemingly unassailable lead to smithereens. With 83 minutes on the clock, and the game heading to extra time, Walter Samuel spared his side's blushes by looping a header over the goalkeeper, and even the defender on the line, from a corner kick. The central defender whipped off his shirt, the celebrations showing what reaching Boca's first Copa Libertadores Final since 1979 meant to the players.

In defending champions Palmeiras, Boca were facing a functional Luiz Felipe Scolari side. 'The one player who leaps out is the playmaker Alex, who is a lovely player,' stated Brazil-based journalist Tim Vickery. 'He was very unfortunate not to go to the World Cup. Scolari ended up taking a young Kaká rather than Alex in 2002. Alex was a gorgeous, gorgeous player, perhaps physically not quite enough for the top level in Europe, although he did very well in Turkey. Intelligent. A chess master who has worked out what is going to happen five moves in advance. César Sampaio, who played in the 1998 World Cup, was functional more than anything else. Galeano was a club legend. Scolari selected a pair of attacking full-backs. Roque Junior was an emerging defender of some class. As was customary with Scolari teams at the time, he had a big-man small-man combination up front with a target-man centre-forward, Marcelo Ramos, and a speed merchant in Euler, nicknamed the "son of the wind".'

Boca took the lead in the first leg at La Bombonera through Arruabarrena who nodded in from close range after 21 minutes, before Pena equalised for the visitors just before half-time. *El Vasco* restored Boca's lead on the hour with his second of the night, the left-back, one of the best in the club's history, finishing in the six-yard box and showing his penchant for big-game performances. Seemingly equal to whatever Boca were able to throw at them, Scolari's side equalised once again after 73 minutes.

Returning home for the second leg with no deficit to overturn meant the Parmalat-backed Palmeiras were massive favourites, yet Scolari, for one, wasn't complacent. 'Some Brazilians tend to write off the rest of the continent but not Scolari,' began Tim Vickery. 'He had complete respect for the opposition and there was no feeling that the job was any more than 50 per cent done.' Although playing at home is an advantage it also adds pressure. Palmeiras had been made to suffer by Deportivo Cali in the 1999 Copa Libertadores Final so the tie was by no means cut and dried.

Five thousand Boca fans followed their idols to São Paulo with the prospect of Boca overcoming the odds to be crowned South American champions. Mauricio Serna, who injured his left knee in a January friendly against River, also travelled to Brazil on crutches to support his team-mates. Forced to suffer for 90 minutes in the intimidating Morumbi stadium, Boca secured a 0-0 draw that eventually resulted in the lottery of a penalty shoot-out.

Bianchi told the players that the key wasn't striking the ball perfectly, it was more a case of handling the pressure of 80,000 pairs of eyes boring a hole in their backs as they strode up to take their kicks, as well as the millions watching the game on TV around the world. Alex and Guillermo Barros Schelotto were as cool as ice, converting the first spot-kicks for their respective sides. The nonchalant Faustino Asprilla was the first man to crumble, his penalty saved by compatriot Córdoba, putting the advantage firmly in Boca's hands.

Riquelme made it 2-1 before Córdoba made his second save of the night, this time from Roque Junior. Palermo converted his kick, exorcising his demons after famously missing three penalties in one match in the 1999 Copa América. Palmeiras' Rogerio scored to make it 3-2 so it was left to Bermúdez to step up and take the decisive kick. *El Patrón* struck his penalty firmly, sending the goalkeeper the wrong way.

Team-mates rushed to pile on the Colombian central defender whose kick had won the title for Boca; players hugged one another and cried together during emotionally charged celebrations. In the stands, Boca fans bounced ecstatically, setting off flares as their Palmeiras counterparts headed for the exits. The defending champions had lost the title on their patch and Boca were rulers of the continent for the first time in 22 years. 'For Palmeiras, it wasn't a humiliating defeat to lose on penalties to one of the great names of South American football,' opined Tim Vickery. 'The main disappointment and frustration is that you can't go to the Intercontinental Cup. Palmeiras would've given anything to be there taking on Real Madrid.'

Given Boca's exploits in the Copa Libertadores, it was only natural that their domestic campaign would suffer. The club were unable to fight on two fronts and, with two national titles already in his pocket, Bianchi knew that his side would ultimately be judged on success garnered on international soil. Boca finished seventh in the Clausura, which ran from February to July, with a strong River Plate bagging their second consecutive title.

In the 13th game of the season, Boca travelled to Rosario to face Newell's. The match was abandoned after just 16 minutes when fireworks, coming from the end where the Boca fans were situated, were aimed in the direction of the opposition goalkeeper. After an agreement between the two captains, the referee called a halt to proceedings with the remaining minutes set to be played out the following week. Boca had Aníbal Matellán sent off after 32 minutes and, capitalising on their numerical advantage, Newell's scored the winner courtesy of Manso after 53 minutes. Boca were later punished for their role in the debacle with the deduction of three points.

With the Copa Libertadores securely in the trophy cabinet and a slot in the Intercontinental Cup in late November in the diary, Boca were able to turn their attention back to domestic matters, in the form of the Apertura championship. Arruabarrena and Samuel, stalwarts from the glorious Copa Libertadores campaign, had departed for Europe. Boca started the campaign in fearsome form, posting 15 games unbeaten including a 1-1 draw at El Monumental. With a healthy position in the league, Boca headed to Tokyo in confident mood, ready to face the mighty Real Madrid in a duel to see who the best side on the planet was.

The Boca delegation arrived earlier than their opponents and embarked on a charm offensive, making public appearances, posing for photographs and signing autographs. The majority of neutrals were firmly behind them, as the underdogs. On 28 November Boca entered the National Stadium in the Japanese capital. After the unsavoury episodes of the 1960s and 1970s, and declining interest in the competition, the Intercontinental Cup had undergone a rebirth after moving to Tokyo and was now sponsored by car giant, Toyota.

Real Madrid boss Vicente Del Bosque fielded an incredibly strong XI featuring the likes of Iker Casillas, Fernando Hierro, Roberto Carlos, Guti and Raúl. *Los Blancos* had won two of the last three Champions League titles and had recently acquired the world's most expensive player, Luís Figo. Boca lined up in a deep-lying 4-3-1-2 formation, which effectively became a 7-0-3 out of possession. The defensive block was meant to give licence to a front two of Palermo and Delgado, signed from Racing at the start of the year. Riquelme as the *enganche*, was the hook that would link the rest of the team to the attacking duo.

After just two minutes Serna passed the ball to José Basualdo, who in turn fed the dynamic Delgado who timed his run perfectly to spring the offside trap. The in-form Delgado, selected by Bianchi ahead of Guillermo Barros Schelotto, reached the byeline and centred the ball to

Palermo, who burst into the box to get on the end of the cross and put Boca 1-0 up. It was the fastest goal in the history of the competition.

Four minutes later Palermo doubled his tally, inexplicably giving Boca a 2-0 lead. After a Madrid attack broke down on the edge of Boca's box, Battaglia picked up the loose ball and fed Riquelme. The maestro sprayed a long pass with the perfect amount of backspin so it bounced up in just the right spot for Palermo to fire past Casillas for the second time in six minutes.

Both goals exposed Geremi and the right-hand side of Real Madrid's backline. The Spaniards' star-studded and vastly experienced line-up looked shell-shocked; Boca fans turned up the volume, revelling in their moment in the global spotlight. Moments later a long diagonal pass from Hierro found Roberto Carlos who expertly controlled the ball, first on his chest then on his thigh, before crashing a shot off the crossbar with his weaker right foot. It was a stark warning of the fragility of Boca's lead.

After 12 minutes Figo, escaping the clutches of man-marker Aníbal Matellán, whipped in a cross from the right-hand side. A misjudged header from Ibarra fell to Roberto Carlos and the marauding Brazilian full-back wouldn't be denied a second time. His unstoppable shot, this time with his stronger left foot, left Córdoba with no chance.

As the game wore on Madrid continued to push for an equaliser. Riquelme's ball mastery proved instrumental in keeping the European champions at bay, a free kick stinging Casillas's palms a gentle reminder he had more than enough quality to hurt them. At times it appeared that the ball was glued to the number ten's boots as he toyed with the Madrid defence, taking the sting out of their attacks and winning free kicks at vital moments. After a seemingly interminable wait, Colombian referee Óscar Ruiz blew his whistle to signify the end of the game, sending the 10,000 Boca fans – a record-breaking number that had travelled from Buenos Aires and beyond – into dreamland. Palermo, named as man of the match, was gifted a car from the sponsors as a reward.

The triumph ended a wait of almost a quarter-century since Toto Lorenzo's men had defeated Borussia Mönchengladbach to become world champions. 'The Intercontinental Cup against Real Madrid is remembered as the most important one because of the huge stars we were playing against,' stated Francisco Aure of Boca in English. 'The victory against the feared, and impossible opponent for most earthly teams, Real Madrid, without a doubt returned Boca to the status of a team on the world level,' added Sebastián Sellaro. 'Everything that the club achieved in the late 1970s was brought to light again with an unexpected victory in front of the eyes of the football world.'

Bianchi had boosted his players' confidence, and each member of the squad played a role in the Madrid victory and the success garnered in the year 2000. 'Riquelme and Palermo played the match of their life,' according to Aure. 'Aníbal Matellán used to play at centre-back but played left-back and, aged just 22, had to control Figo in Tokyo. As we say in Argentina, "he erased him from the pitch". Thanks, in part, to that match, Matellán was later transferred to Europe. Jorge Bermúdez was such a warrior in defence, as was Hugo Ibarra, arguably the best right-back ever in Argentine football. Some players had important specific moments: Samuel, who scored the decisive goal against América at the Estadio Azteca; Arruabarrena, who scored a brace versus Palmeiras; back-up strikers Barijho and Moreno scored many goals while Palermo was recovering from his injury.'

An exhausted Boca understandably stumbled in the league upon returning home to Buenos Aires. A 1-0 victory over San Lorenzo was followed up by consecutive defeats which allowed River, looking to become *tricampeón*, to take the title race down to the wire. Boca were two points clear of their sworn enemy going into the final day, and River drew with Huracán whereas Boca were victorious at home to Estudiantes, a 74th-minute winner from substitute Matías Arce securing Boca's 25th league title less than three weeks after the triumph in Tokyo. It was a howler from the visitors' goalkeeper, who let a routine shot from Arce slip through his grasp, yet very few people in La Bombonera cared. The goalscorer sunk to his knees on the ticker-tape-infested pitch as an avalanche of fans swarmed towards their heroes and began climbing the fence separating the stands from the pitch.

The unprecedented haul of three major trophies within the space of six months took Bianchi's Boca to a new plateau and represented the most successful calendar year in the club's illustrious history. It is often said that success is hard to gain, but even harder to maintain, yet more glory was just around the corner.

Chapter Eleven

2001

AFTER SUCH a dream start to the new millennium, Boca had a seemingly impossible task on their hands in replicating the success garnered in 2000. As a result, Carlos Bianchi suggested that 2001 would be a year of transition, his prediction influenced by the departure of several key figures. In the wake of the Triple Crown, both Gustavo Barros Schelotto and Martín Palermo followed in the footsteps of Rodolfo Arruabarrena and Diego Cagna in joining Villarreal's ever-expanding colony of ex-Boca stars.

The gulf between European and South American sides was widening as each year passed, with many players seeking the financial and sporting prestige that came with Champions League football. Player sales became key to the economic model adopted by Boca president Mauricio Macri and other Argentine clubs, with any success merely putting players in the shop window.

Sensing that the squad was weaker on paper, Bianchi placed all of Boca's eggs in the Copa Libertadores basket. In the Torneo Clausura, which ran alongside the continental competition, Boca used more than 30 players during the 19 matches, resting key men and rotating the squad to ensure freshness for the midweek games against the cream of South America. The final league table showed a third-place finish, one which flatters at a glance: Boca finished 17 points behind champions San Lorenzo.

The one game Boca did perhaps take seriously was a satisfying 3-0 home win over River Plate. Hugo Ibarra opened the scoring, cutting inside on his weaker left foot and memorably drilling home from outside the box. Guillermo Barros Schelotto sealed the victory with a late penalty, yet it was Riquelme who grabbed the headlines. Román saw a 71st-minute penalty saved but after he successfully turned in the rebound he took his celebration straight over to the directors' boxes. His brooding glare firmly focused on Macri, Riquelme placed his hands behind his ears, reminding the president exactly who the star of the show was. Riquelme claimed the celebration was for the benefit of his daughter, and that he was mimicking *Topo Gigio*, a mouse puppet from an Italian television show of which she was a fan. Yet it was strongly suspected that the gesture was in response to a dispute between the player and the club over the terms of a new contract, in the wake of serious interest from European clubs.

Boca navigated the group stage of the Copa Libertadores with ease, winning their group – containing CD Cobreloa of Chile, Bolivia's Oriente Petrolero and Colombia's Deportivo Cali – with 15 points, only losing the last game when qualification was already assured.

In the last 16, Boca faced Colombian side Junior and took an early lead in the sweaty Caribbean port city of Barranquilla. After just six minutes Chelo Delgado – whose attacking importance was growing following Palermo's sale – pounced and scored after the defender committed the cardinal sin of playing the ball across the face of the goal.

Junior hit back with two first-half goals of their own, taking a slender advantage into the break. Riquelme drew Boca level with a rare header after 64 minutes, and then played a crucial role in what would prove to be the winner. After 80 minutes Delgado, with his shin pads scruffily protruding from his low-slung socks, played a one-two with Riquelme who hit a lovely reverse pass. Delgado scuffed the ball but fortunately had a second bite at the cherry and finished from close range to make it 3-2.

Junior visited La Bombonera the following week and got off to the best possible start, taking the lead after just two minutes to silence the home crowd; Guillermo Barros Schelotto hit back seven minutes later with a perfectly executed volley from just outside the six-yard box. In the 84th minute Clemente Rodríguez was sent off along with Junior's Zambrano, and the game ended 1-1. It wasn't exactly plain sailing but the key statistic was that Boca were through to the last eight. The dream was still alive.

The quarter-final pitted Boca against Vasco da Gama, Copa Libertadores champions in 1998, with the first leg scheduled in Rio de Janeiro. The only goal of the game came from a set-piece, Guillermo Barros Schelotto bundling home a Riquelme corner to secure a vital victory on Brazilian soil.

In the return leg, Boca produced their most impressive home display of the campaign, comfortably dispatching Vasco 3-0 to advance to the final four. Boca blitzed the Brazilians in a whirlwind opening 30 minutes. Aníbal Matellán opened the account after 11 minutes, with Guillermo Barros Schelotto doubling the lead from the penalty spot after 20 minutes. On the half-hour mark, Boca sprung the offside trap, Guillermo rifling the ball into the roof of the net with the instep of his right boot after a centre from the left.

The semi-final was a repeat of the previous year's final, against Palmeiras, who had knocked out compatriots São

Caetano and Cruzeiro en route to the final four. Attacking midfielder Alex, who later became captain of Turkish giants Fenerbahçe, drew first blood for the Brazilians after 18 minutes, silencing La Bombonera. Guillermo Barros Schelotto equalised after 42 minutes, Boca's number seven smashing a penalty straight down the throat of Palmeiras stopper Marcos after the Paraguayan referee had pointed to the spot.

The second half was almost a carbon copy of the first, with Palmeiras starting brightly only to be pegged back by a dogged Boca. After 54 minutes Fabio Junior gave Palmeiras the lead for the second time in the game, yet just one minute later a stubborn Boca equalised once again through Antonio Barijho. Boca's number nine poked the ball home from close range amidst a ticker-tape-infested penalty area and, with a show of urgency, Riquelme, whose clever trickery set up the goal, plucked the ball from the net and headed to the centre circle in a deliberate rush to restart the game at the earliest opportunity.

Going into the game at Palmeiras' Palestra Italia the odds were stacked against Boca. Delgado, missing from the first leg after suffering an injury on international duty, was doubtful. Barijho, sent off after 77 minutes along with Palmeiras' Fernando, was suspended. And Guillermo Barros Schelotto, withdrawn at half-time of the first leg, would miss the crucial decider through injury.

Despite this, Boca made a stunning start to the second leg, taking a two-goal lead within the first quarter of an hour. Walter Gaitán struck first, after gratefully tapping in the goalkeeper's parry, before Riquelme drilled the ball low and into the corner from the edge of the 18-yard box, recreating the *Topo Gigio* celebration that had caused so much hysteria. Fabio Junior provided a lifeline for Palmeiras after 37 minutes, yet the Brazilians gave themselves a mountain to climb when Alexandre was dismissed after 45 minutes.

However, luck was on their side when, on 66 minutes, Bermúdez diverted the ball into his own net. When Matellán was sent off after 85 minutes a nervous end awaited Boca. The game eventually went to penalty kicks. The influential Alex was the first to step up for Palmeiras, although he saw his effort saved by Óscar Córdoba. Riquelme, then Lopes, converted to make it 1-1 before Cristian Traverso missed for Boca. Córdoba produced more heroics to deny Basilio, and the next three penalties all hit the back of the net including one by Bermúdez, atoning for his own goal. With Boca leading 3-2, Arce stepped up for Palmeiras knowing he needed to score to keep Brazilian hopes alive. He missed, sending Boca through to the final.

Cruz Azul had already eliminated River Plate and Rosario Central and were hoping to claim an impressive trio of Argentine scalps. Mexican teams had been competing in the Copa Libertadores since 1998, invited to participate primarily for financial reasons, yet *Los Cementeros* were the first to reach the prestigious final.

The first leg was played out in front of more than 100,000 in the Estadio Azteca, the venue for the 1986 World Cup Final. In what was becoming somewhat of a habit, Riquelme underlined his importance to the club with yet another man-of-the-match display and it was his pass that led to the game's only goal, scored by Delgado in the 79th minute. The crowd in the cavernous arena – aside from the respectable Boca contingent, many of whom that had made the arduous journey from Buenos Aires, one that is greater in distance than London to Mumbai – fell silent. Ibarra almost made it 2-0 at the death, but his tame shot trickled inches wide.

Back in La Bombonera for the second leg, the Mexicans took the lead just before half-time, Palencia scoring from close range after a Cruz Azul corner. Boca failed to reply in the second half, leading to penalties once again. With smoke from firecrackers filling the air, Riquelme stepped up first for the home side and coolly converted his kick. Palencia, the scorer of the game's only goal, matched Boca's number ten to make it 1-1. Mauricio Serna scored Boca's second before Córdoba saved Pablo Galdames's effort. Delgado made it three in three for Boca and when José Hernández blazed his effort high and wide the Argentine side were in the driving seat.

Jorge Bermúdez, the player whose kick had won the cup for Boca in the Morumbi in 2000, once again had the chance to be the hero, yet cannoned his penalty off the crossbar to give Cruz Azul a glimmer of hope. However, Julio César Pinheiro missed, confirming Boca had retained their trophy and were kings of the continent once again. Less than five months after Bianchi became the club's most successful coach with six major honours, Juan Carlos Lorenzo, who had won five during his tenure, passed away aged 79.

In becoming continental *bicampeón*, and repeating the feat of 1977 and 1978, Boca recorded victories in Mexico, Brazil, Bolivia, Chile, and Colombia; Bianchi's men were true Latin American road warriors. Since those back-to-back triumphs towards the end of the 1970s, only São Paulo had managed to retain their Copa Libertadores crown. That Boca had done it again and increased their overall haul to four, was an amazing achievement, especially at the outset of the era when South American teams were becoming increasingly preyed upon by their more powerful and richer European counterparts.

The Torneo Apertura kicked off in August, and Boca were once again weakened by the transfer market. Ibarra, Bermúdez, and Aníbal Matellán all headed for the bright lights of Europe, joining Porto, Olympiacos and Schalke

04 respectively. Their replacements – Jorge Martínez, Rolando Schiavi, and Jorginho – were capable yet of inferior quality and failed to excite the demanding fan base. In a bizarre marketing move, Boca also signed Japanese player Naohiro Takahara but he would only make six appearances throughout the campaign.

The 11th fixture of the Torneo Apertura saw Boca travel to Córdoba to face Talleres in the Estadio Kempes, Bianchi handing a debut to 17-year-old youth-team prodigy Carlos Tevez. The match took place on Mother's Day, and to celebrate the occasion Boca removed the sponsor, Quilmes, from the front of the shirt and replaced it with the name of each player's mother, in the same font as the logo of the popular Argentine beer.

What was supposed to be a nice gesture, caused controversy in the Tevez household. The debutant's shirt displayed the name of Fabiana, his estranged biological mother, rather than Adriana, his auntie who had raised him and who he considered to be his mother. The shirts were the highlight of a drab game, Tevez substituted five minutes after the hosts scored what proved to be the winner. Although it was the youngster's only contribution of the campaign, the tenacious talent from Fuerte Apache would become a fan favourite before too long.

With just a few games of the Apertura remaining, Boca's focus switched to the Intercontinental Cup and another sojourn to Tokyo. Awaiting in the opposite corner were Bayern Munich who had defeated Spanish side Valencia in the San Siro to lift the Champions League trophy.

Bayern, under Ottmar Hitzfeld, weren't extraordinary compared to Real Madrid's *galácticos*, but still featured the likes of Oliver Kahn, Willy Sagnol, Samuel Kuffour, Bixente Lizarazu, Owen Hargreaves, Claudio Pizarro and Giovane Élber. Although just 364 days had passed since

Boca's memorable victory over the Spaniards, the team had changed dramatically. From the back four, Ibarra, Bermúdez, and Matellán had all been sold, whilst Cristian Traverso was instead deployed in midfield. The injured Sebastián Battaglia wasn't in the squad; José Basualdo and Palermo had also departed.

Kahn, captaining the German side, produced several vital saves during the match, the pick of the bunch coming after 29 minutes when he denied Guillermo Barros Schelotto. Boca looked to be facing an uphill struggle when Delgado was dismissed for two yellow-card offences after 46 minutes, the second brandished by Kim Milton Nielsen for simulation.

After 90 goalless minutes, the game went to extra time, the war of attrition lacking the quality and spark of the previous final. After 109 minutes Bayern's Swiss substitute Ciriaco Sforza swung in a corner which Córdoba came for but failed to take. In a goalmouth scramble, the ball was headed down and cleared off the line before Kuffour struck from close range to give Bayern the lead with just 11 minutes remaining. The Boca contingent protested, primarily for a foul on Clemente Rodríguez, and felt the goal shouldn't have stood. In general, Boca felt hard done to by the Danish referee throughout the evening. After the final whistle blew Riquelme sat forlornly on the grass, in tears.

Upon returning to conclude the Apertura season, Boca lost to Banfield and drew with Vélez. On 16 December Independiente visited La Bombonera for what would be Bianchi's last game and the final home game of the season. Fans sang the name of the departing coach throughout the 5-3 victory, Boca's goals coming from Barijho, Schiavi, Riquelme (2), and Guillermo Barros Schelotto.

Bianchi had announced his imminent departure in a press conference back in September, confirming that he wouldn't be renewing his contract which expired on 31 December, ending his cycle in the Boca dugout. *El Virrey* was disgruntled by the continued player sales which were compounded by the incoming players, reportedly not Bianchi's choices and not the required quality to replace their predecessors.

During Bianchi's stewardship Boca had won three national league titles, two Copas Libertadores, and the Intercontinental Cup, clocking up a ridiculous amount of air miles including two trips to Tokyo and one to Mexico City in the Copa Libertadores. It was mightily impressive – especially given that the squad was repeatedly decimated by player sales – to maintain such a high level of performance and achievement.

Off the pitch, the club were performing at a high level and turning into a money-making machine. Boca could count on over 60,000 paying members, and the stature of the club was confirmed with the opening of a museum on 3 April 2001, the 96th anniversary of the club's foundation. The Museo de la Pasión Boquense would harness the club's illustrious history and worldwide appeal, attracting the hordes of tourists flooding the neighbourhood of La Boca daily.

The performance of Boca Juniors was in stark contrast to the crisis engulfing the rest of the country. Problems of old began to mount as Argentina entered into a recession in 1999 and Fernando de la Rúa, promising to revive the economy, was elected president in December of that year. In July 2001 De la Rúa implemented austerity measures – including slashing state salaries and pensions – at the behest of the International Monetary Fund (IMF). Increasing unemployment and widespread discontent led to strikes and, in November 2001, many Argentines withdrew their money from banks, fearing the collapse of the system. The government responded by effectively freezing accounts for 12 months and, with unemployment pushing 20 per cent and anger and poverty rising, unions called a strike on 13

December 2001. Six days later a State of Emergency was declared to stem the protests yet within days the president and his economic minister resigned amidst the chaos.

In what felt like an afterthought, Boca fulfilled their last fixture of the Apertura campaign on 5 February 2002, seven weeks after Bianchi's last game, sharing a 2-2 draw with Newell's Old Boys in Rosario. Boca finished third in the championship, with Racing picking up their first domestic title after an excruciating 35-year wait. After the three-and-a-half-year tenure of Bianchi, the club were forced to move into a new era.

Chapter Twelve

2003

IN THE wake of Carlos Bianchi's departure, Boca turned to tranquil Uruguayan Óscar Tabárez, the architect of the 1992 title triumph and the only man, aside from *El Virrey*, to have led Boca to a league title since Silvio Marzolini in 1981. It was hoped that *El Maestro*'s pedigree and calmness could provide a smooth transition to maintain the momentum created by his popular predecessor.

Boca went unbeaten in the first five fixtures of the 2002 Clausura before losing 3-0 to River Plate at La Bombonera. A late red card for Cristian Traverso, playing in his last tournament before heading to Mexico, compounded the misery for Tabárez in the first *Superclásico* since his return. A run of consecutive victories, in which Héctor Bracamonte scored six goals in as many games, gave the Boca fans faint hope but just two wins from the last six extinguished any chances and the team ultimately finished third, eight points behind champions River.

Boca exited the 2002 Copa Libertadores at the quarter-final stage at the hands of eventual winners Olimpia, the 1-0 defeat in Asunción the last action of Juan Román Riquelme before his move to La Liga. Tabárez brought Hugo Ibarra back to the club for the 2002 Apertura, along with several new signings, to strengthen the squad following the departures of key figures Riquelme, Traverso, and Mauricio Serna.

Halfway through the tournament, after Boca had been eliminated from the inaugural Copa Sudamericana at the first hurdle, Tabárez's men found themselves eight points adrift of Independiente. Five successive victories, including a 2-1 win at El Monumental thanks to a Marcelo Delgado brace, set up a crucial match with the league leaders in the penultimate round of the season.

Boca headed to Avellaneda just three points behind *Los Rojos*, having gradually chipped away at their opponents' lead. A win for the boys from Calle Brandsen would put both teams on equal points going into the final day of the season. Captain Guillermo Barros Schelotto had Boca fans dreaming when, after 38 minutes, he scored from eight yards to give his side the lead. Lucas Pusineri equalised with just minutes to spare to make it 1-1 and, with both sides winning on the final day, the title was Independiente's.

Two days before Christmas 2002 Macri swallowed his pride and Bianchi returned, less than 12 months after his exit. The reign of Tabárez had been far from a disaster yet Bianchi was seen as the figure to restore glory to the club. During tough negotiations, *El Virrey* secured a three-year contract to return to La Bombonera. Bianchi's men set a strong pace in the 2003 Clausura, amassing 19 points from the first 24 available, whilst qualifying from a Copa Libertadores group containing Deportivo Independiente Medellín, SC Barcelona, and Colo Colo. Boca then qualified for the semi-final after eliminating Brazilian side Paysandú and Chilean outfit CD Cobreloa.

Back on the domestic front, Boca hosted River at La Bombonera in a crucial clash that would help determine where the championship would head. Two goals down at half-time, Boca hit back with a brace from Guillermo Barros Schelotto in a typically feisty affair which saw River receive two red cards. A 4-0 demolition of Huracán in the following fixture, featuring a Bracamonte hat-trick, sent Boca to the top of the table with just four fixtures remaining.

Bianchi's men eased past América in the last four of the Copa Libertadores, kicking the tie off with a 2-0 win at La Bombonera, the goals coming from a Rolando Schiavi header and an 89th-minute effort from Carlos Tevez. In the second leg in Cali, Tevez scored two within the first 22 minutes to put the tie to bed: one from a corner kick; the second a cool finish following a rapid counter-attack. Spot-kicks from Schiavi and Delgado gave the night a resounding finish and the 6-0 aggregate scoreline was a sign that Bianchi's men were in the ascendancy.

In between the two legs against the Colombians, Boca could only draw 2-2 at home with lowly Arsenal, and in the next league fixture lost 3-1 to Talleres in Córdoba, the home side racing into a 3-0 lead after just 23 minutes. The wheels were coming off the domestic campaign but, with a Copa Libertadores final on the horizon, it was time to prioritise at a decisive moment.

In the opposite corner were Santos who Boca famously faced in their first-ever continental final exactly 40 years earlier. The Brazilians were managed by Émerson Leão, the former international goalkeeper, who had a young side at his disposal, the oldest player being 27 years old. Teenage sensations Diego and Robinho lined up alongside Alex, who would later feature for Chelsea in the Premier League. Renato, who won six trophies in a seven-year spell with Sevilla, Léo, who later represented Benfica, and Ricardo Oliveira, who is still playing now aged 40, were the other standouts for Santos.

Santos's run to the final was 'really romantic', according to South American football expert Tim Vickery. 'The first group stage game they played wasn't even on Brazilian TV, and they played so well. It was like "wow" and the whole country rose to them.' Leão's men topped their group with 14 points and eliminated Nacional, Cruz Azul and Deportivo Independiente Medellín without losing a single game.

Led out by captain Diego Cagna, who had returned to the club from Villarreal, the players emerged from the tunnel at La Bombonera to a cacophony of noise created by fireworks and the vocal cords of the Boca faithful, ticker-tape and smoke from the stands reducing visibility and adding to the atmosphere. Delgado scored after 32 minutes with a strike from 20 yards, the ecstatic player rushing to the technical area to celebrate with Riquelme, sitting on Boca's bench as a show of support despite now being contracted to another club.

Delgado was proving a real thorn in Santos's side. Too quick for Reginaldo Araújo, Chelo evaded his marker and drew a foul, the Brazilian's second yellow card forcing him to head for an early bath. Delgado took the free kick himself, swinging the ball into the dangerous no-man's land between the defence and Fábio Costa. Players from either side attempted to attack the ball yet it bounced off the turf without a single touch and into the net past the forlorn goalkeeper.

Boca travelled to Sao Paolo's Morumbi stadium with an all-Argentine squad for the second leg, yet without one of their key players, Guillermo Barros Schelotto, who was forced off after 53 minutes of the first encounter against the Brazilians. The twin scored a hat-trick in the round of 16 versus Paysandú but missed the semi-final and was now missing for the crucial return with Santos. On the wrong side of 30, injuries were now beginning to catch up with the man from La Plata. Tevez gave Boca the lead after 20 minutes, sweeping the ball into the deep net after superb link-up play with Sebastián Battaglia. Trailing 3-0 on aggregate, Santos now had a proverbial mountain to climb.

Alex gave the Brazilians hope, smashing a long-range strike in off the post after 75 minutes, and Santos now had 15 minutes to find the two goals that would force extra time. Leão's side pushed forward relentlessly in search of a second and Boca exploited their gung-ho approach and high defensive line. Tevez sprung the trap and freed Delgado, leaving him alone in the Santos half with just the goalkeeper for company. As Fábio Costa approached, more than 40 yards off his line, Chelo simply passed the ball into the empty net from distance for his ninth goal of the competition. A 95th-minute penalty from Schiavi, after a reckless two-footed lunge from the hapless goalkeeper, finished the scoring and allowed Boca to repeat the feat from 2000: a lap of honour in the Morumbi.

The triumph represented Boca's fifth Copa Libertadores title, and third in four years. For Bianchi it was his fourth time winning the coveted title, making him the competition's most successful coach, pulling him clear of Osvaldo Zubeldía. Without Riquelme and a natural replacement as *enganche*, Bianchi adapted his system and instead operated with three mobile and interchangeable forwards in Tevez, Delgado, and Guillermo Barros Schelotto.

For Tim Vickery, the outcome of the final wasn't necessarily a surprise. '[Santos] were an inexperienced side and, in a way, an inexperienced club, that had hardly played in the Copa Libertadores since the mid-1960s,' began Vickery. 'They had problems at centre-back and were emotionally inexperienced; the occasion was too much for them.' Boca, on the other hand, were a different proposition altogether. 'Bianchi had a well-organised team with enough flashes of individual talent. They were a streetwise team that caught form at the right time,' stated Vickery. 'After the defeat of Paysandú in the round of 16 first leg, Boca really caught fire. They found the right position for Tevez because in the earlier games there was an attempt to shoehorn him into being a Riquelme substitute. After that defeat at home, he played up front and it was the making of him and the making of that team.'

Tevez was the standout star, named not only the best player in the Copa Libertadores but also South American Footballer of the Year for 2003. The hugely popular forward was a product of the *potrero* in the mould of Diego Maradona, and proudly displayed a noticeable scar across his neck, a result of a childhood accident, which he refused to have rectified. It was part of his humble character, as were his relentless performances on a football pitch. 'The club distributed a VHS video by mail to their members to show the big work done in the academy, showing many talents from the lower divisions, including a 14-year-old named Carlos Tevez who was a star from the ninth division in 1998,' remembered Buenos Aires-based journalist and member of the Boca in English team, Francisco Aure, about Tevez's emergence. 'Surprisingly he started a match in 2001, but after Oscar Tabárez replaced Bianchi in 2002, he turned into a regular starter despite having only recently turned 18 years old.'

Boca were back in league action just four days later, closing out the Clausura campaign shorn of all of the exhausted Copa Libertadores stars, including Bianchi who was absent from the dugout. A defeat may have been expected in this context, yet few could have predicted the 7-2 thrashing at the hands of Rosario Central. Boca finished the league season in second position, four points behind River.

The priority for the second half of the year was the Intercontinental Cup, yet this would take place one week after the end of the Apertura, in mid-December, so there was still scope to focus fully on the domestic league until then. Delgado had since left for Cruz Azul, and right-back Ibarra departed for Europe once again, this time to Monaco. Replacing the mainstays of the recent triumphs, with varying degrees of success, were three foreigners: Brazilian Pedro Iarley and Colombians Fabián Vargas and Luis Perea.

Bianchi's side won their first five fixtures of the 2003 Apertura, scoring 14 goals and conceding just two. The rulers of the continent were clearly in no mood to take their foot off the throttle. Nine points from the next 15 were won, before the first defeat of the season, 1-0, away at Newell's. A goalless draw at home to Independiente preceded a 2-0 win at El Monumental. Battaglia headed a free kick across the goalkeeper on 37 minutes and, seven minutes after the restart, Iarley doubled Boca's lead and ensured the points would be heading back to La Boca.

Another derby followed as Boca hosted San Lorenzo. With the visitors down to ten men, Iarley scored the only goal of the game on the hour mark, the number ten coolly sliding the ball past the goalkeeper from inside the box. Boca won just one of the last four fixtures but the win over San Lorenzo proved vital: Bianchi's men were champions and finished three points ahead of the men from Boedo. The Midas touch of *El Virrey* had done it again.

The well-rested squad, many of whom missed the last league game and therefore hadn't played for two weeks, headed to the happy stomping ground of Japan, albeit this time in Yokohama instead of Tokyo, for the Intercontinental Cup. Awaiting them were the mighty AC Milan, who had become European champions after defeating countrymen Juventus at Old Trafford.

After playing Real Madrid and Bayern Munich in 2000 and 2001 respectively, Boca were facing another heavyweight of European football. Carlo Ancelotti had a star-studded squad at his disposal and was able to select the likes of Cafu, Andrea Pirlo, Clarence Seedorf, Kaká, and Andriy Shevchenko. Whereas Boca had to continuously rebuild following each success, Milan could even call on two players who had played in the same competition against Bianchi's Vélez nine years earlier: the vastly experienced Paolo Maldini and Alessandro Costacurta.

Battaglia, sporting a bandage on his head following an earlier clash, surrendered possession to Pirlo after 23 minutes. The playmaker found Danish forward Jon Dahl Tomasson, who slid the ball through the legs of Roberto *Pato* Abbondanzieri to give the Italians the lead. Five minutes later Dida made a save from compatriot Iarley after the Brazilian got his toe on the end of a Guillermo Barros Schelotto cross. However, the ball fell to grateful 23-year-old Matías Donnet who was free to finish from close range.

With neither side able to add to the scoring, the game went to penalty kicks. Pirlo opened proceedings yet saw his kick saved by Pato, diving to his right. Schiavi smashed the ball past Dida: first blood to Boca. Pato went the right way once again, yet couldn't keep out Rui Costa's effort. When Battaglia had his penalty saved by Milan's Brazilian goalkeeper – his last kick in a Boca shirt before his move to Villarreal – the score was even after two penalties apiece.

Another heavyweight name, this time Seedorf, missed for Milan, sending the ball high over the crossbar. Donnet, the Argentine repatriated from Venezia, emphatically converted his spot-kick to make it 2-1 to Boca, the pendulum swinging back in favour of the South American champions. The accomplished Costacurta then scuffed his kick, the experienced man perhaps ruffled by Abbondanzieri's mind games in the build-up to the 12-yard duel. Raúl Cascini successfully converted his kick, making it 3-1 to Boca, crowning the new kings of world football. The Italians, who had won the Champions League on penalties, weren't so fortunate in the land of the rising sun.

Cascini was an unlikely hero. The 32-year-old from San Fernando debuted for Boca in July 2002 after a 12-year professional career in which he had represented Platense, Independiente, Estudiantes, and Toulouse. In scoring the winning penalty against Milan, the attacking midfielder became the author of one of Boca's most historically important goals and won his first piece of silverware.

What made the success since the turn of the century all the more impressive was the club's business model, set against a depressed national economy and a shift in the global football transfer market which European sides now dominated. 'The player sales were part of Macri's view on how to administrate a club: like a company,' stated Francisco Aure. It was, therefore, a testament to the management, particularly Bianchi's, to keep the club performing at the highest level. 'It always was a team effort but Bianchi made it possible for new heroes to emerge,' said Aure. 'Donnet, for example, was an average playmaker who had a fantastic match against Milan in 2003. Abbondanzieri was the backup to Oscar Córdoba in 2000. Bianchi let him play the 2001 Clausura while Córdoba kept goal in the Copa Libertadores, and when Córdoba left Abbondanzieri inherited the gloves.'

Other players also came to the fore. 'Delgado was a substitute in 2000 and turned into a star in 2003. Schiavi, who joined in 2001, captained the team shortly after. There is Cascini, Tevez, and Battaglia who established themselves during those years. Some players left after 2000, yes, but I wouldn't say the team was ever weakened because of that. The new signings or youngsters proved to be equal or better.'

The record-breaking Bianchi now became the first manager to have won the Intercontinental Cup on three occasions and remains the only man ever to have achieved that feat. The scourge of Milan, Bianchi beat the Italian giants in 1994 with Vélez in lifting the trophy for the first time and had now done it again. Boca repeated the success of 2000 in winning the triple crown of the three most prestigious competitions up for grabs in the calendar year: the domestic championship, Copa Libertadores and, the icing on the cake, the Intercontinental Cup. Very few teams had ever enjoyed such a concentrated period of success, the most golden of eras in the club's illustrious history.

Chapter Thirteen

425 Days

THE CHAMPIONS of Argentina, South America, and the world were straight back in action during the first half of 2004, with the defence of two of their crowns the top priorities. The Torneo Clausura and Copa Libertadores kicked off in February and Boca started both defences in fine fettle.

Carlos Bianchi's men topped a Copa Libertadores group which featured Deportivo Cali, Bolívar and Colo Colo, and by the end of April were unbeaten in 12 league games. Sporting Cristal were eliminated in the last 16 of the continental competition, 5-3 on aggregate, before River Plate visited La Bombonera in round 14 of the Clausura.

Fernando Cavenaghi gave River a half-time lead and just after the break Boca defender José María Calvo was dismissed by referee Sergio Pezzotta. Any chance of a comeback was dashed when, on 82 minutes, Carlos Tevez joined Calvo when Pezzotta flashed his red card once again. From thereon in the league form collapsed, with just five points won from the last available 15.

In the last eight of the Copa Libertadores Boca edged out Brazilian side São Caetano on penalties after more than

180 minutes of open play failed to separate the two sides. Goalkeeper Roberto Abbondanzieri was the hero, saving two spot-kicks and converting the crucial one himself to set up a powder-keg semi-final clash with recently crowned Clausura champions River.

On 10 June the first leg took place at La Bombonera with no away fans as a security measure. Despite the absence of a benched Tevez, defender Rolando Schiavi opened the scoring for Boca after 28 minutes. Three minutes later the tie exploded as Raúl Cascini and Marcelo Gallardo were both red-carded. Before half-time River were reduced to nine men when Ariel Garcé was given his marching orders. A strong River side containing the likes of Javier Mascherano, Maxi López and Lucho González hit the crossbar and were unlucky not to score, yet on the overall balance of play, Boca deserved the narrow victory.

The sides met one week later at El Monumental and an adventurous River set up in a bold 3-4-3 formation. Within the space of five minutes, Boca's Fabián Vargas was sent off for a second bookable offence and Lucho González scored for the hosts with a sweetly struck shot from 20 yards. The pendulum swung back in Boca's favour when River's Rubens Sambueza was red-carded for dissent on 84 minutes, a decision which even appeared to bemuse Bianchi. In the protests, an incensed River manager Leo Astrada, as well as his assistant and the physio, Gabriel Macaya, who was allegedly punched by Guillermo Barros Schelotto, were sent to the stands. Ricardo Rojas hobbled off with an injury and River, who had already used their three substitutes, had to finish the game with nine men.

After 87 minutes Bianchi rolled the dice, replacing Diego Cagna, struggling with cramp, with Franco Cángele. One minute later the recently introduced striker made an impact, driving down the left-hand side before crossing for Tevez with his very first action. *El Apache* smashed the ball into the roof of the net with his left foot from the edge of the six-yard box, silencing the crowd and then instinctively removing his number nine shirt in celebration. Several of his ecstatic team-mates enveloped the forward and when he broke free, he mimicked a chicken with his arms. The referee immediately brandished a red card, repeating the chicken gesture to Tevez so he was in no doubt as to why he had been punished. The derogatory nickname for River, the *gallinas* (chickens), stems from an incident in 1966 when River gave up a two-goal lead to lose 4-2 to Peñarol in the Copa Libertadores Final. Back home, in a subsequent league fixture against River, Banfield fans threw a live chicken on to the pitch to taunt their rivals, and the tag stuck. The referee deemed Tevez's gesture to be incendiary.

For Boca fans, it only served to heighten their love for the youngster from Fuerte Apache. 'When Tevez appeared it was a sign, an omen,' said Sebastián Sellaro of Somos Boca. 'Another "different" player we were going to enjoy watching wear blue-and-gold. We could feel that this small, brave, and intrepid young footballer was going to fill us with joy. His power, strength and liveliness in the penalty area made comparisons with Maradona inevitable. The famous "chicken" celebration in Núñez was a perfect portrait of the most genuine Tevez, without fear of anything, born in a humble neighbourhood and acting only as his heart commanded. This demonstration was pure love for Boca and the renunciation of a rival.'

The drama, however, wasn't over. The stretched game, now nine versus nine on a full-sized pitch, gave River a chance for one last push. Deep into injury time Cristian Nasuti made it 2-1 for the home side on the night, levelling the aggregate score at 2-2. Penalties, something which Boca had become accustomed to in recent years, were required yet again, the final ingredient in one of the most classic of all the *Superclásicos.*

Both sides converted their first four penalties, with Schiavi, Pablo Álvarez, Pablo Ledesma and Nicolás Burdisso finding the net for Boca. Abbondanzieri came to the fore yet again, repelling a poor effort from Maxi López that was fairly central and at the perfect height for a goalkeeper. Javier Villarreal, the battler from Córdoba, scored the crucial penalty to send Boca to their fourth Copa Libertadores final in five years. Abbondanzieri kissed his goalkeeping counterpart on the cheek in a quick show of solidarity before rushing to celebrate with his team-mates.

Just six days later Boca hosted Once Caldas in the final first leg at La Bombonera. The humble Colombians had only been founded just over 40 years earlier and had just two domestic titles to their name. It was real David versus Goliath territory. Without the suspended Tevez, however, Boca were toothless, and the defensively resolute Colombians were able to defy the odds and escape Buenos Aires with a goalless draw.

The following week Boca travelled to Manizales, a small city in the middle of the Andean mountain range, for the return leg. Bianchi's side were caught napping in Colombia's coffee capital, Once Caldas taking the lead after just seven minutes through Jhon Viáfara who later played in England for both Portsmouth and Southampton. Seven minutes into the second half Boca finally managed to break down the stubborn Colombians, Burdisso powerfully heading in a Cángele free kick to equalise. No more goals meant the lottery of penalty kicks once again.

Boca got off to the best possible start in the shoot-out, *Pato* Abbondanzieri saving Once Caldas' first effort from 12 yards. However, Schiavi missed his kick before Elkin Soto made it 1-0 to the Colombians. Cascini saw his kick saved, then *Pato* made yet another stop. Burdisso, whose goal forced penalties, missed his kick then Jorge Agudelo scored to make it 2-0 to Once Caldas. Cángele saw his penalty saved and Boca were out of luck.

Bianchi's side, so ruthless in numerous penalty shoot-outs, failed to score a single kick in Colombia. It was astonishing that Boca were able to overcome a hurdle as difficult as River over two legs, and then lose to a team as unfancied as Once Caldas. The Colombians enjoyed their greatest-ever moment, and since triumphing in 2004 have won just two more honours in the ensuing 16 years. 'It was very odd but, for many, the consolation was that the cup was won by eliminating River in their stadium,' began Sebastián Sellaro. 'The pressure and attrition experienced in the semi-final led the group, perhaps, to have lived it as a title despite it not being the final. Everything was missing: the luck of a champion and the infallibility in penalty shoot-outs. The night in Manizales was the height of imperfection.'

Following the shock defeat, Bianchi departed. His relationship with the club's directors was deteriorating and the shrewd coach sensed that a major rebuild was required. Bianchi, now aged 55, pitched up at Atlético Madrid but the union was unsuccessful and years of inactivity would follow.

Much was expected in the second half of 2004. Tevez came home from the Olympics in Athens with a gold medal, having scored the winner in the final. His new strike partner, Martín Palermo, returned to his spiritual home after an underwhelming spell in Europe. Bianchi's replacement was Miguel Ángel Brindisi, a key figure in the 1981 Metropolitano title-winning team.

In September 2004 Boca lost another final on penalties, this time the Recopa Sudamericana, which pitted the 2003 champions of the Copa Libertadores against the Copa Sudamericana winners, Cienciano. The Peruvians were the surprise victors in Fort Lauderdale, Florida. On 7 November, in round 14 of the Torneo Apertura, Boca lost 2-0 to River at El Monumental. During a run in which the side failed to score in more than 600 minutes of football, an unwelcomed professional-era club record, Brindisi's brief three-month reign was brought to an end. In what proved to be a domestic campaign of flux, Boca finished eighth in the league, ten points behind champions Newell's.

San Lorenzo, Cerro Porteño, and Internacional were beaten en route to the Copa Sudamericana final in December and Brindisi's replacement, Jorge *Chino* Benítez, took the side to Bolivia to face Bolívar. In the high altitude of La Paz, Horacio Chiorazzo scored the only goal of the game in the Estadio Hernando Siles to give the home side a slender advantage going into the second leg.

Back in Buenos Aires, Boca turned the tie around in front of a typically fervent crowd at La Bombonera. Palermo rose highest to head the opener after 13 minutes before Tevez doubled the lead and sealed the victory 14 minutes later, side-footing a cut-back from Guillermo Barros Schelotto into the net from 12 yards. Benítez, who had begun working with the youth team towards the end of the 90s, had now won Boca titles as a player and a manager.

A visibly emotional Tevez, playing his last game for the club before joining Corinthians, sank to his knees on the turf and saluted the fans. 'They loved him in Brazil and he was exactly the right kind of player for Corinthians,' remarked Tim Vickery. 'It's a team with a working-class ethic of blood, sweat and sacrifice. So he fitted right into that. He was seen as someone who was gifted but also really prepared to put in a shift so he is loved.' Tevez retained his South American Footballer of the Year award in Brazil, making him the first man since Zico to be named the continent's best player on three occasions. He then headed to Europe, appearing for

Premier League outfits West Ham United, Manchester United and Manchester City, and Juventus in Serie A.

To replace the outgoing Tevez, the club repatriated one of the heroes of the Bianchi era, Marcelo Delgado, from Cruz Azul in Mexico. Twenty-two-year-old forward Rodrigo Palacio joined from Banfield and within two months would make his Argentina debut.

On 3 April 2005, the club's 100th birthday, the side lost 2-0 at Vélez in the Clausura. Despite the result, it was a major moment in the club's history. 'It was truly unforgettable,' began Sebastián Sellaro. 'For us [Somos Boca], as a journalistic medium linked to the club, the date marked a distinct "before and after". On 3 April 2005, we transmitted for more than 24 hours uninterrupted, something that can never be equalled. More than a day dedicated to content purely and exclusively about a football club, an inexplicable passion. No radio station, at least in Argentina, has ever done it.'

In the Copa Libertadores, Benítez's men eased through the group before knocking out Colombia's Junior in the last 16 to set up a quarter-final clash with Chivas Guadalajara. A resounding 4-0 defeat in Mexico – with all goals coming in the space of 22 disastrous minutes – gave Boca an impossible mountain to climb in the second leg.

Events took an ugly turn in La Bombonera. After 75 minutes, with the score goalless, Palermo and Chivas's Adolfo Bautista were red-carded, the Boca forward punching the Mexican following provocation. As Bautista was leaving, with police protection, a fan entered the field, punching him before attempting to hide in the stands. The assailant was later arrested, but that was the least of the club's worries. As Bautista passed the Boca bench a disgruntled Benítez spat on his face; Delgado spent the night at the police station after an altercation with an officer. Projectiles rained down from the stands, peppering the visiting goalkeeper. After four minutes of chaos, the Uruguayan referee had no choice but to abandon the match. The scandal was a real black mark on the history of the club, and no way to celebrate the centenary year.

Palermo and Benítez were both suspended by Conmebol, and the club was hit with a three-game stadium ban. After just six months, a combination of poor results and the unsporting act against the Mexicans brought Benítez's reign to an end. One month after the scandal Boca closed out a terrible domestic campaign, in which 40 players were used en route to a 15th-place finish. The final fixture summed up the season. Losing 3-2 away to Almagro, the match was abandoned due to disturbances in the stands. Both sides were subsequently awarded a defeat by a tribunal.

Major changes were required in order to salvage what remained of the centenary year. Alfio *Coco* Basile, a veteran with 30 years of management experience, was appointed in July. Basile had won an international title with Racing in 1988 before leading Argentina to two Copas América and the King Fahd Cup between 1991 and 1993. At La Bombonera, Basile moulded a great team in the classic Boca 4-3-1-2 formation – two strong central defenders, three all-round midfielders, an *enganche*, and two forwards – and was about to embark on the most successful spell of his career.

Basile added Jorge *Ruso* Ribolzi, an attacking midfielder who won five titles with the club in the late 1970s and early 1980s to his back-room team. After retiring, Ribolzi began studying in 1985 at the AFA's 'Escuela de Técnicos'. 'One of the best things that happened to me was getting the call to be part of Basile's technical staff,' began Ribolzi. 'I have massive respect and admiration for *Coco*. We weren't friends beforehand, but from this point on, and forever, we are going to have this friendship. He was a great trainer, one who taught me a lot, not just in football but in life also. It was a beautiful phase.'

The squad was shaken up. Federico *Pocho* Insúa and Daniel *Cata* Díaz – both of whom would be ever-presents in the Apertura – came in from Independiente and Colón respectively. Sebastián Battaglia returned from Villarreal; Daniel Bilos and Juan Krupoviesa provided further reinforcement for the squad. Cristian Traverso and Aníbal Matellán, who had both returned in mid-2004, both departed, having won seven titles each over two spells with Boca. Traverso retired, whereas Matellán joined Getafe in Spain.

Basile's side picked up five points from the first available nine with the fourth fixture of the league schedule – a 3-0 home win over Instituto – bookended by the two legs of the 2005 Recopa Sudamericana. Boca had two motivations to lift the trophy: the previous Recopa had seen a defeat on penalties to Cienciano and the opponents were Once Caldas, who had shocked South American football in beating Boca for the 2004 Copa Libertadores. Revenge, of sorts, was on the cards.

Boca flew out of the traps in the first leg at La Bombonera, winning 3-1 with all three goals coming in the first 18 minutes. The Colombians took an early lead in the second leg, bringing them back into the tie, but a sending off on 44 minutes reduced them to ten men and put the ball back in Boca's court. Schiavi equalised on the hour and, on 76 minutes, Once Caldas took a 2-1 lead despite now being down to nine men. Battaglia also saw red but Boca hung on for the aggregate victory. The Recopa was Boca's 14th international title, and the Basile reign was up and running with an early trophy.

After a defeat to San Lorenzo in early September, Boca embarked on a five-match winning streak before a forgettable goalless draw with River at El Monumental. Basile's side stumbled somewhat, winning just one of the next four fixtures, yet were able to peak at the vital moment. Title rivals Gimnasia drew each of their final four fixtures, whilst Boca won them all, producing an eight-point swing. From five points behind Boca won the Apertura title with a three-point cushion. Rodrigo Palacio was Boca's top scorer with 10 in 17; youth-team product Fernando Gago, and new signings Insúa and Bilos, were standout performers.

Four days after the domestic coronation Boca had the chance to lift yet another international title: the Copa Sudamericana. Cerro Porteño, Internacional and Universidad Católica were vanquished along the way to the final against UNAM. A 1-1 draw in the Mexican capital in the first leg poised the return in La Bombonera perfectly.

Palermo gave Boca a half-time lead but the Mexicans equalised after 54 minutes to take the tie to penalties. Abbondanzieri got Boca off to the best possible start in saving UNAM's first effort, but Guillermo Barros Schelotto saw his kick repelled. Gonzalo Pineda and Boca's creative hub, Insúa, were up next for their respective sides and both converted successfully. *Pato* saved yet another penalty, but Palermo missed his kick. After six penalties the score was just 1-1.

Both sides netted their next two, taking the shoot-out to sudden death. UNAM cracked. Gerardo Galindo missed for the Mexicans before the confident Abbondanzieri complemented his goalkeeping heroics by scoring the winning kick to seal the cup for Boca. A centenary year which had begun so badly now saw Basile's Boca with three titles in just five months, a fitting end to the celebration of the club's rich history.

For Boca, it was yet another title won on penalty kicks. 'Penalties are not as tied to luck and fortune as many people think,' stated Sebastián Sellaro of Somos Boca. 'Various factors are present at this stressful moment: concentration, attitude, psychological preparation, fatigue, physical condition, and intuition to name but a few. But, I think it's very unfair that people think Boca won so many titles on penalties. Boca thrashed their opponents in three of the six Copa Libertadores successes and only won one of the three Intercontinental Cups on penalties.'

After the exhilarating end to 2005, the following year began rather slowly. Boca picked up just five points from the first 15 available in the Clausura championship but, with no continental distractions, built up a head of steam and went the rest of the campaign unbeaten.

In round 11 River visited La Bombonera and at half-time were leading 1-0. Abbondanzieri was red-carded after a foul on Marcelo Gallardo and, when Daniel Montenegro was bearing down on goal in the 82nd minute *Los Millonarios* had a real chance to seal the points. That was until Krupoviesa intervened, felling the attacking midfielder with a shocking knee-high lunge which gave the referee no option but to reduce Boca to nine men. Still, the tackle would prove to be a crucial intervention and, despite the numerical disadvantage, a late Palermo penalty rescued a point for Basile's men.

The lively derby clash was the last appearance of Guillermo Barros Schelotto in the blue-and-gold shirt. The 33-year-old was used less frequently by Basile, the rapid rise of Rodrigo Palacio the final nail in the coffin of his Boca career. After 16 major honours, the twin from La Plata joined Columbus Crew of Major League Soccer (MLS).

Boca drew the following match, 1-1 away to Newell's, but won seven of the last seven games to seal the championship dominantly, eight points clear of Lanús. The league was sewn up on the turf of fellow *grande* Independiente in the penultimate fixture. Palacio and Palermo, who scored almost half of Boca's goals in this championship and were synonymous with the Basile era, grabbed the goals in a 2-0 win. 'The team of 2005/06 had everything: football ability, personality, and experienced players that knew how to play in the style *Coco* wanted to implement,' stated Ribolzi. 'Palermo and Palacio were truly fearsome. It's a dream to have been part of Palermo's journey to becoming Boca's all-time leading scorer. Palacio was quick and intelligent; it was a team that was equal in all areas of the pitch.'

Sebastián Sellaro also waxed lyrical about the 'Pa-Pa' partnership. 'In Palacio, Palermo found what he had had years earlier with Guillermo Barros Schelotto and Marcelo Delgado,' began the Somos Boca journalist. 'Rodrigo arrived and revolutionised Boca's attack, giving Palermo the hope and certainty that he would continue converting goals. Thanks to this new offensive partnership, that terrorised rival defences and goalkeepers, Boca continued collecting titles. I do not doubt that Palacio is one of the most important forwards in the history of the institution.'

Despite the absence of the departed Abbondanzieri, Insúa and Bilos, Basile's side started the 2006 Apertura in fine form. However, the opening day victory over Banfield was bittersweet for one of the club's favourite sons. Four days before the August clash, Palermo's newborn son, Stéfano, had died after complications during childbirth. On an emotionally charged afternoon, the prolific forward insisted on playing. After 58 minutes he opened the scoring before being enveloped by his team-mates. Battaglia doubled the lead nine minutes later then, on 75 minutes, Palermo grabbed his second to make it 3-0 before sinking to the turf. His work done, he was replaced four minutes later to rapturous applause, the love and sympathy from the fans in the stands palpable.

Victories over Rosario Central, Independiente and San Lorenzo – a 7-1 destruction in front of their fans, the first time Boca had scored seven in a league match in more than 20 years – saw Boca maintain their 100 per cent start to the season. The club was then a victim of its own success. The Argentine national team went to the 2006 World Cup in Germany with the realistic ambition of winning the tournament. The fervour was heightened when *La Albiceleste* destroyed Serbia – who had only conceded one goal in ten matches during qualification – 6-0, with one of the finest team goals that the tournament has ever witnessed. The joy was short-lived. With Riquelme withdrawn prematurely, Argentina were eliminated by the hosts in the quarter-final, on penalty kicks. The knock-on effect was that national coach José Pékerman left, and Basile, in the best moment of his career, was summoned to fill the vacant post.

Before taking up the national-team job, Basile stayed to lead Boca in the Recopa Sudamericana against the reigning Copa Libertadores champions São Paulo. Macri negotiated with AFA president Julio Grondona to allow the coach to remain in charge for the two-legged competition. Thiago Ribeiro gave the Brazilians a half-time lead in La Bombonera but a second-half Palacio brace meant Boca took a lead to the Morumbi. One week later, Júnior put the home side ahead before Palacio and Palermo gave Boca a 2-1 advantage with goals either side of the break. São Paulo grabbed a late equaliser but couldn't find the additional goal required to bring them back into the tie. For the third time in their history, the Recopa was Boca's.

For Basile, it was his fifth title in just 425 days, and the perfect way to sign off from what was an unforgettable trophy-laden year. 'After a turbulent start the team settled down and came to terms with Basile's ideas,' stated Sebastián Sellaro. 'After that, they couldn't stop doing laps of honour. The players remember him as a great motivator, a carrier of constant joy that supported the group and stood up for them.

Unfortunately, and inexplicably, he went to the national team halfway through a season and a super successful cycle was stopped. Had he stayed, there surely would have been many more conquests.'

Ribolzi, on a caretaker basis, led the side to a 2-0 home win over Estudiantes in the league, the irrepressible partnership of Palacio and Palermo once again coming up with the goods. 'It was a dream to wear the Boca shirt and win five titles, and then to be part of the coaching staff and win so much,' remarked Ribolzi. 'This love for Boca is something I'll carry with me forever.'

Three days after the Recopa had been lifted in Brazil, Basile's successor, Ricardo La Volpe, took control of his first game when Boca welcomed Godoy Cruz to La Bombonera on 17 September. Former goalkeeper La Volpe, a member of Argentina's World Cup-winning squad in 1978, had hung up his gloves in Mexico before starting his coaching career. Over 23 years, La Volpe managed seven different Mexican clubs as well as the national team, becoming one of the most influential managers in Mexico's football history.

However, La Volpe wasn't Boca's first choice to replace Basile. The timing of the approach from the AFA was problematic as the best coaches were already ensconced in roles at other clubs. Having not managed since leading Argentina to a gold medal at the 2004 Olympics, Marcelo Bielsa continued with his hiatus, while Miguel Ángel Russo decided to remain at Vélez and honour his contract.

The afternoon of La Volpe's debut as coach started in a celebratory mood as the players, as well as outgoing hero Basile, paraded the Recopa trophy around the pitch at La Bombonera. There was little else to cheer that day. Despite coming under heavy fire Godoy Cruz held out for a goalless draw. La Volpe committed the cardinal sin of wearing a red tie, a colour associated with River Plate.

La Volpe's first victory came in the following fixture, a 1-0 win at Nueva Chicago in which his side scraped through, despite failing to perform, to hold on to the top spot. A 3-2 win at home to Vélez, when Boca were down 2-0 after 70 minutes, was much improved and wildly celebrated. Boca's coach, this time sensibly wearing a blue tie, looked mightily relieved.

Boca travelled to El Monumental for La Volpe's first *Superclásico* in the hot seat. One of his non-negotiable philosophies, playing out from the back, led to River's first goal in a 3-1 defeat. The 22-match unbeaten run was over but seven wins and a draw from the next eight games put Boca in a strong position – four points ahead of nearest challengers, Estudiantes – going into the last two rounds of the championship.

The penultimate fixture saw Boca travel to Córdoba to face Belgrano, knowing a victory would seal the title with a game to spare. Instead, a 1-0 defeat, and a point for Estudiantes at Argentinos Juniors, took the race to the final day. Still, Boca's cushion of three points meant that the destiny of the title remained in their hands. La Volpe's men just had to equal or better the result of their rivals from La Plata.

Palermo settled Boca's nerves after 30 minutes of the final day, at home to Lanús, with the expectant fans in attendance ready to party. However, the away side equalised just before half-time, scoring the winner after 57 minutes to inexplicably beat Boca on their turf. A 2-0 win over Arsenal for Estudiantes meant the sides finished the season level on points. Despite having a better goal difference, having scored more goals, and a better head-to-head record after winning the league clash, Boca were forced into a one-off play-off to determine the destination of the championship.

What was effectively a final took place at the stadium of Vélez in Liniers. As he had done on so many occasions,

Palermo gave Boca the lead, converting a Pablo Ledesma cross from close range after just four minutes. Both sides were reduced to ten men after 38 minutes and, in the second half, Estudiantes took control, scoring in the 54th and 80th minutes to snatch victory, and the title, from the jaws of defeat. It was the third successive match in which Boca had had the title in their hands, only for it to agonisingly slip away.

The bid for the first *tricampeonato* in the club's history was up in smoke and one man, in particular, was deemed culpable. La Volpe failed to respect the classic style of Boca and reneged on his promise not to continuously tinker with tactics, confusing the players who failed to understand why the game plan and formation changed so often. Rather than focusing on their strengths, La Volpe was more concerned with adapting to the opponents. It was the mindset of a small club and wasn't in keeping with the tradition of an institution with the reputation of Boca Juniors.

After the league capitulation, and an early exit from the Copa Sudamericana, La Volpe's resignation was entirely predictable. The moustachioed coach headed to Vélez before returning to Mexico where, despite being Argentine, his style seemed to fit. In what amounted to a game of managerial musical chairs, his replacement came from Vélez. Six months earlier Boca had failed with an attempt to lure Russo to La Bombonera but this time the approach was successful. Early in 2007, the new coach would take up his position, aided by a returning icon.

Chapter Fourteen

Riquelme's Return

JUAN ROMÁN Riquelme joined La Liga giants FC Barcelona in July 2002 and, like Maradona, his spell at the Camp Nou failed to produce the desired results. Riquelme arrived in the Catalan capital during a time of real churn when the club were saying goodbye to the likes of Rivaldo, Sergi Barjuán and Abelardo Fernández; Louis Van Gaal was simultaneously returning for his second spell in the hot seat.

The enigmatic playmaker, who cost Barcelona €11m, found no room in the rigid plans of the pragmatic Dutchman, his game-time severely restricted by a man known for favouring systems and processes over individual creativity. During the club's worst season in 15 years, both Van Gaal and president Joan Gaspart departed the club within the space of 16 days in early 2003.

The disastrous campaign preceded the election of Joan Laporta and the glory years under Frank Rijkaard and, later, Pep Guardiola, yet for Riquelme there was no reverse in fortune despite the winds of change blowing through the club. With Barça exceeding their limit on foreign players following the acquisition of Ronaldinho, a two-year loan deal with Villarreal was arranged and, in the summer of 2003, Riquelme relocated 290km along the coast to the small city in the Valencian Community.

Although Riquelme had thrived in the Boca goldfish bowl, when it came to Spanish football he was perfectly suited to the modest outfit. Riquelme blossomed at El Madrigal, where expectations are lower, the limelight and pressure not as intense as at the Camp Nou or La Bombonera. Although it hadn't worked out for the playmaker in Barcelona, the Spanish league, where technique trumps physicality, seemed tailor-made for his more artistic strengths to flourish.

After an excellent campaign in 2004/05, in which Riquelme's 15 goals propelled the club to a third-place finish, the loan deal was made permanent and a four-year contract was signed. With Manuel Pellegrini's team built around Riquelme, the Yellow Submarine ventured into the uncharted waters of the Champions League in 2005/06, where they reached the semi-final. Riquelme mesmerised Europe playing for an unfancied side with no prior history of excelling at such a high level, putting Villarreal firmly on the map.

What should have been a high point for Riquelme proved to be the beginning of the end of his time in Europe. Trailing Arsenal 1-0 on aggregate deep into the semi-final second leg, Villarreal were awarded a penalty. Riquelme, who had calmly netted numerous crucial spot-kicks for Boca, faced Jens Lehmann from 12 yards, the German international saving the uncharacteristically tame effort. Villarreal were out and Riquelme was denied the chance to face Barcelona in the final and gain revenge on the club which had discarded him.

After the disappointment of the 2006 World Cup, where the number ten was expected to star for an Argentina side with realistic ambitions of winning the trophy, Riquelme returned to Villarreal but his love affair had ended with the missed penalty kick. The relationship between player and Pellegrini soured and Riquelme played just 13 times in the first half of the 2006/07 season. Given his ability and transformative powers, the Spanish club had pandered to Riquelme when things were going well, yet grew tired when they felt their commitment wasn't being reciprocated. Pellegrini had the full backing of the club president to sideline the star.

After four and a half sweet and sour years in European football, Riquelme returned to La Bombonera, initially on loan, in January 2007. Aged 28, the player was returning to Argentine football in his physical prime but, for a player with Riquelme's characteristics, what mattered most was the grey matter between his ears, and how motivated he was to achieve more, having already won everything the South American game had to offer.

Under the tutelage of former Estudiantes midfielder Miguel Ángel Russo, who lifted the 2005 Clausura title with Vélez Sarsfield, Boca finished second in the 2007 Clausura but the first half of the calendar year was all about the Copa Libertadores. On paper the group phase looked straightforward: Boca were drawn with Toluca (Mexico), Cienciano (Peru) and Bolívar (Bolivia). The home matches were navigated with ease and saw Boca take maximum points in Buenos Aires, scoring 11 and conceding zero. However, the away form proved a struggle. Against three opponents based at high altitude, Boca took just one point from nine and failed to register a single goal. Boca finished second in the group behind Toluca and just one point ahead of Cienciano, progressing to the knockout phase.

In the first leg of the last 16 an inspired Riquelme led Boca to a 3-0 home win over Vélez – awkwardly managed by Ricardo La Volpe, Russo's predecessor – opening the scoring himself after nine minutes, a stunning curling effort into the top corner from a Palermo lay-off. Boca lost the return leg 3-1 yet Riquelme scored a *gol olímpico* (a goal straight from a corner) after 32 minutes and Boca progressed to the last eight.

Boca needed a late Palermo goal to salvage a draw at home to Libertad in the first leg of the quarter-final. Atoning for his penalty miss at La Bombonera, Riquelme opened the scoring for Boca 62 minutes into the return leg in Paraguay, with a virtuoso effort. Receiving the ball on the edge of the centre circle with his back to goal, Riquelme spun his defender and attacked the space before finishing from 20 yards. Rodrigo Palacio's close-range finish nine minutes later sealed Boca's passage to the final four.

Boca enjoyed a solid start to the semi-final first leg against Cúcuta, taking a 1-0 lead after 27 minutes thanks to Pablo Ledesma. The Colombians equalised before half-time before adding two more in the second half, taking a two-goal cushion to La Bombonera.

The return fixture will be remembered for years to come by those present. Just before half-time a Riquelme free kick gave Boca a lifeline and Palermo wiped out Cúcuta's lead after 55 minutes. The remaining time on the clock represented a straight shoot-out for the chance to appear in the final. Boca were in the ascendancy and at this point it felt as if there would only be one winner. After 81 minutes Sebastián Battaglia nodded in a Riquelme corner and the Colombians were unable to respond. On a foggy night in La Bombonera, Boca had memorably advanced to their fifth Copa Libertadores final in eight years.

Six nights after the Cúcuta victory, Grêmio arrived at La Bombonera to contest the first portion of the Copa Libertadores final. Seemingly picking up where they had left off the previous week, Russo's side scored after 18 minutes. A Riquelme free kick found Palermo, wearing the captain's armband, and he centred it to Palacio to tap the ball into the empty net from a couple of yards out. Twelve minutes into the second half Sandro Goiano was dismissed after his foot connected high on Éver Banega's chest and, rather than sticking with a one-goal cushion, Boca twisted and doubled their lead after 73 minutes courtesy of the majestic Riquelme who, after himself being fouled, lashed in a free kick from 25 yards. The celebration showed exactly how much it meant to him, and that the fire was still burning bright after his spell in Europe. Any questions about his commitment and motivation evaporated into the cold night sky. A miserable night for Grêmio was complete when, after 89 minutes, they scored an own goal to make it 3-0 to Boca.

The Argentine side underlined their dominance in the second leg, beating the Brazilians 2-0 in their back yard, although Grêmio hit the crossbar in the first half, and former Boca man Rolando Schiavi hit the post with a header in the second period. With 68 minutes on the clock Riquelme, the undisputed star of the tournament, made it 4-0 on aggregate to Boca, with a mind-blowing goal that combined teamwork and individual brilliance. It was the essence of Russo's Boca, a pragmatic side built in the image of their manager yet one able to accommodate a mercurial number ten. Riquelme, drifting in the final third in search of a pocket of space, found one and, fed by Ibarra, unleashed an unstoppable shot from the corner of the 18-yard-box, across the goalkeeper and into the far side of the net. Riquelme was perhaps the only player in world football at that moment that would have attempted something so audacious. The goal's protagonist was held aloft by his team-mates as if they were carrying a king on his throne.

Riquelme's second goal, his eighth in 11 Copa Libertadores games, came from a counter-attack. With Boca holding a three-versus-two advantage, Riquelme drove with the ball before laying it off. When the goalkeeper fumbled Palacio's shot Riquelme was on hand to finish the rebound. The club's sixth Copa Libertadores title nudged Boca ahead of Peñarol in the pecking order and just one behind Independiente. For Riquelme, the flame still flickered and his love for football, and Boca, remained. This wasn't another story of a South American player returning home and going through the motions.

The emphatic 5-0 scoreline, the largest in the history of two-legged Copa Libertadores finals, was a surprise, but that the trophy ended up in the cabinet on Calle Brandsen perhaps wasn't. 'Grêmio were down in the Brazilian second division in 2005 so were pretty inexperienced,' began Rio de Janeiro-based journalist Tim Vickery. 'They got relegated and went back up and that momentum carried them into the next season and they qualified for the Copa Libertadores. Then they reach the final, although it perhaps came a couple of years too soon for the club. There was a huge chasm between those two sides, technically, emotionally, and in terms of big-match experience.'

Although Riquelme hails from a country which shares a traditionally fierce rivalry with their neighbours, his legacy in Brazil is strong. 'There is an annual youth tournament in São Paulo at the start of every year, a big tournament with lots of teams,' stated Vickery. 'One year there were 11 players from the 100 teams with the Christian name of "Riquelme" which tells you something.' The player's popularity across the continent perhaps stems from his style of play which was different to that of many of his peers. 'He's almost like someone stepping out of a black-and-white photo,' said Vickery. 'He represents an old-fashioned form of South American football that lots of people still remember with great affection.'

Diego Tomasi, an author of a book about Riquelme, was effusive with praise about the star's performance in the 2007

Copa Libertadores. 'He produced one of the most influential and outstanding individual performances in the history of modern football,' began Tomasi. 'In terms of Argentine players, only Maradona in the 1986 World Cup has reached a higher peak. Additionally, Riquelme performed excellently, alongside Lionel Messi, at the 2007 Copa América and Argentina were unlucky to lose the final to Brazil.' Gabriel Aguero, founder of the Boca in English Twitter account and podcast, is equally complimentary. 'Riquelme's form in 2007 was magnificent and many argue that Boca won that Libertadores exclusively because of him,' said Aguero. 'He was Boca's top scorer with eight goals and, now, is Boca's top scorer in Copa Libertadores history with 25 goals in 73 matches. Years later he would be recognised as the Copa Libertadores' greatest-ever player.'

Riquelme didn't feature in the 2007 Apertura, which ran from August to December, spending six months in the footballing wilderness whilst Boca negotiated with Villarreal over a permanent transfer following the expiration of the loan agreement. Without their talisman, Boca finished fourth in a domestic championship which was won by Lanús for the first time in their history.

Riquelme also missed Boca's appearance at the FIFA Club World Cup, a new, expanded format which replaced the Intercontinental Cup. The 2007 Copa Libertadores champions faced CAF Champions League winners ESS in the semi-final after the Tunisians had overcome Mexican side Pachuca in the last eight. Back in Japan, where Boca had previously enjoyed two Intercontinental Cup successes, a 37th-minute Neri Cardozo goal in Tokyo was enough to send *Los Xeneizes* through to the final.

Milan, who Boca had defeated on penalties to lift the 2003 Intercontinental Cup, were the opponents after the Italians had seen off Urawa Red Diamonds with a Clarence

Seedorf goal. Predictably, and by design, the competition boiled down to a South America versus Europe face-off to determine the world champions of club football.

The two sides met in Yokohama's International Stadium, where they had clashed four years earlier, on 16 December 2007 in front of a crowd of almost 70,000. Deadly marksman Filippo Inzaghi scored the game's first goal after 20 minutes from customarily close range before wheeling away in trademark style, celebrating as if it were the first and last goal of his career. Boca hit back immediately. Palacio, complete with iconic rat's tail, outfoxed the legendary *Rossoneri* defence and headed past Dida following a clever short-corner routine.

However, the Italians blitzed Boca in a 20-minute second-half spell, scoring three times through Alessandro Nesta, Kaká, arguably the best player in the world at the time, and Inzaghi's second of the night. A late own goal from Massimo Ambrosini made the score 4-2 but, in truth, Boca were outclassed by the European champions.

Boca kicked off the 2008 Clausura without Russo, replaced by Carlos Ischia who had previously been part of Carlos Bianchi's technical staff and was therefore familiar to the club and several players. 'Russo's time at Boca in 2007 is considered as a successful stint,' began Gabriel Aguero. 'Any time the club captures the Copa Libertadores is considered a success. Russo departed after the loss to Milan because the president, Pedro Pompilio, wanted to impose a new strength and conditioning coach, Alfredo Altieri, who worked with Bianchi during his second stint at Boca. Russo wasn't having it, and decided to walk away from the club.'

After his hiatus, Riquelme signed a permanent deal, putting pen to paper on a massive contract that made him the highest-paid player in Argentine football history. The agreement also stipulated that he would play the final season for free. Despite beating River 1-0 at La Bombonera, Boca finished second in the Clausura table, four points behind their great rivals. The Copa Libertadores crown was lost as Brazilian side Fluminense prevailed 5-3 on aggregate in the semi-final.

With the 2008 Apertura campaign still in its infancy, Boca lifted the Recopa Sudamericana after beating fellow Argentine side Arsenal 5-3 on aggregate. In the first leg, Palermo scored his 194th goal for the club, equalling the professional-era club record set by Francisco Varallo.

On 30 October, the death of president Pompilio sent shockwaves throughout the *Boquense* family. Pompilio, whose involvement with the club spanned more than two decades, had succeeded Mauricio Macri in December 2007 but lasted less than a year in the job before succumbing to heart problems. The 58-year-old was Boca's 31st president but the first to die whilst at the helm of the club. In the first fixture following Pompilio's death, at home to San Lorenzo, Riquelme scored the only goal of the game from a free kick. In an emotionally charged celebration, Riquelme revealed a T-shirt with 'thanks for everything, Pedro' written on it, in front of the directors' boxes where Pompilio's family were situated. The fallen president's legacy is the Complejo Pedro Pompilio, also known as the Casa Amarilla, the club's training base. 'Pompilio's death had a significant impact as he was admired by almost everyone within the club, and the fans,' stated Gabriel Aguero. 'After working for many years in Macri's administration, Pompilio showed a lot of promise.'

Macri, who had been comfortably re-elected in 1999 and 2003, completed 12 years as Boca president before leaving to pursue his political ambition and, upon his departure from La Bombonera in 2007, he became the Mayor of Buenos Aires. He oversaw much success on and off the pitch and raised commercial revenue and the awareness of the Boca Juniors brand across the globe. His administration created a youth system which would provide players for the first team but with an explicit, ultimate aim of providing an income stream by selling the most promising stars abroad. Between 1995 and 2007 Boca recouped close to £100m, with the sales of Éver Banega and Fernando Gago, to Valencia and Real Madrid respectively, accounting for approximately a third of that figure.

It was always suspected that Macri was using Boca as a platform from which to launch his political career, an idea which ultimately came to fruition. During his tenure, there were whispers of corruption and the Tandil man was accused of gentrifying the club's fan base. Although the external political climate played a part, the club's *barra brava* grew richer and more influential during his time as president. For many, Macri's centre-right political stance was always massively at odds with Boca's image as a working-class club, regardless of any positive achievements his regime may have overseen.

For Gabriel Aguero, his tenure was undoubtedly a success. 'Macri certainly left a big legacy with the club, a legacy that probably will never be replicated,' he began. 'Having won a plethora of league titles, two Copas Libertadores, and an Intercontinental Cup, Macri showed he was able to surround himself with people who knew about football, while he managed the financial aspects of the club. With both sets of knowledge, it's easy to see why he was so successful. He could keep and renovate a squad, while being advised which players to go after.'

As Mayor of Buenos Aires, he was re-elected in 2011 and, in November 2015, Macri was elected President of the Nation with 51.34 per cent of the votes. After four years in the Casa Rosada, the divisive figure lost the 2019 election to the *Frente de Todos* coalition, featuring former president Cristina Fernández de Kirchner.

After the 2008 Apertura schedule was completed, three teams – Boca, San Lorenzo, and Tigre – were tied on points at the top of the table. Rather than using the common methods of goal difference, goals scored, or head-to-head, the three sides were forced into a three-way play-off to determine the champions.

Three days after San Lorenzo had kicked off the mini-tournament by beating Tigre 2-1, Boca faced the side from Boedo at the home of Racing, on 20 December. Lucas Viatri opened the scoring in the dying embers of the first half, heading in a Riquelme corner in front of the ecstatic Boca fans. San Lorenzo equalised on the hour before Palacio restored Boca's lead on 76 minutes, finishing off a quick move which began with a long kick from goalkeeper Javier García. Two red cards in seven minutes for San Lorenzo dramatically reduced their chances of getting back into the game, and Boca sealed the 3-1 victory with a stoppage-time goal from substitute Cristian Chávez.

Seventy-two hours later Boca were back at Racing's ground, this time to face Tigre in the final decider of the three-way tournament. Unlike the actual championship itself, the mini-tournament would be settled on goal difference, meaning Tigre needed to win by at least two clear goals. The injured Riquelme, who had limped off after 68 minutes of the San Lorenzo clash, was missing and his absence told as Boca slipped to a 1-0 defeat. It was a strange way to celebrate a triumph but, despite the result on the day, Boca were champions once again. The title represented the first success of the Jorge Amor Ameal regime, the new president having succeeded Pompilio following his untimely passing.

For many fans, the success was made sweeter by the fact that River Plate finished bottom of the table, although they were given a reprieve due to the *promedios* system. Never had the gap – 25 points – between the two rivals been so large, even more staggering given the short championship format of just 19 games.

The first half of 2009 was distinctly forgettable for Boca, who finished 14th in the league and were eliminated from the Copa Libertadores – the 50th edition of the continental competition – at the last-16 stage. The second half of the year wasn't much better, despite the return of Alfio Basile: Boca finished 11th in the table and exited the Copa Sudamericana at the first hurdle. Basile lasted just 21 games, of which he won only seven, and was unable to repeat the success of 2005/06.

The new year failed to bring luck and the slump continued in 2010. Two men – Abel Alves and Roberto Pompei – occupied the hot seat during the Clausura. Boca had no continental campaign to focus on yet couldn't produce the goods on home soil, finishing 16th, their worst season since the institutional problems that dogged the club during the mid-1980s. In the three years since Boca had lifted the Copa Libertadores in 2007, the club had changed

In round 14 of the Clausura campaign, Pompei's first match in the dugout, Boca trounced Arsenal 4-0 at La Bombonera. In the ninth minute, Riquelme played a one-two with Nicolás Gaitán before rolling the ball to Palermo who finished from close range to give Boca a 1-0 lead. It was the forward's 219th goal in Boca's colours, and made him the club's all-time leading scorer, beating Roberto Cherro's record which had stood for more than 70 years.

The celebrations in the wake of the goal, however, highlighted the deterioration of the personal relationship between Riquelme and Palermo, two key figures behind most of Boca's success since the late 1990s. Rather than embracing the person for whom he had laid on so many goals, Riquelme peeled off on his own, almost to remind the fans that he was the most important member of the duo.

Palermo looked bemused, belatedly celebrating with teammates and then in front of the fans, before rushing back to the centre circle to resume business.

There are many versions as to what caused the chasm between the two icons. 'One of the most popular takes is that Palermo came to Pablo Migliore's defence after Riquelme questioned him after the 2008 Copa Libertadores exit to Fluminense where Migliore committed a grave error which cost Boca big time,' said Gabriel Aguero. Francisco Aure believes it may have involved the club's hooligan element and Diego Maradona. 'There's a story that Palermo had a close relationship with the *barra brava,* although it was never verified,' began the Buenos Aires-based journalist. 'The *barra brava* supported Maradona in his arguments with Riquelme and when he was coaching the national team Maradona supported Palermo too, taking him to the World Cup in South Africa.' Diego Tomasi has a different take: 'The relationship between Riquelme and Palermo on the field of play was one of the most fruitful in Argentine football; they complemented each other perfectly. A certain view of the world, and soccer, distanced one from the other and Román's confrontations with the club leadership, media, and the *barra brava* became more evident in opposition to Martín's ties. But nothing erases the history of the relationship, a story full of glory and goals.'

Boca finished 12th in the 2010 Apertura, the fourth successive campaign in which the club had finished in the bottom half of the table. Without Riquelme, who missed six months after surgery on his left knee, the club continued to wallow. Manager Claudio Borghi, who won the 2010 Clausura with Argentinos Juniors, failed to see out the season, lasting just 12 games and leaving after a 1-0 loss to River. Borghi had stubbornly tried to implement a three-man defensive line, as he had successfully done with Argentinos, and his experiment failed. Pompei stepped in as caretaker once more but the club were slipping closer and closer to the lower reaches of the *promedios* table and needed a change of fortune, and fast.

Julio César Falcioni, the former goalkeeper who had led Banfield to the first title in their history in 2009, was appointed Boca manager in December 2010. His tenure got off to the worst possible start with a 4-1 loss to Godoy Cruz at La Bombonera on the opening day of the 2011 Clausura. The new head coach responded by dropping Riquelme, electing to pack the midfield with workhorses who lacked guile yet would do the defensive work his system required. Rather than taking it lying down, Riquelme sniped openly about his new boss. In just the third game of the season, a goalless stalemate with All Boys, Falcioni was booed at La Bombonera.

After five games Falcioni's men had won just once and had four points from a possible 15 on the board. Riquelme returned to the side in round six, a 2-0 defeat at home to Olimpo. The number ten proved decisive the following week, scoring the only goal of the game with a free kick away to Colón. A miserable run of three successive defeats, and 463 minutes without breaching the opponents' net, was over. Falcioni and Riquelme appeared to have struck an uneasy truce.

The final game of the season proved to be Palermo's swansong, the record-breaker hanging up his boots after a distinguished career in which he scored 236 goals for Boca in 404 games. Fittingly, his final game came in his home city, Boca drawing 1-1 with Gimnasia in La Plata. In the wake of his retirement, Palermo cited his poor relationship with Riquelme, and his unwillingness to share a dressing room with him, as one of the key factors in his decision.

In what was an inconsistent season, Boca ultimately finished seventh. River, despite finishing ninth, were forced into a relegation play-off with Belgrano due to the *promedios* system which was ironically designed to protect the *grandes*. River lost the two-legged affair against the team from Córdoba and were relegated to the second tier for the first time in their history.

Although the majority of Boca fans revelled in the demise of River Plate, the lack of a *Superclásico* gave the 2011 Apertura a strange feel. Falcioni strengthened his defence ahead of the campaign, bringing in goalkeeper Agustín Orión, who had previously won the championship with San Lorenzo and Estudiantes. Rolando Schiavi, who had featured in Boca's triple crown success of 2003, and subsequently won the 2009 Copa Libertadores on a peculiar short-term loan to Estudiantes, returned to the club from Newell's Old Boys and was a rock at the back despite his advancing years. Facundo Roncaglia, a youth-team product who had been out on loan to Espanyol and Estudiantes over the last two years, also returned.

Defensively the results were spectacular; Boca conceded just six goals in 19 games and went the whole campaign unbeaten. Offensively, Boca sorely missed the retired Palermo and scored just 1.32 goals per game. Darío Cvitanich, on loan from Ajax, was the team's top scorer with a meagre five.

The workmanlike team was built on a solid base and the formidable Boca finished 12 points clear of the rest of the field, their first league title in three years. Few could have predicted that Falcioni's team would perform in such an efficient manner.

On 4 December 2011 Daniel Angelici, who had the backing of Mauricio Macri, was elected president following a record turnout of almost 25,000 voting members. One week later Sebastián Battaglia played his last game for the club. Battaglia had debuted for them in May 1998 and won

17 major honours, more than any other player in the history of Boca Juniors.

After a three-year absence from South America's top table, Boca returned to the Copa Libertadores in early 2012. They finished fourth in the 2012 Clausura and were in with a chance of winning the title going into the last three games. However, one point from the last available nine, including a 3-0 home defeat to eventual champions Arsenal, put paid to any title aspirations.

Along with Fluminense, Boca breezed through their Copa Libertadores group, but the opening fixture further ruptured an uneasy relationship. Although it was Valentine's Day, there was no love lost on 14 February. Boca drew 0-0 in Venezuela, against Zamora, and Riquelme and Falcioni openly clashed in the dressing room following the match. The player disagreed with the coach's tactics, preferring a more expressive style of play, and Falcioni threatened to quit on the plane journey home. Falcioni and Riquelme made a pact which was a mere Band-Aid on a wound that would reopen before long.

In the knockout phase, Boca bested Unión Española, group stage foes Fluminense, and Universidad de Chile en route to a final against Brazilian side Corinthians. After a 1-1 draw at La Bombonera, Boca lost the second leg 2-0, repeating the mistake from 2008 when they failed to take a lead to Brazil.

Success in the Copa Argentina – the only previous iteration of the competition was also won by Boca back in 1969 – provided the club with some cheer to end the first half of the year. The revamped and expanded cup now featured 186 teams from the top five tiers of Argentine football, with every province in the land represented. The new format also saw games played at neutral venues in the final phase. Boca defeated Santamarina, Central Córdoba, Olimpo, Rosario

Central, and Deportivo Merlo on the journey to the final, playing games in Salta, San Juan, and Catamarca. This gave Boca fans in all corners of the republic the chance to see their heroes in action.

The final, delayed until August due to Boca's participation in the Copa Libertadores, saw Boca defeat Racing 2-1 in San Juan with goals from Santiago Silva and Lucas Viatri. Of the six matches Boca won in the lead-up to lifting the trophy, four were settled on penalty kicks. The most memorable shoot-out came in the semi-final versus Deportivo Merlo, Riquelme effortlessly clipping a panenka down the centre of the goal. The crowd chanted his name – *Riqueeeeelme, Riqueeeeelme, Riqueeeeelme* – as he picked the ball out of the net and kissed it before dropping it to the floor. Despite not breaking into a smile, it was a symbolic gesture that suggested he still loved the sport.

The second half of 2012 saw the implementation of a new idea from the AFA: the Apertura and Clausura championships were renamed Inicial and Final. As before, each tournament would declare an official champion, then the two would face off to declare a 'Super Champion'. Riquelme decided to sit out this period, emotionally announcing after the Copa Libertadores final defeat to Corinthians that he wouldn't be continuing in the Boca shirt. Two years remained on his current contract and, in public at least, both Falcioni and president Angelici left the door open for his return. During his absence, he often trained, whilst speculation linked him with moves to Brazil, the Middle East, and elsewhere.

On 28 October Boca travelled to El Monumental to face River, who had returned to the top flight at the first time of asking following a year in the Primera B Nacional. Boca fans marched miles across the city towards the stadium in a fierce show of force, letting off flares and firecrackers, bringing Avenida Libertador to a standstill. It was far from a friendly reunion – 25 people were hospitalised that day – and within a matter of months fans would be banned from Argentine top-flight games.

River took the lead, with Orión badly fluffing a harmless Leo Ponzio free kick; Rodrigo Mora doubled the home side's advantage. A dream return to *Superclásico* action looked to be on the cards for River but Santiago Silva pulled a goal back for Boca from the penalty spot before Walter Erviti grabbed a last-gasp equaliser to ensure that the spoils were shared.

For coaches Matías Almeyda and Falcioni, it would be their last derby and both would soon be gone. Boca finished the season in sixth position, River were two points back in eighth. Falcioni was booed by the Boca fans in the last match of the season, a 2-1 home win over Godoy Cruz, and it was deemed the overall performance of his team was unacceptable. His position was untenable. 'Many fans identify Falcioni's teams as being very solid defensively but poor going forward which is worrying considering the players that he had at his disposal,' began Gabriel Aguero. 'He won the 2011 Apertura title with 12 wins, seven draws, and that team conceded the least amount of goals in the history of a short tournament [six]. He ultimately left the club due to poor relationships with a majority of the squad.'

With Falcioni gone, Boca attempted to turn back the clock by more than a decade. Carlos Bianchi returned to the dugout and Riquelme, after much speculation, emerged from his hibernation to don the number ten jersey once more. The two, who had enjoyed so much success in the early part of the 2000s, were unable to recreate the magic that had seen them conquer the world together. Boca finished second bottom of the 2013 Torneo Final table, winning just three games all season. A run of 12 games without recording a victory summed up the miserable campaign.

When the now 35-year-old Riquelme did feature it didn't make too much of a difference. In his five appearances, Boca won just two, and the side had a better points-per-game average without him. The cups also failed to provide a welcome distraction; Boca exited the Copa Libertadores and Copa Argentina at the last 16 and quarter-final stage respectively.

The poor campaign led to major personnel changes. More than a dozen players departed and amongst those joining the club were Emmanuel Gigliotti and the returning Fernando Gago after spells with Real Madrid, Roma, and Valencia, and Daniel Díaz. Riquelme managed 12 appearances and two goals. The performance was much improved and after 15 rounds Boca were still in the title hunt. Yet just two points from the final four games, including a defeat to Arsenal who finished above Boca, consigned Bianchi's men to a seventh-place finish. The league table was deceptive: Boca finished just four points behind champions San Lorenzo.

Boca started the 2014 Torneo Final poorly, winning just three of the first nine games. In round ten, River won 2-1 at La Bombonera, a stunning Riquelme free kick, arguably the best of his career, sandwiched in between goals from future Premier League player Manuel Lanzini and Ramiro Funes Mori.

In the penultimate match of the season, Lanús were guests at La Bombonera, a game which would prove to be the last time Riquelme pulled the famous blue-and-gold jersey over his head. The magisterial number ten appeared visibly moved as the teams lined up for the pre-match formalities, whilst a brass band played the national anthem behind them. Every silky touch was greeted with cheers from the fans braving the rain, as Riquelme rolled back the years to produce one last great performance. The *coup de grâce* came in the 65th minute. A pass was sent in Riquelme's direction and he flicked his right boot as if he were about to control it. Instead, he dummied the ball and it went through the legs of the Lanús player marking him and on to Emmanuel Gigliotti. The stadium trembled. Riquelme was replaced after 88 minutes to allow him to soak up the adulation one last time. Bianchi's side amassed 20 points from the last available 24 to finish second behind River, who won the title just three years after their relegation to the second tier.

In the wake of the campaign, Riquelme signed a contract with his original boyhood club, Argentinos Juniors. On 20 July a happy and proud looking Riquelme was unveiled at a press conference at the Panamericano Hotel in the Argentine capital. Argentinos, competing in the Primera B Nacional, were one of ten teams promoted to the top flight at the end of that season, part of an AFA reshuffle to increase the Primera División to 30 teams.

Having led his first love to a promotion, Riquelme officially announced his retirement from professional football on 25 January 2015. The man from Don Turcuato, a master of dictating the tempo of football matches throughout his career, had converted himself from a shy, skinny kid into the biggest idol Boca Juniors had ever known. The last of the great number tens won four league championships, the Copa Libertadores on three occasions, and the 2000 Intercontinental Cup amongst a plethora of other team and individual gongs. With 206 appearances at La Bombonera, no player has played more games for the club at their iconic home. In those games, he managed 56 goals, a record of better than one in four.

Whenever things weren't going well, Riquelme's detractors assumed he was lazy and uninterested due to his languid style. Yet when Boca were winning it seemed like Riquelme was an artist, the football pitch his canvas; a conductor leading the orchestra with every stroke of his masterful right foot. 'In his first spell at the club [1996–2002] he is athletic, fast, and dynamic,' analysed Diego Tomasi. 'In the second spell [2007–2014] he's not only a leader on the field but also off it. He's much wiser and although he's slower his capacity to protect the ball, when to accelerate and when to pause, is unbeatable.'

His days wowing crowds on the grass over, Riquelme was now free to enjoy *asados* – Argentinean barbecues – with friends, something which he said he was looking forward to after hanging up his boots. The much-needed break would reinvigorate Riquelme's love for football and in 2019 he would be back at Boca in an altogether different capacity.

Chapter Fifteen

Twin Peaks

FOLLOWING THE 2014 World Cup, in which Argentina lost the final to Germany, the *Transición* championship commenced in August. Without Riquelme, Bianchi's side lost two of the first three matches. In round four, a 3-1 defeat away to Estudiantes, in which Boca were 3-0 down at half-time, was the final stand for the record-breaking coach. A day later president Daniel Angelici took the painful decision to rescind his contract.

Over three spells and 427 games, *El Virrey* produced a win rate of 51 per cent and remains the most successful manager in the club's history. The flame might have been extinguished but there is no erasing the legacy that Bianchi, now 65, left at La Bombonera. 'I believe Bianchi's third stint as head coach of Boca Juniors was a disappointment for two reasons,' began Gabriel Aguero of Boca in English. 'Firstly, because of a very poor squad, he wasn't given the reinforcements he had asked for, and secondly because his first-team selections were poor. Leandro Paredes, now an established player in Europe, was given very little playing time under Bianchi.'

Rodolfo Arruabarrena, who had joined Boca as an 11-year-old before winning three titles as a player at the outset of Bianchi's first spell, replaced his former boss in the hot seat. Upon hanging up his boots in 2011, Arruabarrena started his managerial career with Tigre before crossing the Río de la Plata to take control of Nacional. After sacking a man so synonymous with Boca's glory years, and with elections scheduled for the following year, Angelici knew he had to get this appointment right, and settled for a man who had risen through the club's youth ranks and was popular with the fan base. However, he wasn't the first choice for the role. Another much-loved former star, Guillermo Barros Schelotto, was performing well as manager of Lanús, having won the 2013 Copa Sudamericana, although his acquisition wasn't possible at that moment.

Under *El Vasco*, the form improved. Having lost three of the first four games, his side lost just three of the remaining 15, rising from 17th when he took over to a respectable fifth-place finish, ten points behind champions Racing. As the *Transición* schedule was coming to a close, in November, Arruabarrena's side faced River Plate in the Copa Sudamericana semi-final. Boca had knocked out Rosario Central, Deportivo Capiatá, and Cerro Porteño to set up the final-four *Superclásico*.

The first leg at La Bombonera, a war of attrition with few moments of quality, left the tie wide open for the second leg. After just two minutes at El Monumental Boca had a great chance to take the driving seat in their very first attack. However, Emmanuel Gigliotti, who had arrived from Colón halfway through 2013, saw his penalty saved by Marcelo Barovero. After 16 minutes River took the lead through Leonardo Pisculichi, the only goal of the game, and Arruabarrena's side finished with ten men following the late dismissal of Daniel Díaz. River went on to win the tournament and lift their first international title in 17 years.

Arruabarrena's side were unbeaten in the first 12 league games of the 2015 championship – named in honour of recently passed former AFA president Julio Grondona – winning eight and drawing four. One of those victories was a 2-0 home win over fellow unbeaten side River Plate on 3 May, the first of three *Superclásicos* in ten days. Goalless going into the last six minutes of regulation time, the match was settled by two substitutes, relatively recent arrivals Cristian Pavón and Pablo Pérez, and Boca held on to the top spot in the league. Four days later the two rivals faced off in the first leg of the Copa Libertadores round of 16.

Having accumulated the same amount of points in 2013/14, Boca and Vélez had been forced into a one-off clash to determine which of them would take part in the 2015 version of South America's premier competition. Boca edged the match in Mar del Plata with a *golazo* from Nicolás Colazo. *Los Xeneizes* steamrollered the group stage, winning all six matches and scoring 19 and conceding just two in the process. Their reward was being drawn against their fierce rivals in the last 16, the first time the two had met in the Copa Libertadores since 2004.

The first leg, at El Monumental, appeared to be heading for a 0-0 stalemate until referee Germán Delfino awarded a questionable penalty to the home side, which was converted by Uruguayan midfielder Carlos Sánchez. Delfino sent off River's hot-headed Colombian Teo Gutiérrez but, crucially, River had a lead to take to La Bombonera.

After the half-time break in the second leg the River players, who had edged the goalless first 45 minutes, were in the tunnel waiting to re-enter the pitch when they were attacked with a homemade pepper spray smuggled into the stadium by a supporter with links to Boca's *barra brava*.

After 50 minutes of chaos – which saw projectiles attack the River contingent – the match was eventually abandoned. Four River players were hospitalised and Conmebol handed down heavy punishment to Boca, eliminating them from the competition, issuing a large fine, and forcing the club to play the next four home games behind closed doors. The club's fans were also banned from attending the next four away games in the continental competition.

Just one year after away fans had been banned from Argentine stadiums, in response to the escalating violence that plagued the sport, it seemed the lesson had failed to be heeded. Incredibly, River went on to win the Copa Libertadores, just four years after they had been relegated to the second division.

The hangover from the shameful disqualification saw Boca lose the following two league fixtures, before bouncing back to beat Newell's 4-0, and Sarmiento de Junín 1-0 away from home. The following match, at home to Quilmes on 18 July, saw the return of Carlos Tevez after more than a decade away from the club. Tevez always stated that he would return to Boca in decent shape and he was more than true to his word. The 31-year-old was in excellent physical condition and, after scoring 29 goals to lead Juventus to a Serie A and Coppa Italia double, could have realistically had his pick of moves but chose to follow his heart.

Days after a packed and expectant La Bombonera saw Carlitos unveiled, he helped his new team-mates to a 2-1 win over Quilmes on his second debut. Jonathan Calleri, who had signed from All Boys one year earlier, scored the winner. An efficient Boca won ten of the next 12 games, a run that included a 1-0 win over River at El Monumental. In the first derby since the pepper-spray incident Nicolás Lodeiro, who replaced the injured Fernando Gago after just 30 seconds, scored the winner on 19 minutes.

Boca were six points clear at the top of the table going into the penultimate round of the season, knowing just one point from the final two games would be enough to seal the championship. After 42 minutes of the home clash with Tigre, a Lodeiro corner was powerfully headed in by Luciano Monzón. Boca were champions for the first time in four years, and could even afford to lose the final match and still finish three points ahead of San Lorenzo. Arruabarrena joined the exclusive list of men who had won the title as both player and coach.

Three days later *El Vasco* led the side to another triumph, adding a 65th star to the club's crest. The Copa Argentina, which started with 272 hopeful sides, had been whittled down to just two: Boca Juniors and Rosario Central. Córdoba's Estadio Kempes was designated as the venue where the battle would take place.

In a tough game, Rosario Central made Boca work for their victory. Lodeiro sent the goalkeeper the wrong way from the penalty spot after 54 minutes and the festivities truly commenced when, with a minute of regulation time remaining, Andrés Chávez tapped the ball home from close range. It was Boca's third Copa Argentina in just its fifth edition, and for returning hero Tevez it was the second domestic double in six months.

The AFA continued to tinker as part of their grand restructuring plan. The 2016 top flight retained 30 teams, but this time they were split into two groups of 15. After a 0-0 draw away at Temperley on the opening day of the season, a physically underprepared and error-strewn Boca were trounced 4-0 in the Supercopa Argentina at the hands of San Lorenzo. A 1-0 defeat to Atlético Tucumán at La Bombonera followed before two league wins.

A 1-0 defeat away to Racing, on 28 February, followed a goalless draw in the Copa Libertadores. Angelici wielded the axe once again, and Arruabarrena was fired after 15 months in charge. Despite securing a historic double at the end of 2015, *El Vasco* paid for the poor start to the new season, and it was perhaps clear that, with a much-changed squad, he was unable to repeat the magic of the previous year. The defeats to River in the 2014 Copa Sudamericana and the 2015 Copa Libertadores scandal stained his résumé, and his side lacked a defined playing style.

Finally, Angelici, who had been re-elected four months earlier with almost 44 per cent of the votes, was able to land Guillermo Barros Schelotto. The twin had joined Sicilian side Palermo in Serie A after the expiration of his contract with Lanús but was forced to leave after just a month, having failed to secure the required UEFA-recognised coaching licence. Barros Schelotto oversaw a goalless draw at home to Racing in the Copa Libertadores in his first game on the bench, which was followed by another stalemate in the league at El Monumental.

A 1-1 draw away to Bolívar meant that Barros Schelotto had to wait until the fourth attempt to record his first victory as Boca boss, in a league game against Unión. The outfit from Santa Fe took the lead on 58 minutes but Lodeiro deceived the goalkeeper to level the score five minutes later from out wide. When it looked like another draw was on the cards after an uninspiring performance, Tevez scored the winner on 89 minutes, bundling the ball home from close range after pinball in the penalty area. The passionate forward celebrated as if it were a championship-clinching wonder strike, and so did the fans in the stands, who had pushed the team on in the closing stages of the game.

Boca won two and lost two of the next four league outings but were much more consistent on the continent. Three wins from the final three games – including a 6-2 triumph over

Deportivo Cali at La Bombonera – ensured qualification to the next phase of the Copa Libertadores.

Boca failed to win any of their final five league games, finishing in a miserable tenth position in their zonal group. There was still time, however, for more unthinkably bad news. After eliminating Cerro Porteño and Nacional, *Los Xeneizes* were drawn against Independiente del Valle in the Copa Libertadores semi-final in July. Regardless of their poor form, and even though the Ecuadorian minnows had already eliminated River, it was a clash the Argentine giants were supposed to win easily.

Pablo Pérez looked to have set Boca on their way when he opened the scoring after just 12 minutes of the first leg, but as the game wore on, the high altitude of Quito began to take its toll on the side from sea-level Buenos Aires. Independiente del Valle scored two in the last half hour and had something to defend at La Bombonera.

As in the first leg, Boca started brightly, Pavón scoring after just three minutes to level the tie on aggregate. On home soil, surely progression was now a given. The Ecuadorians had other ideas, equalising on 25 minutes to go into the half-time break at 1-1. Inexplicably, two goals in two minutes for the visitors not long after the restart gave them a 5-2 aggregate lead with 40 minutes in which to defend it. Luck seemed to be further in their favour when Lodeiro saw a 70th-minute penalty saved and Pavón's late goal was merely a consolation.

It was a defeat that would look better with time: Independiente del Valle won the 2019 Copa Sudamericana, the first major honour in their 60-year history. 'The Ecuadorian club was beginning to form a team that would later be important in several international tournaments, most notably the Copa Sudamericana,' stated Lucas Guerrero from Muy Boca, an independent multimedia platform, who doesn't believe it was a disaster. 'Boca should have been winning 2-0 in Ecuador but had a valid goal disallowed. And then Boca were winning at La Bombonera, a stadium where the club is typically strong. Barros Schelotto's team just needed more time.'

After three months without domestic football, due to an internal crisis within the AFA, the 2016/17 championship got underway at the end of August. Barros Schelotto finally had the chance to put his stamp on the squad, shipping out eight players and bringing in the likes of Santiago Vergini (Getafe), Gino Peruzzi (Catania), Wilmar Barrios (Tolima), Walter Bou (Gimnasia), Ricky Centurión (Racing), and Darío Benedetto (Club América).

The new-look side won just four of the first eight league fixtures before crashing out of the Copa Argentina at the quarter-final stage, losing 2-1 to Rosario Central in Córdoba. From thereon in the form picked up. In the build-up to the first *Superclásico* of the season, Boca picked up ten points from the available 12, heading to El Monumental in buoyant mood. Bou gave Boca the lead after 13 minutes after excellent work from Tevez, although River scored twice to take a 2-1 lead into the dressing room at half-time.

Pouncing on a goalkeeping error, Tevez equalised after 61 minutes before kissing the badge on his shirt. In the absence of away fans, you could hear every joyous shout from the Boca players and staff. If Tevez's first goal was opportunism, the second was pure class. Following intricate work from Centurión and Pavón, the ball fell to Boca's number ten and captain, who curled it in off the post from 20 yards. In the fourth minute of time added on, Centurión lifted the ball over the hapless Augusto Batalla, who had rushed miles out of his goal, to score. An ecstatic Barros Schelotto jumped into the arms of goalkeeper Axel Werner, celebrating an excellent attacking display which bore signs that his plans were gradually coming to fruition.

In the following match, at home to Colón, Barros Schelotto's side scored four once again in a comfortable victory. Tevez scored Boca's second, although it proved to be his last action before a record-breaking move to Chinese football. A couple of months before his 33rd birthday, Shanghai Shenhua paid a reported US$11m for his transfer, offering him a two-year contract allegedly worth a staggering US$82m.

Barros Schelotto's side won five of the next nine after the summer break before tasting their own medicine in a 3-1 home defeat at the hands of River in May. It was the last reverse the side would suffer. A 3-0 win over Independiente at La Bombonera, and a comfortable 4-0 win on the road at Aldosivi, put the title within touching distance. On Tuesday, 20 June, when Banfield lost to San Lorenzo at the Nuevo Gasómetro, it was confirmed: Boca were champions. The following night the newly crowned kings of Argentine football drew 2-2 at Olimpo, taking a 2-0 lead through Centurión and Benedetto before being pegged back by the Bahía Blanca outfit.

The party could truly begin on the final day of the season when Unión visited La Bombonera. A packed stadium saw festivities take place before and after the match, and throughout the 90 minutes. Benedetto opened the scoring after 12 minutes, capitalising on a poor kick from the goalkeeper before sliding the ball home from a tight angle. The prolific marksman, the league's top scorer, scored his second of the night and 21st of the season just after the break, striking the ball first time from the edge of the box. Unión scored after 58 minutes but it proved nothing more than a consolation and couldn't dampen spirits in any case. Barros Schelotto, with his twin brother Gustavo alongside him on the bench, was now a champion with Boca as a coach, adding to the 16 titles he won as a player.

The rebranded Superliga kicked off in late August 2017, with the title-winning squad bolstered by the acquisition of tireless Uruguayan midfielder Nahitan Nández from Peñarol, defender Paolo Goltz, and Colombian attacking midfielder Edwin Cardona. The champions won the first seven matches then beat River 2-1 at El Monumental, a match in which Cardona scored a stunning free kick but was later sent off. River equalised before pocket-rocket Nández won the match with a volley from 12 yards. In March, River would gain revenge, beating Boca 2-0 in Mendoza to win the Supercopa Argentina.

In January 2018, after a year in China, Tevez returned for the third and final act of his Boca career, staying true to his word of ending his career in the blue-and-gold jersey. Although Tevez's bank balance was healthier, he wasn't in the best sporting shape after what had effectively been a holiday: the forward only played 16 matches and reportedly spent more time on the golf course than on the football pitch.

The absence of Gago and Benedetto, who only made 15 appearances between them all season after suffering serious injuries, hampered Boca who were only able to win eight of the 13 games after the return of the ineffectual Tevez. Going into the penultimate fixture, away to Gimnasia, a point was all that was needed to secure the *bicampeonato*. Barros Schelotto, at the home of his former club, was made to suffer, as Boca led twice only to be pegged back by the side from La Plata. As the final whistle blew the required point had been secured and Boca were champions once again.

In the first half of 2018, whilst securing the title, Boca had laboured in their Copa Libertadores group, finishing second behind a dominant Palmeiras but, more importantly, progressing to the knockout phase. Ahead of the business end of the continental competition, and the start of the 2018/19 Superliga, Boca signed Esteban Andrada, the

27-year-old goalkeeper from Arsenal who was known to Barros Schelotto from their time together at Lanús. Defender Carlos Izquierdoz was acquired from Mexican football; Mauro Zárate, the veteran forward who had played in the Middle East, England and Italy was a surprise signing but would go on to make more Superliga appearances than any other player during the season. Flying Colombian winger Sebastián Villa joined from Tolima.

Boca took 24 points from 13 league games, a run that included a 2-0 loss at River in September. However, the club were able to progress relatively comfortably through the latter stages of the Copa Libertadores. Paraguay's Libertad were beaten 6-2 on aggregate before Cruzeiro were knocked out in the quarter-final after a 3-1 win for Boca over two legs.

In the first leg of the semi-final a late Benedetto brace against Palmeiras, who had won 2-0 at La Bombonera in the group phase, gave Boca an excellent advantage going into the second leg in Brazil. The first, a header, came on 83 minutes and was the forward's first goal in almost a year following a serious injury lay-off. Back in the groove, the second oozed class. With his back to goal, Benedetto allowed the ball to run across his body before dragging it back, totally taking the defender out of the game and creating the space to unleash a strike from 25 yards.

Benedetto was crucial once again in Brazil. Ramón Ábila had given Boca the lead after just 18 minutes but two goals in seven second-half minutes brought Palmeiras back into the tie. On 70 minutes Benedetto extinguished Brazilian hopes, making it 2-2 on the night, and 4-2 on aggregate, once again striking the ball across the goalkeeper from 25 yards. Boca were through to the final and, in the opposite corner, River Plate awaited. It would prove to be one of the most infamous *Superclásicos* of all time and dominate global sporting media throughout November and December 2018.

Chapter Sixteen

La Gran Final

EVEN ON the cusp of summer, November is typically one of the wettest months of the year in Buenos Aires. The heavens opening and dumping short bursts of torrential rainfall on the Argentine capital is nothing new, yet even if Nostradamus himself had been a weatherman he would have failed to forecast the deluge of biblical proportions that fell from the sky in the early hours of 10 November 2018. Thunderstorms dropped four centimetres of rain on the port city in the space of two hours. Images of a waterlogged pitch at La Bombonera, water cascading from one steep tier to another, circulated as rapidly via social media as the rain itself fell.

There was no other choice: the game would have to be postponed. Rain-soaked fans, already creating an atmosphere inside the blue-and-gold temple of football, were sent home following an announcement on the public address system. The unpredictable weather would set the tone for the chaos, unprecedented even by *Superclásico* standards, which would engulf the tie. The rain ultimately passed but the storm would continue to gather force.

The 2018 Copa Libertadores Final between Boca and River Plate was labelled by many as the biggest club match in the history of South American football. Some wondered if it would be too big. Too much, logistically, for the city of Buenos Aires to handle two potentially explosive matches in as many weeks. Too much, emotionally, for the respective fan bases. In the distant Misiones province, hundreds of miles from Boca and River's traditional heartlands, two friends argued about which club was the most prestigious. The feud resulted in one of the protagonists burning down the house of the other, showing just how deep passion runs when it comes to the rivalry. Boca and River had, of course, met in numerous important clashes before but the magnitude of this occasion just felt different.

Twenty-four hours later the rain had cleared and, even though the sponge-like pitch retained some surface water, *La Gran Final* was ready to commence on Sunday, 11 November. Boca were the domestic force approaching the tie, having won the two most recent national championships, and sat above River in the Superliga table. The form of both sides going into the first leg was patchy but, as the old cliché goes, league form goes out of the window when it comes to cup games, even more so in derby matches.

Boca lined up with Agustín Rossi in goal behind a back four, from left to right, of Lucas Olaza, Lisandro Magallán, Carlos Izquierdoz, and Leonardo Jara. The midfield trio of Wilmar Barrios, Nahitan Nández, and captain Pablo Pérez supported a front three of Sebastián Villa, Cristian Pavón, and Ramón *Wanchope* Ábila. Boca's strong, experienced, yet perhaps unbalanced, substitutes bench included Fernando Gago and three forwards: Darío Benedetto, Carlos Tevez, and Mauro Zárate. Matías Biscay, River's second in command, took charge as manager Marcelo Gallardo was suspended for flouting a touchline ban in the semi-final.

In front of a hostile Bombonera replete with raucous fans, referee Roberto Tobar blew his whistle to kick off proceedings at 4pm. Boca came out firing, winning two corners in the first 120 seconds. After just six minutes, River stated their intent when Gonzalo *Pity* Martínez's left-footed free kick forced a smart save from Rossi. The subsequent corner should have seen River take the lead, although Lucas Martínez sent a free header wide of Rossi's upright. The away side began to settle as the first half wore on, although their attempts to play the ball on the floor were hampered by the sodden surface.

Pavón injured his hamstring trying to execute a one-two after just 22 minutes, the distraught forward pounding the Bombonera turf in frustration before leaving the pitch in tears. His replacement, Benedetto, had been prolific since signing from Mexican giants Club América but had endured a miserable 2018 in which he recovered from a ruptured anterior cruciate ligament injury, only to later suffer from Achilles and hamstring issues. His lack of match fitness was the reason he started the game on the bench.

After 34 minutes, Boca took the lead, causing an avalanche as the lower section of the *Popular Norte* surged towards the fence that separates the fans from the pitch. River goalkeeper Franco Armani kept Ábila's first effort at bay, in a somewhat unorthodox fashion with his chest, although the Boca forward reacted quicker than anyone in the penalty area to slam home the rebound. The Argentine international stopper should perhaps have done better at his near post yet the ferocity of the shot from such close range would have troubled the world's best.

A team is never more vulnerable than immediately after they have scored themselves and River capitalised on this, equalising just 90 seconds after the opener through Lucas Pratto, who ironically had started his career in the *azul y oro*. Despite a poor first touch, the ball seemingly sticking underneath his feet, Pratto was able to dig it out of the turf and send it across Rossi and into the far corner before celebrating his effort with gusto in front of an eerily quiet Bombonera.

Benedetto restored the home side's lead on the stroke of half-time, forcing the respective managers to rip up their planned team talks. Boca's Colombia forward Villa, operating from the right-hand side, lofted a dangerous free kick into the penalty area which *Pipa* expertly guided into the net with a powerful header. River hit back on the hour mark and, although Pratto claimed to have scored his second goal, replays showed the ball skimmed off the head of the unfortunate Izquierdoz before nestling in the net. The defender's glum expression indicated that it was indeed an own goal.

Guillermo Barros Schelotto introduced Tevez after 75 minutes, hoping the forward's experience and big-game nous could swing the tie in Boca's favour. In the closing sequence of the game, *El Apache* broke free of the River defence, riding a challenge and laying the ball on a plate for Benedetto. *Pipa's* effort was brilliantly saved by Armani, who closed down the angle and spread himself expertly. As Tobar put the whistle to his lips to signify the end of the game, the look on Benedetto's face signalled that he knew he had fluffed a major opportunity to give his side the upper hand.

With just six yellow cards shown by the Chilean referee, it was a relatively tame affair by *Superclásico* standards. Several players were just one yellow card away from missing the second leg and perhaps holding back some of the customary enthusiasm for the tackle, with only River's Rafael Santos Borré unfortunate enough to be ruled out of the return clash.

On the Thursday evening before the scheduled second leg, Boca Juniors held an open training session at La Bombonera, packing the stadium and even having to close the doors such was the demand for entry. Capacity was breached, with fans sneaking in and seeking every vantage point possible. The fans were bidding farewell to the players: despite the relative proximity of River's stadium, it would be the last time the Boca faithful would see their heroes in the flesh before the big game.

On the afternoon of 24 November 2018, just a few hours before the scheduled kick-off, the Boca team bus was heading towards El Monumental. Thousands of River fans were already inside the stadium, creating a festival-like atmosphere under a blue Buenos Aires sky, a stark difference to the weather that afflicted the first leg. Many River fans remained outside the stadium and when Boca's bus passed through the throng on Avenida Monroe, a well-known pre-match haunt of the *Millonarios* faithful just blocks from the stadium, all hell broke loose.

The bus, carrying Boca's players and technical staff, was attacked by projectiles which smashed through several windows. Youngster Gonzalo Lamardo and Pablo Pérez were hospitalised after shards of glass went into their eyes. The police – who numbered more than 2,000 in one of the biggest operations of its kind in Argentine history – allegedly used military-grade tear gas to disperse the troublesome crowd, although an unfortunate side effect of this unnecessary tactic was that the fumes seeped into the vehicle, causing several players to vomit and require treatment from the club doctor. The driver passed out, and a Boca director had to take the wheel to steer the bus to the relative safety of the stadium.

Mirroring the first leg, when Boca fans were informed of the postponement due to the rain, El Monumental was almost full when River's fans received the announcement that the game wouldn't be going ahead as originally planned. Confusion reigned as events unfolded outside. Cones and balls were already laid out for River's pre-match warm-up, such were the expectations so close to kick-off that the game would proceed. The kick-off time was pushed back four times before it was eventually decided that the game wouldn't be going ahead at all. With networks jammed as thousands of fans turned to their phones in search of answers, an impromptu game of Chinese whispers spread around the bowl-like structure like a Mexican wave.

The presidents of the two clubs were in unison at the decision to postpone the game. Rumours suggested that FIFA president Gianni Infantino, who had flown in from Switzerland especially for the game, threatened Boca with disqualification if they didn't play, although it wasn't in his jurisdiction as a Conmebol tournament. Upon entering and leaving the stadium with a bloated security detail, Infantino was given a less than pleasant reception.

The rescheduled game was set for the following day – 25 November at 5pm – and, three hours before kick-off, 2,000 expectant River fans had already entered the stadium. Then, in another twist of fate, the game was postponed once again, pending a further announcement after Boca had presented a formal press release demanding the game be played in equal conditions.

On the Tuesday following the cancelled second leg, Alejandro Domínguez, Conmebol president since January 2016, announced that the match would be played on neutral territory outside Argentina. Prior fears that the game was just too big for Argentina to handle had come to fruition. Neither side was satisfied; everyone involved lost out. River were robbed of home advantage and, they hoped, a victorious trophy parade in front of their fans. The so-called Millionaires were hit with a US$400,000 fine for their part in the ugly scenes that marred the afternoon of 24 November. Boca sought further postponements, threatening legal action and demanding that they be awarded the cup by default, taking their fight to the Court of Arbitration for Sport (CAS). Argentine football, and the reputation of the South American game in general, took a hit when all eyes were watching. The fans, so often an afterthought in modern football, would soon be forced to travel at astronomical expense.

Several world cities – including Doha, Miami, and Medellín – threw their hats in the ring to host the event. Two days later, on 29 November, South American football's governing body, following a meeting at their Asunción headquarters, announced that the second leg of the final would be played in Real Madrid's famous Santiago Bernabeú stadium, 10,000km away on the other side of the Atlantic Ocean. In some quarters, there were calls for River to be disqualified, a fate that had befallen Boca in the 2015 Copa Libertadores, although a counter-argument was that the incidents had happened outside of the club's jurisdiction, too far away from El Monumental for them to be responsible.

According to Conmebol's official press release announcing the news, Madrid was chosen for several key reasons: the security guarantees provided by the city of Madrid and the Spanish state; the neutrality of the venue; the quality of the sporting infrastructure; the existence of a rich football culture; quality of hotels and public transport; and culture of fair play and opposition to violence. Spain is also home to the largest Argentine ex-pat community in the world, there are good direct flights between Buenos Aires and Madrid, and the time difference is not too prohibitive. It may have also cushioned the blow that Real Madrid offered the venue free-of-charge to Conmebol.

The irony of Madrid as a venue for a cup named after the historic figures that liberated South America from the Spanish Empire wasn't lost on quick-witted internet users, who immediately flooded social media networks with memes. In a clever play on words, many jokingly dubbed the competition the *Copa Conquistadores.* Many prominent figures, including Tevez and former Boca coach and World Cup winner César Luis Menotti, were outspoken in their opposition to the switch. 'After the match was suspended at El Monumental everything was a great disappointment,' lamented Lucas Guerrero of Muy Boca. 'We knew that Conmebol wouldn't be able to provide a suitable solution and, in the end, they took the final to Europe purely for economic reasons, which was a real shame.'

The clubs were given an allocation of 25,000 tickets each, 80 per cent of which were earmarked for their European fans. Tickets were also available to Real Madrid club members, who sold out their allocation in no time at all, and the so-called 'FIFA family'. Many neutral footballers and celebrities were in attendance, intrigued by the occasion. Boca, still unhappy, pressed ahead with their efforts to postpone the game whilst hoping for River to be disqualified, yet their complaints fell on deaf ears and the game ultimately went ahead.

The Madrid clash was the 26th meeting of the two sides in South America's premier cup competition, Boca leading their great rivals 10-7, with eight draws. If the tie was big news before the first leg, interest in the second leg in the Spanish capital Madrid – taking place on 9 December – had skyrocketed to unimaginable levels. The 72,000-capacity crowd at the Santiago Bernabeú couldn't quite believe their luck in managing to source tickets for such a historic clash.

Esteban Andrada, now back to full fitness, edged out the unfortunate Rossi in goal, whilst Julio Buffarini took the right-back berth from Jara. Benedetto, another player who was struggling for match sharpness ahead of the first leg, was selected in favour of Ábila to spearhead Boca's attack. The injury that forced Pavón from the field during the first fixture had cleared sufficiently to allow the winger to participate. The wide man was included in Barros Schelotto's squad and given a chance to prove himself with a late fitness test, the four-week gap between the two matches providing him with vital recovery time. Otherwise, Boca were unchanged from the first leg.

Two of the chances Boca carved out in the first half fell to the tenacious Pérez. The first effort was saved by Armani, the second drifted agonisingly wide following heroic body-on-the-line work by River's defence. Boca looked reasonably comfortable in the first half, allowing River to hold the ball whilst looking to launch counter-attacks. Villa and Pavón, the two wide forwards in a 4-3-3 formation, worked tirelessly to retain Boca's defensive shape.

Boca scored on the stroke of half-time through Benedetto. Following the breakdown of a River attack, Boca countered with breakneck speed, Nández eventually sliding the ball into the path of Benedetto who skipped past the challenge of one River defender before opening his body up and stroking the ball to Armani's left. The comical tongue-out celebration that followed became somewhat of a trademark and would be repeated following subsequent goals from the forward.

Boca's intensity dropped in the second period and the game changed during four key minutes around the hour mark. After 58 minutes River brought on the gifted yet mercurial Juan Fernando Quintero, the Colombian introduced to pick the locks of a well-drilled and stubborn Boca defence. Four minutes later Boca made their own change: Benedetto was replaced by Ábila. In truth, neither of the Boca forwards were fully fit, yet the new arrival was even less suited to the counter attacking game Boca were employing on the night.

Pratto – operating as a lone striker due to the absence of the injured Ignacio Scocco – drew River level after 68 minutes following excellent interplay, the quick exchange of passes befuddling the Boca backline. It felt only natural that the interminable tie would go to extra time and live for at least 30 minutes longer.

Merely 90 seconds after the restart a pivotal moment occurred. Barrios, who had picked up a booking towards the end of regulation time, was shown his second yellow card by Andrés Cunha. Just yards from the Uruguayan referee, Barrios left the ground with both feet and made a stamping motion. Even though contact from the studs was minimal, the referee had no option but to dismiss the Colombian midfielder. The result, now, somehow felt inevitable. Quintero, who had already launched a couple of unsuccessful range-finders in Andrada's direction, made a decisive contribution in the 109th minute. Controlling the ball on the edge of Boca's 18-yard box, the Colombian unleashed an unstoppable shot which crashed off the underside of the crossbar and into the net, leaving the Boca stopper with no chance.

River began to dominate as the game wore on and for Boca, it was time to stick or twist. With Andrada up for a corner in the dying embers of the match, River broke, Martínez racing away to roll the ball into the empty net to make it 3-1. Not even the introduction of Tevez, the fourth substitute to come on in extra time, could swing the tie in Boca's favour. Fernando Gago, another ageing club icon who emerged from the bench, was forced off with an injury leaving Boca down to nine men. The tear in his right Achilles tendon would signal the end of his time wearing the *azul y oro*, before a move to Vélez Sarsfield in the middle of 2019.

Aside from the defeat, the major disappointment of the final was that the action on the grass was overshadowed by events off the field, leaving a somewhat sour taste in the mouths of the majority of observers. Although the Madrid tie featured two of South America's key footballing superpowers, it lacked almost everything else usually associated with the beautiful game on the continent. South American football is often held up as the antidote to the sanitisation of modern football but the Madrid second leg couldn't have been any more polished.

Boca understandably felt hard done to in the wake of the defeat and fans had every right to peddle conspiracy theories. Whilst Barros Schelotto's side had been knocking out Fluminense in the semi-final, River prevailed in another Argentina-Brazil clash, eliminating Grêmio in controversial circumstances. In the second leg, Gallardo flouted a touchline ban given for bringing his team out late for the second half of the first leg and River were gifted a questionable VAR-assisted penalty in the fifth minute of time added on. 'Boca had a great team going into the final, sparking a lot of hope,' stated Lucas Guerrero. 'But it is also true that there were many controversies that complicated the tournament and took away a bit of genuine emotion. I don't think anyone could have predicted the importance of a Copa Libertadores Final between Boca and River. However, the incidents that happened meant we were discussing other things and not football. Unfortunately, the second leg should not have been played. The precedent was clear: in the face of aggression from rival fans the game should have been suspended. Why was it different this time? Because of the economic importance of the final? So River's leadership and Conmebol could retain a good relationship? We will never know, but it was a shame for everyone, including River fans.'

On 4 February 2020, more than a year after the final, CAS released their ruling in response to Boca's appeal against the decision of December 2018. River, already hit with a large fine, would have to play two Copa Libertadores matches behind closed doors. CAS, however, announced that they wouldn't recommend the disqualification of River from the 2018 competition, suggesting that such a punishment would be excessive. Boca, ejected from the same tournament in 2015 following the pepper-spray incident, were right to feel aggrieved.

In analysing the defeat Barros Schelotto may look back on some tactical mistakes made in the second leg. The unbalanced substitutes' bench left Boca shorn of genuine options in key areas, something that would bite them later in the game. Three forwards – Tevez, Ábila, and Zárate – were never realistically all going to be used and, with the ageing Fernando Gago also selected, it meant Boca lacked real options in central midfield and wide areas. The manager, however, was magnanimous in defeat and all but ruled out the idea of any further complaints from his part.

Within days of the defeat, the last final to be played over two legs before it changed to a one-off showpiece event, it was announced that Barros Schelotto, following a meeting with president Daniel Angelici, was to leave the pressure cooker of La Bombonera to head for the less intrusive MLS, a well-trodden path he had also followed as a player. 'Guillermo won two consecutive Argentine titles, something that hadn't been done since Basile's Boca in 2006,' stated Guerrero when analysing the twin's spell as Boca manager. 'He consolidated players that would go on to have a global profile, such as Benedetto, Pavón, Rodrigo Bentancur, Barrios, and Nández. His team was very offensive and defeated River twice at El Monumental, on one occasion scoring four goals, something that hadn't been done since 1995. Nevertheless, this was outweighed by two final defeats to River [Supercopa Argentina and Copa Libertadores] because of the pain it caused the fans. Over time I'm sure this will be forgotten and he'll return to the status of idol because that's what he is.'

Chapter Seventeen

A New Dawn

IN THE wake of Guillermo Barros Schelotto's departure following the devastating Copa Libertadores defeat to River Plate, Boca turned to Gustavo Alfaro. The coaching veteran won promotion to the top tier with both Olimpo and Quilmes in the early 2000s before later leading Arsenal de Sarandí to the 2007 Copa Sudamericana, 2012 Clausura, and 2013 Copa Argentina.

The appointment of the 56-year-old former Atlético de Rafaela midfielder was announced on 2 January 2019 and, 25 days later, the 2018/19 Superliga recommenced after a two-month break. The squad at Alfaro's disposal was much changed, the club putting new sporting director Nicolás Burdisso – a stalwart from Boca's glory years – to work immediately. Pablo Pérez transferred to Independiente, and Lisandro Magallán headed to Dutch giants Ajax. Also saying goodbye to the club were Leonardo Jara, Agustín Rossi, Lucas Olaza and Edwin Cardona. Bolstering the squad were Iván Marcone, Jorman Campuzano, Lisandro López, Marcos Díaz, Kevin Mac Allister – son of Carlos, who played for Boca between 1992 and 1996 – and Junior Alonso.

Alfaro's side lost just once in the remaining 12 games, putting four goals past San Martín de San Juan and San Martín de Tucumán on the road, and beating San Lorenzo 3-0 in a *Clásico* at La Bombonera with goals from Mauro Zárate, Nahitan Nández, and Sebastián Villa. However, the damage had been done in the first half of the season. Alfaro's Boca won 2.25 points per game as opposed to Guillermo Barros Schelotto's 1.85. It was much-improved form but ultimately not enough. The defending champions had given up their crown to Racing, who finished six points ahead of Boca.

At the beginning of May, Alfaro landed his first piece of silverware as Boca boss. In Mendoza, Boca, champions of the 2017/18 Superliga, faced Copa Argentina holders Rosario Central for the right to lift the Supercopa Argentina. After 90 goalless minutes, the match went to penalty kicks.

Each side netted their first five, and the shoot-out moved into sudden death. To a chorus of whistles, midfielder Fabián Rinaudo stepped up for Rosario Central to face Esteban Andrada. The kick was struck fiercely enough, but the diving Boca goalkeeper was able to stretch and meet the ball with his left palm, sending it over the crossbar. Carlos Izquierdoz smashed the ball into the bottom corner, leaving Central's goalkeeper rooted to the spot, before running and jumping into Andrada's arms. Soon enough, the rest of the squad, and the bench, joined in the celebrations in front of the Boca faithful gathered in the Estadio Malvinas Argentinas.

Exactly one month later Boca participated in another final, the Copa Superliga, yet this time had to settle for second best. A new competition from the AFA, created to supplement the low number of league fixtures, featured all the sides from the Argentine top flight in a knockout tournament. Boca beat Godoy Cruz, Vélez Sarsfield and Argentinos Juniors en route to the final in Córdoba's Estadio

Mario Kempes but fell 2-0 to Tigre due to a combination of poor refereeing decisions and wasteful finishing from the forwards.

The 2019/20 Superliga produced a flat opening: a goalless draw with Huracán at La Bombonera, with several key players rested ahead of a Copa Libertadores clash. In the first 15 minutes of the second league fixture, Boca demonstrated the gulf in class against their opponents, scoring twice against Patronato de Paraná on the way to a 2-0 victory. Attention then turned to the Copa Argentina.

After easing past Estudiantes de Río Cuarto in Mar del Plata in April, Boca were drawn against Almagro in the last 32. The two sides met in August, in La Plata, and Boca's XI contained a curious name. Burdisso pulled off a major coup, capturing Italian icon Daniele De Rossi – a friend and former team-mate from their time together in Serie A – on a free transfer. The midfielder, who had spent his entire career to date at boyhood club Roma, turned down numerous more lucrative offers to sign a one-year contract at La Bombonera, driven by a dream to play in Boca's legendary home.

Despite his advancing years, the 2006 World Cup winner was still expected to make a huge impact on Argentine football. After just 28 minutes of his debut, the 36-year-old headed in from a corner to give Boca the lead against Almagro. The veteran produced a superb display, showing his intelligence, experience, and array of passing. Unfortunately, it was to be the highlight of the night. After a 1-1 draw Boca crashed out of the competition, 3-1 on penalties, as three new signings – Alexis Mac Allister, son of Carlos and brother of Kevin, Jan Hurtado, and Eduardo Salvio – all failed to score their spot-kicks.

Without ever exploding into life, Alfaro's side won four and drew two of the next six Superliga fixtures, including a 0-0 stalemate with River Plate which stretched Boca's domestic unbeaten run at El Monumental to almost ten years. The Copa Libertadores semi-final pitted the two arch-rivals against each other once again, in a repeat of the explosive 2018 final. Boca had topped their group – containing Athletico Paranaense, Deportivo Tolima and Jorge Wilstermann – before eliminating group stage opponents Athletico Paranaense and LDU Quito to set up the final-four *Superclásico*.

Just four minutes into the first leg in El Monumental, Brazilian referee Raphael Claus consulted the VAR monitor and awarded River a penalty after Emmanuel Más had felled Rafael Borré. Borré stepped up and successfully converted from 12 yards to give the home side the lead. River doubled their advantage after 69 minutes through Ignacio Fernández and Boca's misery was compounded when Nicolás Capaldo – who missed a gilt-edged chance in the first half – was red-carded late in the game. Once again, River had benefitted from VAR.

Three weeks later the two sides met at La Bombonera for the second leg. Despite the boisterous atmosphere, the cards were always stacked in River's favour. Under Marcelo Gallardo, *Los Millonarios* had lost just once in eight visits to La Boca, and Alfaro's men were an efficient yet low-scoring side.

Salvio appeared to have given Boca a first-half lead but it was chalked off for an alleged handball in the build-up. The home side huffed and puffed and eventually scored after 80 minutes, 19-year-old Venezuelan forward Hurtado netting from close range from a set-piece. Even with ten minutes remaining the celebrations were muted, almost as if all those in attendance were unconvinced Alfaro's men would find a second. River progressed to the final and, unlike the powder-keg moments of 2015 and 2018, there were no notable disturbances on or off the pitch. The 60th edition of South

America's flagship football tournament featured its first one-off final, with Conmebol seeking to make the competition more appealing worldwide, à la Champions League. River lost to Flamengo in late, dramatic fashion at Lima's Estadio Monumental.

Boca won just two of the last six league games to close out 2019, although the barren run did include a 5-1 home win over Arsenal, the only time in the 16 league games leading up to the end of the year that Alfaro's side had managed to score more than twice within 90 minutes. The coach's points per game average had dropped significantly to just 1.81 in the season's Superliga. Combined with the limp exit from the Copa Libertadores, the former goalkeeper's days were numbered.

The final fixture before Christmas, on 8 December, saw Boca lose 1-0 away to Rosario Central. Back in Buenos Aires, members were lining the streets of La Boca, queuing to make their selection for the next president of their beloved club. Christian Gribaudo, a 46-year-old politician, was incumbent Daniel Angelici's continuation candidate and was backed by Diego Maradona on social media.

The other serious runner in the race – a third candidate, José Beraldi, never stood a chance – was Jorge Amor Ameal, president of the club between 2008 and 2011. Crucially, in November, just weeks before members went to the voting booths, Juan Román Riquelme threw his hat in the ring with Ameal, his partner Mario Pergolini, and their *Identidad Xeneize* movement. Not for the first time, Riquelme was directly at odds with Maradona.

The addition of Riquelme into the mix shook the Boca world and proved embarrassing and awkward to the Angelici-Gribaudo axis who would have to ignore or, worse, discredit the club's biggest icon to win the election. Mud was slung from both sides as the battle for votes turned ugly.

When the 38,362 ballot papers were counted Ameal, Pergolini, and Riquelme were announced as clear winners with 52.8 per cent of the votes. Comfortably defeated, Gribaudo had managed to persuade just 30.6 per cent of the voting members and, after almost a quarter-century, the shadow of Macri and his policies no longer lingered over the club. 'Angelici made progress in terms of economics, structure, and marketing,' stated Lucas Guerrero of Muy Boca. 'But he never managed to achieve the full support of the fans. He always spoke like a businessman without understanding the passion that the club generates. His posturing with Conmebol, an organisation which many Boca fans have felt aggrieved by on several occasions, wasn't great. On the balance of it, he does not leave a good image and it's doubtful that he will return to the institution.'

Unsurprisingly, after less than a year, Alfaro was gone. Despite winning the Supercopa, and leaving Boca just a point behind River in the race for the 2019/20 Superliga, the coach's methods were deemed uninspiring and insipid. Under his tenure, the team scored a paltry average of just 1.4 goals per game.

Alfaro's replacement was Miguel Ángel Russo, the 63-year-old who had led Boca to Copa Libertadores glory in 2007 with Riquelme in majestic form. 'Russo made the players feel more comfortable, possibly owing to his more offensive style: the team scored 16 goals in seven games, exploiting the qualities of footballers at his disposal,' said Lucas Guerrero. 'His personality radiated calm and patience and gave more confidence to fans, players, and journalists. He appeared to be dealing with modern football without problems, arriving at Boca having recently led other important teams on the continent such as Millonarios (Colombia), Alianza Lima (Peru), and Cerro Porteño (Paraguay). He was therefore fully active.'

There was little change in the playing staff, with Boca, like many other Argentine clubs, affected by the latest economic crisis to afflict the country. Guillermo *Pol* Fernández, a midfielder who left the club in 2015, returned, signing from Mexican club Cruz Azul. Whilst it is always positive to welcome home youth-team products, it was far from the inspirational signing the fans craved. Leaving the club, meanwhile, was Daniele De Rossi. After just seven appearances, and two completed 90 minutes, De Rossi returned to his homeland for family reasons and retired from professional football altogether. Although his injury-hit and brief spell with Boca wasn't the fairy tale everyone had hoped it would be, the Italian midfielder left with a heavy heart and lots of affection. 'It was a tough year for Boca fans after the defeat against River, and the arrival of De Rossi was a balm for the soul,' began Lucas Guerrero. 'That a world champion and globally recognised player would decide to come to Argentina was something spectacular. Emotionally, and from a marketing perspective, it was positive.'

Russo's first match back in Boca's dugout was an uninspiring 0-0 draw at home to Independiente, watched by a casual-looking Riquelme, sipping yerba mate alongside *Los Diablos Rojos* legend Ricardo Bochini in the directors' box. Boca lost Izquierdoz after just 21 minutes – when the central defender received his second yellow card – and were forced to adapt. Former Boca man Pablo Pérez evened up the numbers on 75 minutes, given his marching orders for a disgraceful studs-up challenge. With just six games remaining Russo's men trailed River Plate by three points.

In round 18 Boca beat Talleres in Córdoba for the first time since 1991, picking up a crucial three points on the road. Sebastián Villa gave Boca the lead after 13 minutes and, after 63 minutes, Tevez doubled the tally. Tevez had looked a shadow of his former self under Alfaro, and since returning from China, but the appointment of Russo gave him a new lease of life in the autumn of his career. Talleres scored in the 80th minute but Boca held on for a 2-1 win.

Pushed on by the fans, and with a faint hope of winning the championship, Boca beat Atlético Tucumán 2-0 at La Bombonera through Franco Soldano and a Ramón Ábila penalty. The following fixture showed the gulf in class between Boca and their opponents Central Córdoba de Santiago. Russo's men ran riot, scoring four despite missing two penalties.

A comfortable 3-0 home win over Godoy Cruz, with goals from Tevez and two from Salvio, made it four wins in four. River, however, were matching Boca stride for stride and retained a three-point cushion with two fixtures remaining. The penultimate league fixture saw a free-scoring Boca, in stark contrast to the Alfaro era, notch four second-half goals in Santa Fe, defeating Colón on a Friday night. The following day River surprisingly drew at home to Defensa y Justicia. With one game remaining the lead was down to one point. River had finally blinked and the title race would go down to the wire.

As if it were written in the stars, Diego Maradona's relegation-threatened Gimnasia were the visitors to La Bombonera on the final day of the season. The awkwardness of the presidential campaign, during which *El Diego* had sided with the losing candidate, was put to one side and, listening to the fans, the administration of the club decided to pay tribute to the Argentine football legend, in the same way many other clubs up and down the country had recently done. Before the game kicked off Maradona was presented with a commemorative plaque containing the latest replica shirt with his name and number on the back.

The fans proudly sang his name and unfurled banners in tribute to their idol and, before the referee blew the whistle to signal the commencing of proceedings, Tevez gave Maradona a good-luck kiss on the lips. 'Maradona is, together with the 1925 European tour and the Bianchi era, the face of Boca in the world,' according to freelance journalist Leandro Cordobez. 'If there are Boca shirts anywhere in the world, if successful players from other countries choose to join Boca, if La Bombonera is a temple of world football, it is because of Maradona. Diego showed the world his love for Boca and for that our club will forever be thankful. Maradona represents values that the Macri era tried to erase, that we are now recovering. A popular, humble club that never gives up. Arrogant, victorious, rebellious. Diego never forgot Boca and Boca will never forget Diego.'

River travelled to Tucumán to face Atlético, knowing all they needed to do was match Boca's result. The ball was still in their court. Gallardo's side fell behind after 19 minutes but equalised after 40 minutes via Matías Suárez. With 45 minutes left in the season and the score goalless at La Bombonera, River were champions as things stood.

With just 18 minutes of normal time remaining, a patient Boca broke down the left-hand side. Colombian full-back Frank Fabra clipped the ball inside to Ábila who, stretching on the floor, managed to poke it towards Tevez. Carlitos took one touch and, from 20 yards, rifled an unstoppable shot down the throat of the opposition goalkeeper, who couldn't keep it out despite getting a hand to it. La Bombonera exploded, a writhing mass of blue-and-gold. Tevez, mimicking a celebration from earlier in his career, scaled the fence separating the fans from the pitch.

With no further goals in Tucumán, despite a nerve-wracking five minutes of time added on, Boca had done the unthinkable, reaching the summit of the league table at the last possible, but most important, moment. As news filtered through to the players from the stands, the festivities began in earnest. Russo, whose side had amassed 19 points from a possible 21, admirably paid tribute to his predecessor Gustavo Alfaro for laying the foundation of the triumph. The club's 34th league title was in the bag, the 69th entry on the club's ever-expanding and star-studded crest.

Tevez's match-winning goal was the culmination of his excellent form since the arrival of Russo, when many thought his powers and motivation for the game had gone for good. 'Tevez has made mistakes since returning to Boca in 2015 and has had some low-level moments, but nobody can take away the honour of being one of the greatest idols in the club's history,' said Lucas Guerrero. 'He was a key figure in the most recent championship and was a hero in the deciding match, confirming that he still has more to give to the club. Tevez is currently the most important player in Argentine football and has hunger for more glory and to accumulate more trophies. He is the emblem of Russo's Boca.'

Francisco Aure, journalist and member of the Boca in English team, shared the sentiment: 'I admired Tevez in Europe and was amazed when he came back. His departure to China was a big upset for all the fans, but he redeemed himself with his performance in early 2020, leading the team to beat River Plate in the run for the Superliga.'

Riquelme, sipping yerba mate as ever, kept his poker face during the celebrations, although a smile cracked in the corner of his mouth. 'The return of Riquelme was an injection of positivity, a breath of fresh air at the club, an umbrella for whatever rain may fall,' said Lucas Guerrero. 'He brings calm and intelligence in the changing and dynamic world of football. Even though he no longer plays, Riquelme is a figure that can take the pressure and knows how to live with it.' Crucially, Riquelme's presence allowed Russo and Tevez to flourish. 'He was key in bringing in Russo, who achieved a joint-best start – tied with Marzolini in the 1981 Metropolitano – to life as a Boca head coach in league championships, registering six wins and a draw,' began Gabriel Aguero, founder of Boca in English. 'Riquelme was also key in confiding in Tevez, who has shown his best form since December 2017.'

Inexplicably, the AFA decided against sending a trophy – original or replica – to La Bombonera for the crucial Gimnasia match. Instead, in their wisdom, it was decided beforehand that should Boca prevail, the trophy would be presented at their first Copa Superliga match, scheduled for mid-March. However, Argentine football was suspended after just one round of the Copa Superliga, due to the COVID-19 crisis that engulfed the globe in 2020. Although in the grand scheme of the pandemic the decision not to enable Boca fans and players to enjoy the magical trophy-lifting moment wasn't the most pressing issue on people's minds, it was another in a long line of bizarre decisions by Argentine football's governing body.

Off the pitch, the new regime has excelled in public relations. German sportswear giants Adidas replaced long-term kit manufacturers Nike, and the spectacular results have been universally popular. La Bombonera received a desperately required facelift, with a bright paint job inside and out giving the classic temple of football the love it deserves. The partitions between the stands and the pitch, opposite the directors' boxes, were removed, immediately improving the matchday experience for thousands of fans. The plans to do the same with the fences behind each goal, however, proved controversial due to their inextricable links to the club's fan culture, the way Tevez celebrated the title-clinching goal a case in point.

The next key task, and one which may determine how the Ameal-Pergolini-Riquelme regime is viewed in years to come, is the redevelopment of La Bombonera. The majority of people linked with the club want to remain at the place they have called home for 80 years, but there are several different options on the table. The board seem to favour the Bombonera 360 project, which will convert the stadium into an enclosed bowl complete with roof. The capacity of the stadium has to be increased to accommodate the members, tens of thousands of whom are unable to source tickets to watch their beloved team play due to demand wildly outstripping supply.

Boca Juniors are in safe hands. With the likes of Ameal, Riquelme, Russo, and Tevez – all of whom have returned to the club and have blue-and-gold blood running through their veins – do not bet against further success in the coming years. More magical nights under the floodlights at La Bombonera, more success, more stars on the club's crest, and the creation of more heroes. The blue-and-gold passion is eternal.

Bibliography

BOOKS

Agüero, F. & Stark, J. (eds), *Fault Lines of Democracy in Post-Transition Latin America* (Miami: North-South Center Press, 1998).

Auyero, J., *Poor People's Politics: Peronist Survival Networks & the Legacy of Evita* (Durham & London: Duke University Press, 2001).

Ballvé, A., Ibarra, A., & Macri, M., *Pasión Y Gestión: Claves Del Ciclo Macri En Boca* (Buenos Aires: Aguilar, 2011).

Burns, J., *Barça: A People's Passion* (London: Bloomsbury, 1998).

Campomar, A., *Golazo: A History of South American Football* (London: Quercus, 2014).

Caparrós, M., *Boquita* (Madrid: Planeta, 2005).

Contento, L., *Esto Es Boca: El Oro Y El Barro* (Buenos Aires: Libro Fútbol, 2017).

Diamond, L., Hartlyn, J., Linz, J.J., & Lipset, S.M. (eds), *Democracy in Developing Countries: Latin America (Second Edition)* (London: Lynne Rienner Publishers, 1999).

Dionisi, D., *50 Impactos Del Fútbol Argentino* (Buenos Aires: Club House, 2016).

Galeano, E., *Football in Sun & Shadow* (New York: Nation Books, 2013).

Hornos, J., *La 12: Violencia, Dinero y Pasión* (Independently Published, 2018).

Kuhn, G., *Soccer vs. The State: Tackling Football and Radical Politics* (Oakland: PM Press, 2011).

Lievesley, G., *Democracy in Latin America: Mobilization, Power and the Search for a New Politics* (Manchester & New York: Manchester University Press, 1999).

Maradona, D., *El Diego* (London: Yellow Jersey Press, 2005, trans. Marcela Mora y Araujo).

Maradona, D., & Arcucci, D., *Touched By God: How We Won the Mexico '86 World Cup* (London: Constable, 2017).

Richards, J., *Superclásico: Inside the Ultimate Derby* (BackPage Press, 2013).

Rosatti, H., *Cien Años De Multitud (Vol. II)* (Buenos Aires: Galerna, 2010).

Simpson, P., & Hess, U., *Who Invented the Stepover? And Other Crucial Football Conundrums* (London: Profile Books, 2013).

Skidmore, T.E., & Smith, P.H., *Modern Latin America (Sixth Edition)* (New York: Oxford University Press, 2005).

Wilson, J., *Angels with Dirty Faces: The Footballing History of Argentina* (London: Orion, 2016).

Wilson, J., *Inverting the Pyramid: The History of Football Tactics* (London: Orion, 2008).

WEBSITES

argentina.as.com
edition.cnn.com
elpais.com
reutersagency.com
www.11v11.com
www.afa.com.ar
www.batimes.com.ar
www.bbc.co.uk
www.bocajuniors.com.ar
www.cariverplate.com.ar
www.casarosada.gob.ar
www.clarin.com
www.cnn.com
www.conmebol.com
www.elgrafico.com
www.espn.co.uk
www.fifa.com
www.historiadeboca.com.ar
www.independent.co.uk
www.infobae.com
www.lanacion.com.ar
www.lavoz.com.ar
www.muyboca.com.ar
www.nytimes.com
www.realmadrid.com
www.rsssf.com
www.si.com
www.soccerway.com
www.theguardian.com
www.uefa.com
www.usatoday.com